The Government of
Education in Britain

The Government of Education in Britain

Keith Fenwick
Peter McBride

Martin Robertson · Oxford

First published in 1981
Martin Robertson, 108 Cowley Road, Oxford OX4 1JF, England

British Library Cataloguing in Publication Data

Fenwick, Keith
     The government of education.
     1. School management and organization — Great
        Britain
     2. Universities and colleges — Great Britain —
        Administration
     I. Title   II. McBride, Peter
     379'.15'0941   LA631.82

     ISBN 0-85520-255-6 (hb)
     ISBN 0-85520-254-8 (pb)

Filmset by Pioneer Associates, East Sussex
Printed and bound by Book Plan, Worcester

Contents

List of Figures and Tables

Preface

The study of the politics and administration of education draws on many academic sources in the arts and social sciences and it is the authors' view that the behaviour of those involved in the provision of education in Britain can be fully understood only in the context of political life generally. A textbook necessarily simplifies the contextual framework it presents and an introductory text must be selective rather than exhaustive in its treatment of particular issues. Our aim has been to pick up major themes in the government of education today and convey to the reader some of the flavour of old and new controversy alongside detail of the administrative system.

Few textbooks try to integrate historical narrative with exposition of the contemporary system and an awareness of current theoretical perspectives; again, in the author's view, to be most nearly fully understood British educational government must be seen as patterned by past as well as present.

Our first explicitly historical chapter is not intended to provide a comprehensive treatment of the education system before 1944, nor to sketch in a tedious chronology. The chapter sets out to highlight some earlier preoccupations in policy and practice the legacies of which are still with us. The current involvement of the Churches in the education system looks back to a long European tradition which has nevertheless had very different twentieth century outcomes in Britain, France or Germany. The expedient religious compromises of the Education Act, 1944, may be tribute to Anglo-Saxon pragmatism but the centuries-long antagonisms which went before suggest rather different doctrinal and political perspectives. The variety of compromise in the different parts of Britain even now confirms the ambiguity in our tradition.

Historical development also serves to correct the impression common amongst beginning students of contemporary educational government that the system is as it is because it must be so. In fact decisions have been taken at particular times which could easily have been different and pointed the system in a different direction. The broad extent and general confirmation of central government's power in education is a very recent phenomenon, contestable in the past by appeal to deep seated political philosophy as well as the vested interests of local authorities. History may turn full circle when the extensive regulating and funding powers of central government which were justified in the 1940's and 1950's by reference to the poor record in education of some local authorities, are used, as now, to damp down local commitment and impose a maximum of uniformity, rather than a uniform minimum. The Education Act, 1902, its interpretation still a matter of controversy amongst historians of education, is another turning point for the development of a local education service in England; Scotland's retention of ad hoc authorities for nearly thirty years more, and Northern Ireland's current use of them, must make it clear that contemporary institutions are as much the product of historical prejudice as of rational analysis.

In looking at contemporary government of education nationally and locally we have also tried to stress the contestable nature of educational decisions. While we do not deny the existence of "educational" arguments or "professional" criteria, neither do we ignore economic and political criteria, and, most importantly, we do not present one set of criteria as superior to the other. Education is now a major service industry and most of the audience for student texts about it have a stake in its survival and expansion; there is nothing wrong in such a stake but it may prejudice the student when he should be detached in his analysis. In the authors' view such detachment may prepare the student better to defend his interest and to promote the cause of education than an easy acceptance of publicist nostrums or of the special pleadings of organised pressure groups.

While we try to guard against painting a picture of an education system in which there is no legitimate place for any but the professional, our two chapters on the institution of school and college show only too clearly the proliferation and increasing complexity of the tasks facing teachers and educational administrators of all kinds. The impact of legislation, of negotiated agreements, and of institutional bureaucracy seems least in the small primary school, greatest in the college of further education, but all institutions have been affected. Paradoxically, at the same time as institutions have been much more fully integrated into an overall system, the individual teacher may have become more isolated by the social fragmentation resulting from accumulation and subdivision of educational tasks.

The superficial uniformity of contemporary educational institutions masks substantial differences in ideological perspective and interest amongst teachers which find partial expression in their national associations. But just as competing demands for educational resources within the education system could be contained while overall expansion continued, so the strains of internal dissent and confusion may be made more manifest in a period of economic retrenchment. Fewer pupils, fewer resources, a "surplus" of teachers, and less public sympathy for education will require at least different management of teacher's associations, at most a realignment of teacher interests.

There can be little doubt that governmental attitudes to education have changed; it is more difficult to assess the acuity of the politician's judgement of the public mood. Our final chapter explores this issue in the context of the debate over curriculum content and control. Nothing could be more critical to an education system; nothing could have been taken more on trust in most of Britain during the post-war period. The obsession with non-doctrinal religious instruction have finally subsided, a literal reading of the legal responsibilities for curriculum gave way to less formal negotiations amongst teachers or between them and examining bodies, in which public representatives were happy to acquiesce. As the association between individual educational and occupational success in the mind of the public has weakened, and as scapegoats for national economic decline have been sought, it is not surprising that education in general, a major consumer of resources, and the curriculum in particular, should again become a target for criticism.

While the emergence of a radical Conservative government in May 1979, during the writing of this book, confirms the trend toward educational dissensus, it has made more difficult the detailing of the administrative system. When possible we have taken into account changes enacted or forecast by a national government committed to substantial changes in the style and content of policy which have major implications for the running of the education service. It would be premature to try and express a considered view of the consequences of policies still under heated debate. The Local Government Act, 1958, introduced major changes in the financing of education, but forecasts of its effects which drew on the most expert educational judgements made at the time, would have proved woefully inadequate;

the same may prove true of the predicted consequences of the Education Act, 1980, and the bill which will, at the time of writing, shortly become the Local Government Act, 1980.

This note of caution is reaffirmed on grounds of principle in our last chapter; while the overall structure of society may change slowly, its particular manifestation in the education system and educational controversy is by no means stable. We hope that readers will find plenty of evidence in the pages that follow to show that the education system we have is the evolving creation of men, their views and their actions, and not some immutable and uncriticisable monolith detached from everyday reality.

K. Fenwick
P. McBride
October 1980

CHAPTER 1

A Historical Introduction

While it can be no more than a truism to say that our current education system is a product of its history, in British education today certain features owe much more to history than to contemporary rationale. It is these features with which the present chapter is concerned. In the course of examining the trend away from denominational domination of education and the development of local and national institutions for the government of the education system, it should be clear that history has often taken different turnings in England, Scotland, Ireland and, to a lesser extent, Wales. If these significant variations do not in themselves make a point, then it had better be spelled out that the chronology of events and the positive choices of government do not represent any automatically self-justifying progression towards an 'ideal system'. Rather, they are choices made in particular social, political and administrative contexts, having, in the event, unforeseen as well as intended consequences, opening up and closing off unexpected avenues for further change. There was nothing inevitable about the abolition of *ad hoc* authorities for education; different compromises with the Churches were possible; it would have been possible to clarify the various responsibilities of national government in education without creating a single Ministry—after all, government relations with the universities were discharged through the Treasury until fifteen years ago. It is to be hoped that this chapter will help to explain some of the features of the contemporary British education system—it does not seek to justify those features.

THE RELIGIOUS QUESTION

The sponsorship of education by the Christian Church has a very long history in Europe. Through parish priests, monasteries, cathedrals and universities, the Church has traditionally sought to inculcate doctrine in all the people, and lettering, grammar and classical studies in some, particularly those destined to join the clergy. The civil power offered little, if any, competition; and the acts of sovereigns in founding schools were seen by themselves and by others as practical expressions of piety. With the Renaissance and the Reformation the higher valuation of a broader classical education, still within the framework of Christianity, led in England to the foundation of many grammar schools, often funded from the estates of local worthies. In Scotland the systematic provision of regular elementary education was attempted by statute in 1696, through the parishes of the established Presbyterian Church. In Ireland the established Church represented the educational domination of an alien and Anglicised minority over a Roman Catholic majority, fuelling religious antagonism with nationalistic fervour; similar Anglican domination in Wales successfully stifled local linguistic and cultural traditions until their re-invigoration by Welsh nonconformity in the nineteenth century.

But division between the different denominations on questions of doctrine and their practical implications for education weakened the religious monopoly and eventually led to its replacement, in England, Scotland and Wales, by a comprehensive, state-funded and state-controlled system of schools which still recognised, in a variety of ways, the historic and residual contributions that the Churches made. In Northern Ireland there still persists a system of state-funded schools critically divided by religious loyalties and mutual denominational suspicion.

The traditional association between the established Anglican Church and the state since the Reformation underlay much of the denominational rivalry and suspicion. In the early nineteenth century loyalty to Church and state were presumed synonymous, manifestly in the civil disabilities which were partly removed by the Test and Corporation Acts of 1828. The Anglicans asserted as their due a privileged position in many fields, including education, a view which (in the course of the century) they had to modify in the face of the growing political strength of nonconformity and the insufficiency of their financial resources to realise their aspirations unaided. Nonconformists combined to oppose state-backed provision of sectarian education in England and Wales, and their unity was cemented by guarantees that the new board schools after 1870 would be restricted to non-denominational religious education. It was at this same time that the established and the independent Presbyterian churches of Scotland handed over their schools to the state; in this instance the dissenters were Roman Catholics and Protestant episcopalians, who retained their schools until the Education Act of 1918 guaranteed their denominational character within a state system. In Ireland a different solution to the denominational problem in elementary education was attempted, with the establishment in 1831 of the Commissioners of National Education. The Commissioners were empowered to disburse the funds provided by Parliament on the erection of schools, the payment of teachers and the publication of textbooks in an attempt to create a system of schools offering a 'combined literary and separate religious education'. It was anticipated that denominations would unite to provide a common secular education with full opportunities for the separate teaching of religious doctrine. In the event each denomination came to provide its own school for secular and religious education. Government intervention in the funding of intermediate or secondary education—in the form of the passage of the Intermediate Education (Ireland) Act 1878—later in the century had more limited ambitions; grants were made to voluntary schools on the basis of pupil success in public examinations set by the Intermediate Education Board, and so again voluntarism and denominationalism in education were consolidated.

At the beginning of the century the rival denominations might all agree that education and religion were indivisible, but radicals were already arguing directly for a secular education. Rather than concede the claims of the established Church in England and Wales, the nonconformists championed secular education by the state. Eventually the Anglicans found themselves arguing, from a position of financial weakness, for access to state schools, leaving the Roman Catholics alone in their determination to maintain the unity of secular and religious education and direct control by the Church.

Government could never ignore the huge contribution made by the denominations, nor the powerful political lobbies they could muster within the major political parties. The original Scottish system of parochial schools, proposed for England and Wales in 1807 by Whitbread and again in 1820 by Brougham, was defeated in Parliament because Anglicans and nonconformists were equally suspicious of the advantage that such a system might give to the other. The first Inspectors, appointed in 1839, were subject to the approval of the Church of England. Every tentative step depended upon its acceptability across the religious divide. Single-school areas, usually Anglican, were a continuing source of irritation to nonconformists—a fact which was only partly acknowledged when in 1860 the Committee of the Privy Council decided to refuse building grants for new schools whose Trust Deeds did not include a conscience clause.

The perceived failure of the combination of Church initiative and government subsidy to provide a national system of elementary schools by the 1860s exacerbated sectarian conflict and shaped the intervention of the state in direct provision of education under the Elementary Education Act 1870. Radicals campaigned for free, compulsory, secular education under popular control, but there was a variety of less revolutionary views among the anti-Church lobby. The National Education Union, representing the denominationalists, demanded support for Church schools from the local rates as well as central government grant. Under a Liberal government, returned to power in 1868, the prospect of secular school boards was called into being, charged ostensibly with filling the gaps left by Churches in the provision of elementary schools. Over the next thirty years a rapidly shifting and expanding population provided many opportunities for the establishment of state elementary schools committed to the conscience clause, a choice between non-denominational religious instruction and none at all and priority for secular instruction. While for many years to come parents in rural areas might still find themselves with no choice other than the local Church school, in general the board school soon usurped the denominational school as the model for the future in England and Wales.

While the school boards south of the border had to leave Church schools to their own devices, in Scotland school boards set up for every parish and burgh were empowered to take over existing parochial schools, financing them, regardless of sponsorship or denominational character, from local taxation. Denominationalists in England perceived the school boards as a threat because determination of the number of school places needed in an area lay in the boards' hands and because the rates paid by Church members supported the board schools but could not be used to support their own Church schools. In the short term more government subsidy was the solution, allied with Church efforts to dominate the school boards' electorally and thus keep their activities in check; in the long term, as the Majority Report of the Cross Commission proposed, the school boards should acquire permissive powers to aid Church schools from the rates. In the event a Conservative Government, traditionally sympathetic to the Church cause, set out first to restrain, then to abolish, the school boards, transferring their powers and their schools to the recently created county boroughs and county councils, which were in turn empowered, for the first time, to fund Church schools from local taxation. Although unsuccessful, the campaign against what was to become the Education Act 1902 brought together the defenders of the school boards and their undoubted achievements, the nonconformists, secularists and the growing trade union and labour movement, souring the prospects of substantial further educational reform for over a generation. Some local authorities in Wales refused to maintain voluntary schools in their areas, but the government responded by allocating funds directly to voluntary schools and by deducting the amount payable in grants to the local authorities concerned (Education (Local Authority Default) Act 1904). When the Liberals regained office in 1906 they made three attempts to redress the grievances of their nonconformist supporters; Birrell's Bill of 1907 — which, not unlike the Scottish solution, proposed the transfer to local authorities of all Church schools and the introduction of limited opportunities for denominational instruction within the local authority system — was defeated by the House of Lords. McKenna's and Runciman's Bills of 1908 featured the transfer of voluntary schools to the local authority or the alternative of contracting out of rate support, but both were withdrawn in response to the protests they aroused. It was, not only the socially powerful Church of England that stood to lose from the reversal of the 1902 Education Act, of course, but also the Roman Catholic Church, whose influence lay among some of the poorer voters whose support the Liberal Party might be seeking.

As the secular impetus towards educational development grew in the twentieth century (uneven in space and time though its growth was), the dilemma for government was the choice between the improbability of legislative change without religious controversy on the one hand and, on the other, the impossibility of structural reform of education without the provision of substantially more financial support, including capital grants, to Church schools. The problem was finally overcome in Scotland with the Education Act 1918, which allowed denominational interests to retain a right of veto over the appointment of teachers in respect of their religious belief or character, while transferring the schools and all financial responsibility for them to the local education authority. Nonconformists in England and Wales, less ready to compromise and embittered by history as some of them were, represented a much larger section of the organised political community. Unless and until the smouldering antagonisms which had burned so fiercely at the beginning of the century finally died away a programme of comprehensive educational reform would have been nothing but a political liability.

In Ireland partition had produced a separate Parliament in Belfast, which was responsible for educational legislation (among other matters) throughout the six counties and had inherited the structures and the schools of nineteenth-century Ireland, with the one difference that the Catholics who formed a majority in the whole island were a minority in the province. The Education Act (Northern Ireland) of 1923 constituted the two county boroughs and the six counties the responsible education authority for their area. Provision was made for the transfer of the very many voluntary schools of different denominations to facilitate the development of unified schemes of elementary, secondary and further education. Because the Government of Ireland Act 1920 forbade the passing of any law which would directly or indirectly establish or endow any religion, the previous system of financial support for a combined literary and separate religious education initiated by the Commissioners nearly a hundred years before could not be maintained. Until the passing of the Education Act (Northern Ireland) in 1930 a settlement could not be devised which would convince the Protestant managers of the desirability of transferring their schools; the refusal of the Roman Catholic Church to yield control of its schools, despite the financial benefits, has led to the present dual system, under which county schools are staffed and attended largely by Protestants, voluntary schools by Roman Catholics.

The growing consensus among educationists inside and outside central government and the local authorities was in favour of the abolition of the two parallel schemes of public education, elementary and secondary (or higher), and their replacement by one coherent progression, primary, secondary, further, through which all children would have the opportunity to make the fullest use of the education system. The new local education authorities had taken their chance, in the first few years after 1902, to provide many secondary schools to supplement the older endowed and grant-aided foundations, but for the vast majority of children schooling still meant the elementary school from five to fourteen years of age. When the Hadow Report of 1926, which recommended secondary education for all from eleven to fifteen in separate establishments, found wide acceptance, denominationalists had to accept the need for change and compromise, and government had been given sound reasons for extending even further its subsidy to Church schools. The 1936 Education Act made possible a continuation of the dual system without crippling the voluntary schools financially. The Act was mainly concerned to raise the school-leaving age to fifteen in September 1939 and only as a consequence to make available, by special agreement, grants of between 50 per cent and 75 per cent of capital expenditure on necessary new school building by the Churches. In return the local authorities took control of most teacher appointments in the new 'special agreement' schools, leaving the managers responsible for appointing 'reserved' teachers for religious instruction.

Under the impetus of war and under the leadership of a President of the Board of Education who valued the educational contribution of the Churches but was prepared to call their bluff on occasion, public discussion of major legislative reforms which would finally settle the religious question and set the pattern of schooling for a generation began in 1941 with the publication of the government Green Paper and issued in the Education Act 1944.

The Act created two main alternative forms of voluntary school, to be known as 'controlled' and 'aided' schools. The former were to be wholly financed by local education authorities, who would also control teaching appointments. Religious education would be based on a non-denominational 'agreed syllabus', as it would be, compulsorily for the first time, in the local authority's own schools. Limited denominational instruction distinctive of the sponsoring body would be allowed if a majority of parents of pupils expressed a wish for it. 'Aided' status would commit voluntary school governors to funding half the cost of any new buildings or external repairs. In return the governors would appoint and dismiss staff, subject to some control by the local education authority. Religious education within the school would be at the discretion of the governors.

The solution had considerable appeal for all parties. Through schools of 'controlled' status the Church of England could rid itself of the enormous financial burden of its historic contribution to the provision of schools throughout the country and yet retain a residual interest. The previously unavoidable denominational bias in many rural single-school areas could now be eliminated. Through schools of 'aided' status Anglicans and, even more, Roman Catholics could obtain substantial financial assistance towards the capital costs of their schools, yet still retain very firm control. Legal guarantees against religious discrimination largely allayed the fears of increasingly powerful teacher unions. (Even so, Roman Catholics were dissatisfied with the fact that there was no provision for assistance with the cost of building new schools except where government action caused a population shift.)

The unanimity of support for the 1944 Education Act as a whole signalled the end of sectarianism as a source of controversy in education; it was with little political difficulty that much wider discretion was given under the Education Act 1953, and in 1959 a 75 per cent capital grant (now 85 per cent) was made available to governors of 'aided' schools, existing or projected, to cater for children at existing primary schools.

Religious dispute is no longer a serious issue in British education except in Northern Ireland, where the proliferation of small, denominationally distinct primary and secondary schools among a poor and scattered population inhibits educational change in many ways. In Scotland a less grudging acceptance of denominationalism has permitted the integrated development of the school system for over sixty years, while England's more recent (and administratively cumbersome) solution serves to set a minimum standard for pluralist local government of education by institutionalising a separate voice at the level of the school that is independent of central government, local education authority and teachers.

THE GROWTH OF THE CENTRAL GOVERNMENT OF EDUCATION

The reluctance of government to take direct responsibility for educational provision in the early part of the nineteenth century reflected not only traditional deference to the Church in educational matters, and a wariness of inter-denominational rivalries, but also contemporary restrictive views of the legitimate functions of government. The example of other countries such as France and

Prussia, where state initiatives had been taken, served to deter rather than to encourage similar initiatives at Westminster. Such countries were seen by many as typically autocratic, reinforcing the conviction that state intervention in education threatened individual freedom. In addition, government interference, it was thought, might sap voluntary initiative; self-help and private enterprise in areas where Church activity was insufficient were seen as the symbols and effective causes of progress. Whether they subscribed to the popular distortion of Adam Smith's views that pictured state intervention as doomed to failure or catastrophe in the face of immutable, natural economic laws of supply and demand, or to the preference for less government rather than tyrannical government expressed by the early socialist Tom Paine, or to simple parsimony in financial and fiscal policy, the voters and legislators of the early nineteenth century were philosophically well armed against demands for government action in the provision of education. Many might argue, in addition, that popular education, far from serving to gentle the masses and stabilise the state, might ferment discontent and facilitate revolt. Although the nineteenth century saw a massive extension of government in form, scope and substance, in no area of domestic policy was this development viewed with greater reluctance than in education. Even John Stuart Mill was to write in the middle of the century: 'A general state education is a mere contrivance for moulding people to be exactly like one another. It establishes a despotism over the mind leading by natural tendency to one over the body.'

Even if none of these principled doubts had been common currency at the beginning of the nineteenth century, consideration of practicability would have caused government to hesitate before embarking on a state system of schooling. In the counties administrative machinery was restricted to the justices; in the towns, to the decayed and corrupt municipal corporations. The first comprehensive administrative structure to be created on Benthamite lines was the combination of the local Boards of Guardians and National Commissioners of the Poor Law a year after the first government grants to schools in 1833. The first grants were paid by the Treasury directly to those promoters of schools who fulfilled numerous conditions, including recommendation by either the National Society or the British and Foreign School Society (respectively, the national representatives of Anglican and non-conformist interest in education). Without staff to scrutinise applications, the Treasury was forced to rely on the two societies to determine need, viability and priority. The grants were in aid of school buildings, and accounts had to be submitted for audit, but there was no Treasury check on the appropriateness of construction, the legal arrangements for the subsequent holding of the property, its maintenance or the standard of education to be provided.

In this half-hearted way government first acknowledged a responsibility for education; even more important, as misgivings grew about the loose control of expenditure, the solution was seen to be the establishment of suitable political and administrative arrangements for supervision rather than the abolition of the grant aid. For this reason a Committee of the Privy Council was established, consisting of the Lord President, the Lord Privy Seal, the Chancellor of the Exchequer and the Home Secretary, whose function would be to supervise and control the disbursement of grant, assisted by a Permanent Secretary. From 1839, when the Committee was first established, procedures for the payment of grant were extended and modified gradually by rules laid down in the minutes which recorded the Committee's decisions. The scope of payments soon included current costs—books and materials, teachers' salaries, training— grant-aided on a capitation basis. Scholarships for fees and maintenance at teacher-training establishments were introduced, along with grant-aided pupil-teacher apprenticeships. The staff of the Education Office grew to forty-one by 1856 and the annual budget to £663,000 in 1857.

The initiative for much of this expansion in scope and scale came from the Committee's first Secretary, James Kay-Shuttleworth. Appointed before the creation of a general civil service, Kay-Shuttleworth had made his reputation as an investigator of social conditions, turning his attention to pauper education immediately before joining the Education Committee. Routine decisions were left to him; controversial matters were referred to the Lord President, who visited the Privy Council Office every day to deal with the business of any of its departments. The Committee itself met about once a month.

The appointment of peripatetic officials to investigate applications for grant, to monitor the use of grants and to inquire into educational matters had been one of the original provisions of the Order in Council that set up the new Privy Council Committee. It proved necessary to allow the Anglican Church a right of veto on appointments before it would allow inspection of its schools, and similar arrangements had to be made with other denominations. By the end of the 1850s there were seven different sets of inspectors for the various groups of school in England and Scotland. Inspectors and administrators, deploying funds voted by Parliament for use at the discretion of the executive rather than acting under any statutory powers, had to tread delicately among denominational sensitivities. As Kay-Shuttleworth's successor put it in the course of discussing improved arrangements for accountability to the House of Commons:

> The public with which the Department deals is not a political but a religious one, and a religious one in fragments. Take each fragment by itself, Church, Wesleyan, Roman Catholic, etc., and talk to any one of their leading men and you see in a moment how they dread and shrink from a system which subjects the congregation to any civic and undenominational power; no matter whether that power be the Vestry, Town Council, Board of Guardians, or the House of Commons. 'Find us the money and leave us to ourselves' is the prayer of each and all of them.

The statutory creation of the post of Vice-President of the Council to be the responsible Minister for education and the bringing together under his control of the staff of the Committee of Council and of the Science and Art Department (formerly controlled by the President of the Board of Trade) did not satisfy the House of Commons that the unpredictable and rapid increase in public expenditure on education was under control. The vast complexity of the grant system, the necessary generality of rules laid down in the form of minutes of committees and the difficulties arising from the fact that responsibility for initiative lay in the hands of promoters of school were all acknowledged by the Education Department. Certain changes were not implemented; for example, the Newcastle Commission, reporting in 1861, successfully proposed that payment of grant should be dependent upon the success of the pupils in examinations, with the intention of encouraging the most efficient expenditure, and that grant should be payable only to the managers of a school in order to encourage them to discharge their responsibilities fully. The Revised Code of 1862, embodying these recommendations, established the principles of the relationship between central government and the schools for the next thirty years, although the original rigours of 'payment by results' were considerably lessened by the 1890s. The direct relationship between teacher and central government was abolished, but the state's effective control over the content and scope of the curriculum reached its highest point during this period.

A similar but separate system of grant aid to promoters of schools had been established in Ireland in 1831 under the auspices of the Chief Secretary for Ireland, and this survived the English reform of the 1860s. Scottish education started to be separately administered with the creation of the local school board system. The Scottish Education Department, set up in 1872, was responsible to a separate committee of the Privy Council for Education in Scotland. Faced with 984 school boards, many of them providing only one school, the Department adopted an assertive educational role that still distinguishes it from its English counterpart.

In England the introduction of school boards created for the first time a substantial, local, popularly elected counterbalance both to national politics and to the denominations. The Elementary Education Act of 1870 also put an end to the denominational veto on the Inspectorate, whose work had already been transformed by the introduction of the Revised Code, necessitating the appointment of Inspectors' Assistants, who undertook much of the routine assessment of pupils. Now the Inspectors could be reorganised more economically on territorial rather than denominational lines. In 1870—1 there were seventy-six Inspectors and twenty-six Inspectors' Assistants; by 1899 the total Inspectorate numbered 352. The departmental staff also expanded while maintaining specialisation in the education of the senior grades and resisting assimilation to the general classes of the civil service.

Despite reform and despite expansion in the provision of schools under the new school boards, central supervision remained more confused and more fragmentary during the last thirty years of the nineteenth century than at any time since before 1839. There was no consensus over the questions of whether the Lord President was in charge of educational policy and the Vice-President was simply his assistant and spokesman in the House of Commons, whether the duties and responsibilities were equally shared, or whether the Vice-President was responsible *de jure* as he was *de facto*. Although one Minister might be in charge, three departments in different locations but with overlapping responsibilities (namely, the Education Department, the Science and Art Department at South Kensington and the Charity Commissioners) went their own way without regard for each other. In theory, the Department of Education was responsible for elementary education, the Science and Art Department for technical science and art education, and the Endowed Schools (later the Charity) Commission for legacies to and endowments of reorganised secondary schools. The main problem lay in the field of secondary education. The Education Department countenanced the growth of 'higher grade' schools under the school boards which were effectively secondary in character. The Endowed Schools Charity Commission had explicit statutory responsibility for assisting the provision of secondary education. Despite the amalgamation of the authorities responsible for elementary and technical education in 1856, the Science and Art Department continued to operate separately, making payments to teachers and pupils for success in examinations which it sponsored. Later grants were made to 'organised science schools'—that is to say, institutions which met the appropriate criteria and which, in the event, included a small number of endowed secondary schools and a larger number of 'higher grade' schools. With the creation of Technical Instruction Committees of county and county borough councils in the last decade of the century, a further complication and source of potential duplication was introduced. It is hardly surprising that the Bryce Commission, reporting in 1895, proposed the creation of a single department under a Board of Education which could supervise and co-ordinate the three main types of education with which government was concerned. For the most part these proposals were implemented by the Board of Education Act 1899 and provided the administrative base for the last truly entrepreneurial Education Secretary, Robert Morant, to reform the structure of control in the localities with the backing of a Conservative Government and to attempt to mould and direct the expansion of secondary education. The 1904 Secondary Education Regulations, prescribing what would be officially recognised as a balanced secondary curriculum, laid great emphasis on English, the arts, mathematics and modern languages. The 1907 Free Place Regulations opened up fee-paying secondary schools to the more able elementary school pupil, and, in response to the recommendations in 1909 of the new Consultative Committee for compulsory day continuation schools, Morant introduced a plan of further education aimed at education for 'industrial citizenship'. Inside the Board Morant created elementary, secondary and technical branches and established a separate Welsh Department from 1907, with its own Permanent Secretary and Inspectorate. This last was all that survived of the proposal for a National Council for Education in Wales that had been put forward at intervals for nearly half a century. Lloyd George had pressed the case for a National Council in the debates on the Education Act 1902. When Augustine Birrell's 1906 Bill attempting to alter the settlement of 1902 was withdrawn, Section 4, which provided for a Council of Education for Wales, fell with it. The Bruce Report of 1920 again advocated a National Council but without success. At the administrative level, however, the distinction was made, and the combination of a Welsh Education Department and Welsh local education authorities were enabled to promote a separate Welsh identity in educational policy. The first Chief Inspector for the Welsh Education Department, O. M. Edwards, was an enthusiastic promoter of Welsh language and culture in the schools: 'the gradual emergence of a bilingual policy was due to the initiative taken by the Welsh Department, through its inspectors, and not by the Local Education Authority' (Davies, 1973, p. 153).

The English and Welsh reforms of 1899 and 1902 did not apply in Ireland and Scotland. The Scottish Education Department set up in 1872 failed for a long time to satisfy Scottish aspirations to a separate identity, since it was located in Whitehall and had the same President, Vice-President and Permanent Secretary as the Education Department for England and Wales. It was 1885 before a Secretary for Scotland (the more elevated rank of Secretary of State was introduced only in 1926) who was also Vice-President of the Scottish Education Department was created, with cross-party agreement. At the same time a separate Permanent Secretary was appointed, who continued to be based in London until 1921, when effective administrative power was finally concentrated in Edinburgh.

In Ireland administrative change was forced on education by partition in 1921 and by the subsequent establishment of a provincial legislature in Ulster, with its own Ministry of Education and Education Department. Such a department could have attempted to create its own distinctive philosophy and practice of education; in the event, after an attempt to set up a unified system which satisfied neither Protestants nor Catholics, on matters of administrative control and religious instruction it yielded to Protestant pressure, and on other questions of educational development, as befitted a politically unshakeable Unionist government, it looked consciously and explicitly to educational policy in England for guidance. If official policy in Northern Ireland had any thrust of its own during the first fifty years of the province's existence, it was in the promotion of local education authorities as the bodies responsible for schools. This policy attracted a very wary but not a dismissive response from the Catholic hierarchy, which feared the anti-Catholic majority on local authorities. The Nationalist Party was even more sceptical and claimed that 'the interests of education and of improved community relations would best be served by the total removal of education from the sphere of local government.'

FROM INSTITUTION TO SYSTEM IN THE LOCAL AREA

The first local bodies to provide education in England, Wales and Ireland were the managing bodies of voluntary elementary schools, often the parish priests, Anglican or Roman Catholic. Only in Scotland were church and state effectively combined by statute, as early as the beginning of the eighteenth century, to fund, provide and monitor the work of schools in each parish. Even then the local landowners, or heritors, who were responsible for providing funds might seek to reduce or avoid responsibilities forced on them by statute and urged on them by the presbyteries. In the larger towns, or burghs, the Reformation brought control of ancient grammar schools within the jurisdiction of the municipalities, though often after a struggle with the leaders of the reformed Kirk. Such town councils discouraged competition for their schools from private establishments of whatever character and even enforced school attendance by threat of fines. South of the border the private endowment of schools for poor scholars was far commoner than public enterprise, and the eighteenth century saw the general decay of such municipal authorities as existed.

When the school boards were established after 1870 there was no clear alternative to the creation of a system of *ad hoc* authorities. The existing system, 'being a mere partnership with educational volunteers, leaves undone all the work which the volunteers do not care to undertake', but it could not be replaced by direct provision by central government for fear of both Whitehall tyranny and the massive problems of administering local detail from the centre. Parishes and municipal boroughs could provide the local unit for administration, and the original intention was that the boards would be indirectly elected by town councils in the borough and by the vestries in the parishes. The strength of opinion in the House of Commons led the Government to accept direct elections by ratepayers, each with votes equal to the number of places on the board and each able to distribute them among as many or as few candidates for election as he or she chose. This cumulative voting procedure was welcomed by minority groups, who were thus helped to secure representation on the boards.

The boards typified nineteenth-century *ad hoc* local administration of services, which included public health, sewage and the Poor Law in addition to education; and the permissive powers granted to the boards characterised the tentative contemporary response to urgent social demands. The Education Department determined whether or not a board was necessary on the basis of information about the deficiency of school places in a locality or petitions from local electors. The size of the board established once a successful case had been made might range from five to fifteen people, depending on the population of the area.

The new local education authorities were empowered to appoint officials and to determine their salaries. The position of Clerk to the Board was the chief administrative office, providing the first opportunity for the slow development of a cadre of local professional administrators in education. The larger school boards needed to delegate some of their functions to subcommittees for finance or building. Some boards delegated much of their authority to bodies of managers, while others maintained close and direct control through their central office. London and Liverpool developed extensive systems of school managers; Leeds preferred not to insert a further lay element between board officials and head teachers. Traditions established in this way under the school boards often survived long after the substitution of county and county borough councils as local education authorities.

Over a thousand school boards were created in Scotland after 1872, many of them, as in England and Wales, assuming responsibility for only one school. The Scottish solution diverged from the English in providing for the inclusion of voluntary schools in the boards' remit and power of financial support from the rates. Although it was not until 1918 that the Roman Catholics were prepared to hand over their schools to public authority, the system of *ad hoc* authorities in Scotland survived the English reform of 1902, and only in 1929 did education become one of the functions of multi-purpose authorities. Attempts to reduce the number of Scottish school boards in 1905 and 1908 failed, but in 1918 *ad hoc* education authorities, elected by proportional representation, were set up for the thirty-eight counties and burghs in Scotland; the 947 school boards were abolished and their 5000 members reduced to under a thousand public representatives on the new committees. This was only an interim and second-best solution for the Scottish Education Department and for the teachers, whose representatives had recommended the eventual absorption of education responsibilities under the counties. Such a proposal was put before Parliament, but the protests of the school boards and the willingness of the teachers' union to consider a transitional solution led to substantial revisions of the Bill by government as it went through Parliament.

Those in favour of the administrative change in Scotland argued that education authorities needed to be responsible for wider areas and more schools if they were to acquire and retain expertise that could adequately support the work of the schools. To such economies of scale would be added economies of co-ordination if the education function were taken over by the existing multi-purpose local authorities (who were already involved in secondary school provision). Whatever the objective validity of such arguments, ranged against them were the vested interests of the existing school boards, large and small, which emphasised the importance of local interest and involvement. The compromise effected by the Education Act (Scotland) 1918 included provision for management committees for schools or groups of schools in an attempt to retain local interest. But interest in management committees died away as it was seen that the new country-side education authorities did not intend to delegate any substantial power to them. Electoral interest in the new education authorities themselves was also limited, and it was some time before government proposals to absorb these *ad hoc* bodies into the county and burgh authorities, advanced in 1928, provoked any substantial opposition. Even so, the integration took place under the Local Government Act 1929.

Scotland had not abandoned the *ad hoc* principle, as had happened in England at the turn of the century; with the unification of local educational control in 1918 in the hands of the *ad hoc* authority and in 1929 in the hands of multi-purpose local authorities, Scotland was again out of step. For the resistance of school boards to extinction, which in Scotland had led to the creation of more or less impotent school management committees, had in England produced authorities for elementary education only from among the larger second-tier councils in county areas, under Part III of the Education Act 1902. Thus the creation of a unified and progressive public education system in many areas was prevented not only by the existence of different codes of regulations for elementary and secondary schools but also by the division of responsibility which fragmented any comprehensive planning process. In the 1940s it was again the intention of the proposers of the Education Bill to abolish two-tier government of education in the counties, and only the pressure of elementary education authorities led to the establishment of excepted districts and divisional executives to articulate local views as the residuary legatees of the Part III authorities. Although the cry has often been for local involvement in the running of schools, Government compromise has always conceded to the shape of existing interests rather than to any logic of participatory democracy.

The new provincial government in Northern Ireland represented the opposing trend, for it placed responsibility for education for the first time in the hands of public local bodies, the county and county borough councils, who were to administer the service either through one education committee for their whole area or through a number of education committees, each for a specific district. The hope was that the many denominational schools would be transferred to the local education authorities, but the political dominance of the Protestant majority of Ulster in nearly all local authorities deterred the Catholics from co-operation. The adequacy of the supply of secondary schools, under the various funding arrangements made prior to partition, left the new local education authorities with little opportunity to assert their role by making new provision. By 1947 only nine of the seventy-five reorganised grammar schools were managed by education authorities, but some 195 new elementary schools had been built and many other transferred schools substantially improved. The Education Act (Northern Ireland) 1947, in its educational provisions, was modelled on the English Education Act of three years before; there was little change in the local administration of education, except for the abolition of the power to set up more than one education committee in a county area.

In all parts of Britain the creation of school boards and then of education committees of local education authorities stimulated the growth of a new profession of educational administrators. The officials of the Board of Education were assimilated to the general classes of the Civil Service in 1919, so that apart from Her Majesty's Inspectorate and the teachers there was no source of expert administrative advice other than the local government officer serving the education committee of counties, county borough and Part III elementary education authorities and members themselves. Although many of the smaller school boards relied on their members for educational expertise, employing clerks for routine administration and seeking appropriate legal advice when necessary, some of the large school boards did employ clerks with a background in education. Glasgow's clerk, William Kennedy, was a teacher of long experience. In London G. H. Croad, a Cambridge graduate who had taught at Rossall School for ten years before becoming an administrator, served as clerk for almost the whole life of the metropolitan school board. Even so, expertise was assumed and often found among the board members themselves, and no employee was likely to be considered an authoritative source of educational judgement.

Education committees set up by local authorities under the permissive powers of the Technical Instruction Act 1889 took a similar view. Beatrice Webb, whose husband played a leading part in the work of the London Technical Education Board, commented in her diary: 'It is, perhaps, a sign that the County Council is still young that the whole direction of its administration is in the hands of the councillors and not relegated to paid servants. There are twenty or thirty men who make a profession of the Council.' In the West Riding of Yorkshire five or six members of the Technical Instruction Committee dominated policy and administration. When their activities expanded to embrace the whole field of public education after the coming into force of the Education Act 1902, they did set about appointing a Director of Education but their choice, a former civil servant from the Board of Education, only lasted a year before an apparent clash of personality and perspective led to his resignation. No replacement was appointed until 1929.

Other authorities were more successful in their appointments, and the educational developments of the early twentieth century are often seen to bear the marks of a pioneering administrator rather than those of a visionary education committee. William Brockington, appointed Director of Education for Leicestershire in 1903 after an earlier career as academic and headmaster, remained in his post for forty-four years, during which time the entire educational system of the county was radically reorganised. During Brockington's working life the status of the chief education officer was clearly established as equal to that of any other local government officer in his capacity as adviser to the education committee and as initiator as well as implementer of many of the educational policies of the local authority.

As the role of the education office expanded, so the function of co-optation subtly changed. Technical Instruction Committees had brought in expertise in this way. The new education committees after 1902 did the same but were likely to co-opt those who, in addition, had a vested interest in the provision of education, the Churches in particular. In strong nonconformist areas such as the West Riding this sort of co-optation was strongly resisted, but in time, as the status of teachers rose, it became common to add their representatives to the committee. Although the wording of present legislation echoes the earlier justification for co-optation, in practice the emphasis is clearly on the representation of interests affected by the policies of the local education authority.

Between the two world wars there were many developments in the provision of education, but they were often marred by the vagaries of public finance, confined to one or a few local education authorities and vulnerable to attack from unsympathetic councils; the Board of Education was only empowered to 'supervise', not to lead or direct. Ideas raced ahead of resources, both financial and political, but perhaps the period served to consolidate much opinion behind the strategic reforms embodied in the Education Act 1944 and to develop some of the administrative mechanisms necessary to the provision of education as a national service. Into this latter category fell the introduction of percentage grant to local education authorities, the establishment of national negotiating arrangements for teachers' salaries, the Burnham Committee and the national co-ordination of school-leaving examinations through the Secondary Schools Examinations Council. The Consultative Committee of the Board of Education, set up under the Education Act 1902, provided a focus for a good deal of thinking about future developments. In 1926 it reported on the 'Education of the Adolescent', advocating the creation of separate schools for those over the age of eleven. In 1938 the Spens Report elaborated on the system of secondary schools which might best serve various needs.

CHAPTER 2

The Central Government

THE STATUTORY POWERS AND DUTIES OF THE SECRETARY OF STATE

The 1944 Education Act created a Minister (since 1964 renamed Secretary of State) whose duty under Section 1 is 'to promote the education of the people of England and Wales and secure the effective execution by local authorities under his control and direction of the national policy for providing a varied and comprehensive educational service in every area'. The Minister's role goes far beyond that assigned to the President of the Board of Education, 'to superintend and co-ordinate' the activities of the local education authorities. At the very least, Section 1 set the tone for a new relationship between local education authorities and the Minister. One criticism levelled at the then President of the Board of Education when he piloted the Bill through Parliament was that he was seeking dictatorial powers; in answer, he argued the necessity of providing an adequate service and the desirability of ensuring reasonable minimum standards throughout the country. Checks on the excessive use of power were built into the Act by assigning to local education authorities their own powers and duties which would require a co-operative working relationship between the central and local agencies if the Act were to be effectively implemented.

The general powers under Section 1 would not have carried much weight in the courts if they had not been reinforced by a host of other quite specific powers vested in the Minister. These included the power to issue regulations concerning school milk and meals (Section 49), the education of pupils requiring special provision (Section 33), the standards of school premises (Section 10) and grants for educational services (Section 100). However, the

21

promulgation of all such regulations must follow a procedure whereby they are placed before Parliament for a period of forty days, during which they may be annulled by an adverse vote of either House of Parliament. As an ultimate sanction of central government, under Section 99 the Minister is able to order a local education authority to fulfil a statutory duty; this order can be enforced through the courts by a writ of mandamus, which must be granted unless technically defective. Section 93 enables the Minister to make direction for a local inquiry, and Section 42 requires local education authorities to submit schemes of further education for his approval as part of the expected programme of post-war development. Section 13 makes the Minister adjudicator on appeals by objectors to local authority plans for the opening or closing of schools. This role has been extended by Education Act No. 1 1968, so that the appeals procedure also operates if there is any significant change in the character of the school. While the Minister is often able in these ways to intervene or to respond to any local controversies and crises brought to his attention, in respect of some parts of educational provision the law makes the Minister both prime mover and financial arbiter of policy carried out by local authorities, which are virtually his agents rather than his partners. Section 62, which enables the Minister to determine the supply and education of teachers, exemplifies this most clearly. (See Postscript for changes introduced by 1980 Education Act.)

One can see within this battery of powers not only executive but also delegated legislative power. In so far as the Minister exercises discretion over appeals, he exercises adjudicatory powers. His power to settle disputes between other 'partners' (Section 67) and his powers under Section 68 to stop a local authority from acting unreasonably could be described as quasi-judicial. However, the legal position of the Minister in exercising discretion has been tested in recent years in the courts, which have concluded that his powers are not absolute but are only to be exercised within the general framework of the law, which gives the courts jurisdiction to ensure that the Minister does not exceed or abuse his statutory authority. A series of recent court actions involving the Enfield and Tameside authorities have shed more light on the scope and character of the Secretary of State's discretion. Most important, in the actions concerning the London Borough of Enfield it was established that the Secretary of State must carry out a meaningful procedure when dealing with appeals against the decisions of local education authorities. In the more recent Tameside case of 1976 it was the view of the Court of Appeal and the House of Lords that the Minister's exercise, under Section 68, of power to intervene where he considered a local authority to be acting unreasonably was itself subject to a test of reasonableness. Lord Denning, in the Court of Appeal, stated that the Minister must direct himself properly in law and that his decisions must be reasonable. The words of Lord Wilberforce in the House of Lords are significant: 'Section 68 is not simply a matter of ministerial discretion. The power given is to review the action of another public body which itself has discretionary powers and duties.' Lord Scarman, also in the Court of Appeal, noted that what was under review was a dispute between two elected authorities, the local authority and the elected government. The local authority was entitled to have its decision treated with the same respect as the Minister's: 'It was not for the Court to substitute its view for the Minister's, but it was also the law that the Minister could not substitute his views for the education authority's, provided the authority had acted reasonably.' This judicial ruling certainly confirms the reality of a 'partnership' between central government and local authority rather than a simple master/servant relationship; it confirms too the effectiveness of the courts as a check on arbitrary executive power.

One commentator (Taylor, 1976) has posed the question: 'Does this judgment significantly reduce the authority of the "senior partner"?' Previously it had been assumed that Section 1 conferred on the Minister the right to determine national policy. Furthermore, it had been assumed that other sections of the Act (for example, Sections 65, 68, 93 and 99) gave him the power to enforce his rights. But as Diplock (Times Law Report, Oct 22nd 1976) puts it: 'The Act does not leave the national policy to be determined by successive Secretaries of State. Where authorities have statutory discretion the Minister cannot substitute his opinion for theirs.' Even so, Taylor concludes, the unqualified statutory duties of a local education authority are few, and it would be a mistake to assume that the powers of the Secretary of State have been seriously diminished by the Tameside case. The Secretary of State has at least three substantial powers vested in him by Parliament—to issue regulations, to settle national policy in cases in which the exercise of local discretion specifically requires ministerial confirmation and to determine policy directly, as exemplified in the reorganisation of teacher education. Indeed, the Minister has been able to rearrange the whole of further and higher education without further legislation.

THE ADMINISTRATIVE STRUCTURE AND STAFFING OF DEPARTMENTS RESPONSIBLE FOR EDUCATION

Sustained by his substantial legal powers, the Secretary of State has at his disposal the official resources of a major policy-making Department. The powers and duties of a Secretary of State are rarely exercised in isolation from his Department, much of the work of which is concerned with advising the Minister and administering decisions directly on his behalf (see Figure 2.1). Diagrammatic illustration or verbal explanation of the current structure of the Department of Education and Science (DES) tells us something about the way in which its work is organised, although the detailed pattern is by no means immutable. Changes are frequently made in line with changing functions and priorities, but the hierarchical organisation—Department, branches, divisions—remains constant. The nomenclature of senior officials may change, as do titles of Ministers, but the hierarchy of rank in the Department follows the proposals of the Fulton Report on the Civil Service. Two major developments followed from this Report in all departments first, the abolition of the division of the Civil Service into three classes, administrative, executive and clerical, allowing increased mobility within the service; second, wider opportunity to enter the service at all levels.

The DES has been the central agency for educational planning in both England and Wales, but in the principality first schooling (in 1970) and then all other aspects of non-university education (in 1978) were devolved to the Welsh Office as adviser to the Secretary of State for Wales. All public education in Scotland, apart from university matters, has come under the Scottish Secretary and Education Department for many years. With the suspension of the separate Parliament and devolved government of Northern Ireland, the Secretary of State for Northern Ireland has taken full responsibility for all aspects of education through the continuing Department of Education in Belfast. All four Secretaries of State are members of the Cabinet, and the Departments necessarily consult one another at

FIG. 2.1 The Department of Education and Science: Organisation at January 1977

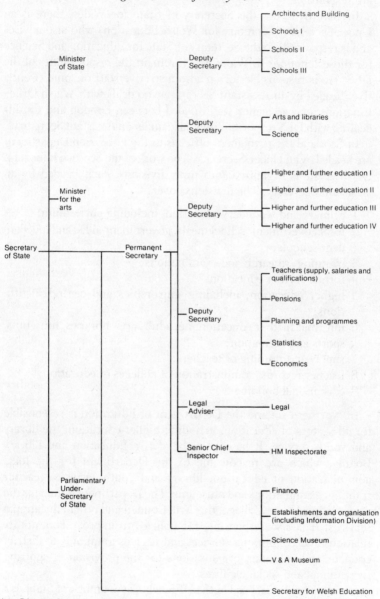

Note: Primary and secondary education in
Wales are the responsibility of the
Secretary of State for Wales.

ministerial and official level on educational matters for which they are responsible.

In Cardiff, under the Secretary of State for Wales, there is an Under-Secretary (Secretary for Welsh Education) who also advises and is responsible to the Secretary of State for Education and Science for those functions in Wales which remain the responsibility of the DES. He is responsible for an administrative staff of some twenty-five, headed by an Assistant Secretary who deals with Welsh Office functions, and a smaller staff divided between London and Cardiff dealing with DES responsibilities, also under an Assistant Secretary.

In Scotland the permanent officials in the Education Department are headed by an Under-Secretary. The work of the Scottish Education Department is organised into nine divisions, each headed by an Assistant Secretary. The divisions cover:

1 primary and secondary education, including curriculum;
2 local government, school meals, government-aided and independent schools;
3 planning, research and examinations;
4 formal further education;
5 higher education, including universities and central institutions;
6 informal further education, i.e. adult, arts, libraries, museums, sports and recreation;
7 supply and training of teachers;
8 teacher records, administration of colleges of education;
9 educational buildings.

In Northern Ireland the Department of Education is responsible for all sectors of education, including higher education, the library and youth service. It has oversight of five Education and Library Boards, which are responsible to the Department for the local administration of education, library and youth services, teacher training, examinations and museums. The Department grant aids the universities, Ulster College, the Arts Council and other educational services. It is also responsible for policies to improve community relations and community service, and it gives grant aids to district councils and voluntary organisations for the provision of sporting recreational and social facilities.

Under the political head of the DES, who, as Secretary of State, is a middle-ranking member of the Cabinet, there are three further offices of political leadership. One Minister of State covers the Department's responsibility for policy towards the arts; another is primarily concerned with policy for schools; and a Parliamentary Under-Secretary takes responsibility for further and higher education. Compared with many departments of state operating in the social field, the DES has only a small staff (about two and a half thousand in 1979). Few executive functions of the education service are carried out directly by the Department, whose officials are largely concerned with reacting to and regulating the initiative of executive bodies such as the local education authorities, or developing policy initiatives which others will have to interpret and carry out. The power of the Secretary of State derives from his influence over resources, his regulating function and his status as the senior partner in the education system who is looked to increasingly for decisive action by the public, rather than from frequent use of his various reserve powers of intervention and direction. His Department does, however, effectively control the building programme and the supply and training of teachers. Although the system of general grant from central government to local authorities prevents the Secretary of State from earmarking any substantial sum to provide for education, he does have a considerable role to play in the annual negotiations which determine the level of financial assistance given to local authorities to enable them to fulfil their responsibilities for the provision of educational services.

The Scottish Education Department, with similar legal powers, has exploited them to the fullest extent to intervene and regulate the activities of the weaker, generally smaller and often submissive local education authorities of Scotland. Until very recently a Code determined in fine detail many of the routine activities of schools, and even now the Schools General (Scotland) Regulations (1975) provide continuing opportunity for traditional departmental leadership.

Welsh tradition in central educational administration is rather different; the Welsh Joint Education Committee, as well as being an examining body and the equivalent of the English regional advisory councils for further education, brings together all the Welsh local education authorities in a forum which can express and convey to the Secretary of State for Wales the direction and force of local feeling about educational policies. If there is a unique tradition in the Welsh Education Office, it is not so much its style of leadership as the commitment of its Inspectorate to the teaching of Welsh language.

The Northern Ireland Department of Education works in a style similar to that of the Scottish Education Department. It is strongly interventionist and even more clearly constitutionally entitled to supervise and direct in detail the activities of the five Education and Library Boards which are the nearest equivalent to local education authorities that Northern Ireland now has. Unable politically to grasp the nettle of denominationally divided schooling, which confirms community divisions, the Department in all other respects, not only since but also before the suspension of Stormont, has followed the English lead in matters of educational policy making.

A major function of the DES and its equivalent national Departments is the planning and influencing of levels and priorities in the distribution of public resources to the education service. The Department has no regional organisation, although some branches are organised on a territorial basis. Work is divided into four main areas: schools and educational building; higher education and further education; civil science, arts and libraries; and educational planning, which involves teacher supply, salaries, statistics and the economic aspects of planning. There are also common service branches for personnel, finance and legal matters. The four main areas are each supervised by a Deputy Secretary and subdivided into branches. The branches are usually headed by an Under-Secretary, who reports to a Deputy Secretary and the Permanent Secretary. Branches are further subdivided into divisions which are the responsibility of Assistant Secretaries. Supporting all the branches are junior officials in descending order of rank, from Principals and Higher Executive Officers to administrative trainees. Planning is jointly undertaken by operational branches, advisory services and the Planning Unit, which constitute the Department of Planning Organisation. A Deputy Secretary and a Chief Inspector form a link between the Department and Inspectorate in the planning process, the former responsible for the Planning Unit's statistics branch and the Department's economic staff, the latter responsible for the Department's contribution to educational research.

The professional commitment of the civil servant members of all these branches to their prime tasks cannot be doubted. One appraisal of the Department (OECD, 1975), which was very critical of many aspects of its educational policy-making and forward planning, nevertheless made it clear that in some respects its performance was unimpeachable:

The Ministry . . . is staffed by a corps of permanent civil servants well trained and experienced in practiced efficiency . . . They exercise, in consequence, influence over the evolution of educational policy in this country at least equal to that of ministries of education that enjoy far more constitutional authority. (p. 28)

The central Department of Education and Science is undoubtedly the most important single force in determining the direction and tempo of educational development. (p. 28)

The permanent officials in the tradition of British civil servants are non-political in their function. In no country, it is safe to say, does the Civil Service govern itself more closely by a code of loyalty to whatever Government is in power. (p. 29)

The British nation has been served by a continuing stream of knowledgeable and experienced officials with strong tradition for discipline, fidelity and morale, and chosen for their individual merits not their political allegiance. (p. 29)

The prestige, acquaintanceship and natural authority of leading civil servants give them a standing in the civil forum often superior to their *de jure* political superiors. They are, in the continental phrase, 'notables' whose opinions must be given special weight, whether or not votes in the next election will be affected. (p. 29)

The Secretary of State and permanent officials have different jobs, but for the most part they work as a team to uphold the public interest as they see it. To suggest that officials exercise an overt political bias or consciously attempt to usurp the power of their political masters would be a crude over-simplification and a distortion of reality. However, this is not to deny the growing power of the Civil Service. It can be argued that as Ministers' burdens increase, their effective powers are diminishing. Since 1945 the average tenure of office of Ministers of Education has been twenty months and that of junior Ministers even less, comparing very unfavourably with the Permanent Secretaries, who may spend half a lifetime in the Department and, on average, have held their office for over six years. Crowther-Hunt points out that there were 50,000 civil servants in 1900 with sixty Ministers, whereas currently there are 750,000 civil servants, controlled by just over a hundred Ministers. He expresses the fear that the calibre of Ministers and other Members of Parliament may have declined, while the expertise and ability of the enlarged Civil Service becomes increasingly formidable.

Whether in respect of cases that must be decided with the Minister's authority or of issues of general policy, the permanent staff of the Department has at its disposal a mass of information—fact and precedent—to deploy in support of certain courses of action and against others. The provision of advice which is at the heart of the work of a senior civil servant necessarily involves judgement and values, professional and personal. How could it be otherwise? And who would want to recruit, train and deploy very able men only to prevent them from giving the Minister the full benefit of their advice? And yet a Cabinet Minister as able and as dominating as Richard Crossman recorded his own sense of frustration with senior officials and his suspicion that they did not respond with alacrity when ministerial decisions conflicted with departmental views.

The sheer volume of work which a new, inadequately prepared and short-lived Secretary for Education has to face may leave him bogged down in the detail of cases and the incessant flow of meetings at the expense of involvement in policy formulation. Thus Ministers are often faced with recommendations that are difficult to dispute in the limited time they have to master a brief that will have taken many highly skilled man hours to prepare. Again, civil servants are situated at every nexus of decision-making and have the advantage of observing the fate of policies across the lifespan of governments and Parliaments. While a Minister is still attempting to come to terms with his new responsibilities, there is an opportunity for permanent officials to resurrect and resubmit their favourite policy options, of whose earlier rejection by the previous administration the incoming regime is kept in ignorance on constitutional grounds. The growing network of inter-departmental committees and linkages, often in association with policies for policy co-ordination and review, may leave a Minister ill-informed and may pre-empt the performance of his traditional function of political brokerage.

Counter to this analysis is posed the continuing loyalty of civil servants to their political masters and the historically attested effectiveness of such Ministers of Education as Sir Edward (now Lord) Boyle and the late Anthony Crosland. The professional loyalty of civil servants is not in doubt, but it seems unwise to rely entirely on the personal characteristics of successive Ministers to shore up a constitutional relationship — total ministerial responsibility and anonymous Civil Service advice — that is, arguably, increasingly ill-suited to present-day administration and political realities. If the expertise and judgement of civil servants is still to be tapped, if Ministers are seriously to engage in policy-making and to be held accountable for it, and if Parliament is to exercise its traditional powers of scrutiny of the executive in effective ways, then some change must come and education has little to lose, much perhaps to gain.

If the Secretary of State cannot positively control all details of the implementation of policies for which he is nominally responsible, he does have a power of veto over all decisions emanating from the Department, and he will try to involve himself in policies which relate to party commitments, the reallocation of resources and issues liable to provoke public controversy.

POLICY-MAKING AND PLANNING

Policy is difficult to define. In one sense it includes routine decisions, the consideration of appeals, the acceptance or rejection of specific closures of schools or changes in instruments and articles of government, as well as the clarification and modification of regulations about building standards or student grants. The impact in aggregate of such decisions may well be profound and long-lasting. Normally, however, when the term 'policy' is used it is presumed to refer to consciously undertaken changes of direction and priority in relation to the service as a whole. These may be exemplified by explicit changes in priority in resource allocation between sectors, the boosting of existing provision (for example, for in-service training) or a deliberate reappraisal of objectives. It is in this latter sense that attention will be focused on policy, although there can be no neat divide between major and minor policy decisions. What may at first appear no more than a routine and small-scale adjustment may be seen in retrospect to have heralded a complete change in the direction of government policy. Conversely, minor modifications in the interpretation of traditional policy may well be misunderstood as the first steps in radical change when, in fact, the decisions in question turn out to be consistent—and are intended to be so—with broad lines of policy in operation for decades.

In the same way it is difficult to locate the source or pinpoint the initiation of new policy. When does a mode of thinking or an ideological approach transform itself into a policy, a policy into specific commitments, commitment into unambiguous action? Certainly, it is not a simple matter of turning expressed views into implemented decisions. For example, when did the Labour Party become committed to comprehensive reorganisation, and at what point did that commitment become a policy? The difficulty in giving a simple answer to such questions illustrates the complexity of the questions posed. Perhaps policy is best summarised as a usually slow development of thinking that is translated gradually into commitment, although this does little more than caution us against precipitate conclusions about particular policy developments. Policy sometimes stems from party commitment reflected in a manifesto. There can be no doubt that the broad movement towards the comprehensive reorganisation of secondary schools in the 1960s was directly, if not uniquely, related to Labour's earlier commitment to abolish the eleven-plus examination but the fact that the Secretary of State sought to bring about the change through a request to local authorities in a circular indicated the discretion he retained over the style of implementation of the policy. It also indicated his appreciation of the significance of other powerful influences on policy. Anthony Crosland, Secretary of State at the time, was deeply aware of the power of the lobby in the education system, particularly the pressure of the local authority associations. He was also fully aware of the constraints placed on a reforming Minister by the legacy of existing school buildings and the decentralised character of educational administration.

Reflecting on one apparent major policy change, the high priority asserted for nursery education and in-service training in the White Paper *Education: A Framework for Expansion* (1972), one might conclude that this was the fulfilment of Conservative promises in the 1970 General Election campaign or the personal priorities of Mrs Thatcher. While this may not be inaccurate, it would leave out of account the climate of opinion created by the Plowden Report (1967) in relation to nursery education or the James Report (1972) on teacher training. The White Paper presented comprehensive forward plans for educational priorities for the following decade. It was instigated and published by a Conservative Government, but the preparation was undertaken by civil servants, who provided all the detailed calculations, information and advice upon which the Secretary of State ultimately determined her strategy. Such information had begun to be gathered and to be deployed under a previous Labour Government and different Secretary of State, and the White Paper may well have owed more to continuing preferences and priorities within the DES itself than to the impact of a new Minister. Only access to the archives will reveal to future historians the extent to which the White Paper manifested the broad priorities of the Department or the personal stamp of a determined and able Minister on neutrally selected information and advice about alternative policy emphases. A policy change may stem from many sources — the campaigns of lobby groups, the findings of research, the recommendations of major reports, the commitments of political parties, the personalities or predilections of different Ministers — but the advice of permanent officials and the respect usually afforded to the informed opinion of the Department are likely always to be major factors in the determination of policy.

Sometimes outside influences will coincide in such a way that certain changes are almost inevitable. Frequently there will be little disagreement between parties about the mainstream of policy for continuation or change. The policies outlined in the 1972 White Paper were hardly challenged by the then Opposition, which, as the Labour Government from 1974—9, modified them in terms of the timing of implementation but then only in response to a general policy of restraint in public expenditure rather than to frustrate the main goals of the White Paper or to reorder its priorities.

By no means is this to say that Ministers never reverse the policy of the previous administration. The present Government's assisted places scheme is the explicit re-introduction of links between state and independent schooling which the direct grant scheme, abolished by Labour, represented. Cabinet economic policy may leave officials with no option but implementation. Fluctuations in the economic condition of the nation may result in the abandonment of or, more likely, delay in the implementation of policies. The postponement in 1968 of the date by which the school-leaving age would be raised to sixteen was a direct consequence of the economic crisis of that year, which also led to the devaluation of the pound sterling. Civil servants are bound to respond to specific policy directives, whether they coincide with their own judgements or not; incoming and outgoing Ministers may well be given the same advice by their officials, which they then accept or reject, but they will not lightly ignore their officials or cast aside the results of careful planning in the Department.

Delays in providing extra resources for nursery education and the in-service training of teachers by the Labour Governments of 1974—9 were excused by reference to contemporary economic difficulties; a reduction in public expenditure, already manifest in education, was a major plank of economic policy in the Conservative Manifesto of 1979 and has consistently dominated the subsequent thinking of the incoming Conservative Secretary of State. Retrenchment is most likely to occur in areas of provision in which there is no statutory responsibility or existing commitment. The statutory responsibility outlined in Section 8 of the 1944 Education Act for the provision of 'sufficient schools and a comprehensive education service for children between the ages of 5 and 16' predetermines the direction of some three-quarters of all expenditure on education; sudden and extensive changes in resource allocation for large parts of the service are hardly possible. It follows that when immediate savings are required because of cut-backs in public expenditure they are most likely to occur in such areas as ancillary services, discretionary grants and non-vocational further education or as the consequence of a delay in the implementation of new policies with major cost implications. To extend retrenchment options further requires legislation, as with the currently proposed relaxation of the duties of local education authorities in respect of school meals.

A feature of educational policy-making is that policy innovations (particularly those which involve a reordering of priorities between sectors) often have a long gestation period. Many Ministers set policies in motion, only to see them come to fruition long after they have left office. By the same token, new Ministers soon appreciate that many areas of policy are well mapped out and that their influence over such policies may be limited to a slight change in emphasis or an increase in the rate of implementation. Labour Ministers between 1964 and 1970 gave high priority to further, higher and teacher education, which became marked in resource allocation by the end of the decade, but such a change required a slow, systematic and consistent re-ordering of expenditure priorities by a series of Ministers. On the other hand, the manner of expansion of higher education was very much influenced by one Minister's initial commitment to the so called 'binary policy', which quickly and dramatically affected the character of higher education to take a form distinctly different from that proposed by the Robbins Committee in 1963.

However they may wish to change the character of the system, all

Ministers are aware of the need to work in partnership within a pluralist system. This may affect the pace of innovation or the tone and style of the presentation of new policy if the co-operation of teachers and local authorities is required for speedy implementation. It is common practice for the Minister to send drafts of key circulars to teachers' unions and local authority associations for consultation before final publication. The government's policy may well be dependent upon co-operation with its powerful partners, and it will be wary of generating collective opposition; this consideration accounts in part for Crosland's tactful 'request' for plans to reorganise secondary education on comprehensive lines in Circular 10/65. Until the 1976 Education Act (repealed in 1979) local authorities could not be compelled to reorganise, but the Department could exert pressure on particular local authorities to secure compliance—for example, by veto of any school building proposals which ran contrary to Government policy. Even then, some local authorities succeeded, openly or covertly, in delaying the full introduction of comprehensive schools until a change of government ended the pressure for reorganisation.

Jeremy Bray (1970) refers to stages and levels of decision-making, suggesting that policy formation should follow a pattern involving a policy review to reappraise and determine long-term goals, which should lead in turn to action programmes or policies to achieve these goals. At the next stage operational decisions would be taken supporting action programmes. The logic of stages and levels of decision-making is a most useful model to follow in developing policy. It can be used to analyse the formation of some past educational policies, but it is as much a prescription for a logical sequence in policy development as a description of normal practice. There are, in fact, many policies, some of major significance, which spring from *ad hoc* decisions by the Minister that follow no obvious pattern but represent a response to immediate political pressure or current economic conditions. Student grants and teachers' salaries are likely to be subject to such forces, yet in these instances *ad hoc* decisions may well set a precedent and become a part of established policy when the political and economic climate is completely different. The Labour Government's decision, outlined in Circular 1/77, to charge students in advanced further education something nearer the full economic cost for courses, which has been more recently confirmed and extended by the Conservative Government elected in 1979, is to be regarded as an austerity measure, but it may be carried forward as conventional policy, without proper analysis now or later of its educational implications, although the initial reason for restriction may have long since disappeared. Mrs Thatcher's decision, taken when she was Secretary of State from 1970—4, to prevent the automatic provision of free school milk for primary school children over the age of seven was possibly part of a broader policy to release resources for other areas of educational expenditure; although bitterly criticised by Labour in Opposition, the policy was continued by the successor Labour Government, with only minor modification. Labour Government policy may be explained by the lack of resources to restore that part of the service; however, it is not difficult to imagine that once the policy has become well established, it will remain, irrespective of economic circumstances.

Education is not normally at the centre of the political arena; there is no contemporary polarisation of opinion equivalent to the denominational issue of the nineteenth and early twentieth centuries, although the last ten years have seen an erosion of the political consensus on educational policy that characterised the first twenty years after the Second World War. No doubt this is because there are substantial policy differences between the parties; education cannot expect to be divorced from the general values and processes that characterise democratic government in Britain.

Educational planning in Britain before the 1960s was piecemeal and haphazard; a White Paper such as *Technical Education* in 1956 was an attempt to isolate a problem, project future development, determine priorities and estimate the cost of proposals. Such exercises did not cover the range of educational activities, nor was there any machinery to evaluate systematically competing demands for resources between departments of state. The tradition, by no means extinct, was to respond to events. Priorities reflected the weight of public demand, the volume of vociferous pressure emanating from a multiplicity of sources, and this was reflected in a series of *ad hoc,* unco-ordinated policies. Planning was based on loose, broad aims, whose detailed interpretation was constantly at the mercy of fluctuating economic conditions.

The Plowden Report (1961) on the management and control of public expenditure moved the government of the day to take the first steps towards creating contemporary machinery for public expenditure planning. Within the DES it was only in 1967 that a small planning branch was established which was ultimately to produce planning papers on output budgeting and on demand for places in higher education up to the 1980s. 1970 saw the introduction of Programme Analysis Review (PAR), a technique for selectively reviewing aspects of policy in terms of specified objectives in order to evaluate existing policy and to consider alternative strategies and their implications. Soon after, in 1971, another development took place which was indicative of the trend towards more systematic planning. The Department's planning branch was replaced by the Department of Planning Organisation, which was to consist of a policy steering committee, policy groups and a full planning unit. The steering committee, chaired by the Permanent Secretary, would include both the most senior officials of the DES and technical and analytical specialists; this team was to determine the nature and scope of planning, to decide on the timing of exercises and ultimately to receive the results of its initiatives before bringing them to the attention of the Minister. There are several policy groups, each headed by the Deputy Secretaries for the respective area of responsibility. These working groups include Inspectors and various economic, statistical and architectural specialists, as well as others who may be co-opted as needed by the group. Each group concentrates on major programmes and policies relating to schools or higher education, and the varied expertise within the group is brought to bear on different facets of policy, working through subgroups. The function of the planning unit, headed by an Under-Secretary, is to service the steering committee and working groups. The coincidence of the introduction of programme budgeting in the Ministry has enabled the Department of Planning Organisation to appreciate more fully the causes of increased expenditure, the cost consequences of existing policy and the cost of both increased demand for and improvement in the standard of services. Furthermore, costs now can be broken down to show their relationship to manpower, building, maintenance and so on. In short, the working groups have a much clearer picture of what policy choices mean financially and of the consequences of such choices for other aspects of expenditure.

So far, we have referred mainly to planning in the DES, but the planning of all public expenditure has been subject to radical change since the late 1960s, when estimates began to be presented as part of a rolling programme that is reviewed annually. The procedures for public expenditure planning and control operate in the following ways.

In early spring Departments submit estimates of projected

expenditure for the next five financial years to the Public Expenditure Survey Committee (PESC), chaired by a Treasury official. The Committee then groups and classifies the mass of projected expenditure into a report, to be completed normally by the middle of the year. There follow, at both ministerial and official levels, negotiations, proposals and counter-proposals, with the Cabinet ultimately resolving disagreement by determining the total level of public expenditure and priorities within it. At the beginning of the following year the results of this exercise are set out in the Annual Expenditure White Paper. Once the pattern for the coming year has been determined, attempts to increase expenditure are unlikely to succeed unless such increases are offset by comparable reductions in the same area of the estimates.

This system of Public Expenditure Survey (PES) is now well established, and the annual White Paper is debated at length in the House of Commons. Such debate may result in modification, but any changes tend to be reflected in the following year's review. The system incorporates the principle of estimating firmly for the coming year and reasonably accurately for the first three years, but the estimates for the final two years are imprecise, broad targets. This gives all concerned not a fixed plan but a firm statement of immediate spending intentions that is related to future calculations of expected demand for expenditure in all areas of government. The approach is flexible, allowing for immediate and long-term planning, which can be reappraised annually across the whole spectrum of government expenditure. It encourages appreciation of the fact that expenditure in one service has ramifications in others. It is a tool for planning the public sector of the economy, which can be re-programmed in the light of experience as more is learned about uncontrollable variables. The machinery acts as a check on spending Departments, enabling both them and politicians to make more informed choices.

Despite the apparent sophistication of this procedure, it is not a mechanism which forces Departments to relate objectives to overall Government policy or to subject departmental expenditure to analysis by objective. It does not provide a means of showing the Department, Parliament or the public how effective existing programmes are in terms of their intended purposes; nor does it attempt to explore cost-related analyses of alternative strategies or to highlight when and how different Departments are pursuing policies with a broadly similar aim, which would be more sensibly co-ordinated into a common programme. Nor, it has been argued, does it provide a very accurate guide to actual Government spending, which is much more sensitive to changes in demand (for example, social security expenditure in relation to unemployment) than to policy changes.

Such deficiencies became the concern of the Central Policy Review Staff, formed in 1970. Its function is to establish Government objectives in given areas of policy, to analyse all programmes which contribute towards such objectives, to trace all relevant allocations of resources and thus to evaluate the effectiveness of policy. The process requires the examination of expenditure in terms of a series of objectives and not simply of departmental budgets. The DES was one of the first Departments to adopt such an approach through the use of PAR. The adoption of these new planning procedures had made it possible for the decisions taken by Ministers to be less arbitrary, more informed and less susceptible to special pleading. Whatever its desirability, this could lead to more effective and systematic central control. The two procedures, PES and PAR, are complementary exercises. The chairman of the PESC also chairs the committee which co-ordinates the Programme Analysis Reviews (PARC) and proposes topics for investigation to be undertaken in Departments. Eventually, findings will be reflected in reports compiled by the relevant Departments and the Treasury for consideration by Cabinet committees; in the long term the data may be brought within the framework of the PES.

Despite improvements in planning procedures introduced in the 1970s, a critique by the Organisation for Economic Co-operation and Development (OECD) submitted in 1975, the Tenth Report of the Expenditure Committee (1976) and the Layfield Report (1976) have in their different ways added to public concern about the inadequacy of planning techniques and procedures in education.

Although impressed by the competence and integrity of civil servants and many of the new techniques for financial planning, the OECD examiners were, however, highly critical of a system which appeared to imply that goals for planning are fixed by tradition, demand and demography. They observed that most planning in our system is about means rather than ends, with an underlying presumption that if intermediate goals are sorted out, long-term goals will look after themselves.

The DES appeared to assume that planning should exclude the consideration of goals with political implications, as these were not the valid domain of paid officials. The examiners noted unnecessary and excessive secrecy, which in their view impaired the co-ordination of effort between 'partners' in the system. When the basis of a policy decision was not fully understood, they argued, it was not likely to be wholeheartedly accepted, and where secrecy obtained accountability diminished. British pride in a decentralised system which involved negotiation with many bodies might be misplaced; it was wrong to conclude that negotiation and participation were the same thing. The fact that we had no committee in Parliament shadowing departmental activities and that officials were not required to justify themselves to parties affected by their decisions was not consistent with full accountability. Accountability, participation and planning in terms of educational objectives stood out as matters of greatest concern in the opinions of the OECD examiners.

The Expenditure Committee reiterated these criticisms about unnecessary secrecy and the lack of involvement of sufficient outside interest groups in long-term planning. They felt that data used by the DES in educational planning should be more widely available and thus subject to discussion and debate. The Committee recommended that a Standing Education Commission, which might include representatives of both sides of industry and other parties interested in education, should be set up to bring more outsiders into the debate about goals and objectives. The Committee echoed the OECD comment that planners in the Department should spend more time on planning educational objectives and should not limit their activities to the allocation of resources. The Committee thought it significant that Parliament was never consulted by the Department or quoted by civil servants in their evidence as a body with which it consulted or negotiated. However, the OECD examiners were satisfied that recognised interest groups were sufficiently consulted, even though the broader public was not involved. The Layfield Committee on local government finance was concerned more specifically with the financial aspects of planning, and most of its comments referred to central government machinery overall rather than the Department of Education in particular. Its Report commented on the difficulty of corporate planning of central and local policies, given the annual renegotiation of the Rate Support Grant (RSG) settlement, the traditional quinquennial settlement of university revenue expenditure, the three-stage planning period for building programmes, the annual allocations of locally determined borrowing power and the varying dates through the financial year when key-sector loan sanction approvals were given. This made it difficult for local authorities to plan their priorities over any extensive period since they lacked full knowledge of resources available to them. For central government the PES of the coming five years did not synchronise with the planning period for different aspects of expenditure in education. Moreover, projected expenditure qualifying for grant in RSG negotiations did not necessarily coincide with previous Public Expenditure White Paper estimates.

The Layfield Committee was particularly concerned that although the function of the PES was to estimate future public expenditure, it was not designed as an effective tool to control it. Layfield concluded that a mechanism was necessary to harmonise the financial planning of local authorities with that of central government. Local authorities needed certainty over a period of years concerning the level of government subsidy and a more integrated timetable for grant determination related to local budgeting. The large number of local authorities created problems of communication and limited the effectiveness of the partnership. Layfield suggested that many of these problems could be offset by a new forum for discussion and negotiation between central and local officials and between Ministers and local authority members.

It is not difficult to pinpoint weaknesses in the system of planning for education. There are undoubtedly anomalies and inadequacies in the machinery for reflecting nationally determined policies in resource allocations or for ensuring that all trends and developments are the consequences of conscious and co-ordinated planning. Co-operation between local and national government is a process of bargaining between partly independent centres of power rather than any straightforward administrative determination of goals and co-ordination of efforts to achieve common purposes. In a 'national system locally administered', a definition which stresses the national—local links established as a partnership by custom as much as by law, it is inevitably difficult to harmonise fully or to plan coherently. Greater local autonomy could rationalise planning within local authority boundaries but might well increase disparities of provision. On the other hand, more precise long-term planning by central government could well erode all genuine discretion exercised by the other partners in education. The implementation of some of the recommendations of recent reports may obviate the most glaring inconsistencies but any fundamental restructuring of national planning for education may well be incompatible with the genuinely decentralised direction of the education service.

CURRICULUM CONTROL AND THE INSPECTORATE

The centre of educational concern must be the curriculum, whether narrowly defined as the available range of classroom subjects and syllabuses or, more widely, as the gamut of knowledge, skills and attitudes transmitted consciously by the school; and yet the distribution of responsibility under English law is widespread and ambiguously delineated. In Scotland the Scottish Education Department has clear overall responsibility; the Scottish Inspectorate takes the lead in curriculum innovation, if anything discouraging grass-roots initiative; and the national Consultative Committee on the Curriculum, staffed by the Department and chaired by its Permanent Secretary, brings together personal appointees of the Secretary of State from among teachers, college and university staff and the Inspectorate. The Welsh Joint Education Committee, policy forum and secondary school examinations board, is much less the instrument of the Welsh Secretary or the Welsh Education Department. The agency relationship of the education and library boards in Northern Ireland would place the provincial Education Department in a strong position to direct on curricular matters, were it not for the expression of a denominationally divided community in two distinct systems of schools. While the Welsh Inspectorate is strongly identified with the promotion of Welsh language teaching, the Irish language is taught only in minority Catholic voluntary schools in Northern Ireland. Most obviously, religious education is a critical element in the curriculum, its links with Irish nationalism reinforced by the different emphases in the teaching of history in state and Catholic schools. Strong central leadership on curriculum matters is unlikely in such emotionally charged circumstances; curricular unification is more likely to accompany or follow institutional integration if and when secondary reorganisation, tentatively encouraged by Labour Secretaries of State, ever takes place.

Statute in England and Wales gives responsibility for the curriculum to the local education authorities and, through them, to the governing bodies of individual schools. For perhaps the last time, in 1944 Parliament was preoccupied with the question of religious education when the Education Bill was under debate, and it is possible that other questions of curriculum were regarded as having been successfully subsumed within the commitment to universal primary and secondary education. Given the statutory protection to the Churches' freedom to instruct in doctrine in their schools, and the county schools' commitment to an agreed syllabus of religious instruction and a daily corporate act of worship, 'secular instruction' was not considered a matter for national government. But the general responsibility of the Minister for the education system, the increasing commitment of resources and the political climate have encouraged the seeking out of ways in which to influence curricular change from the centre. Ministers have had two long-standing instruments at their disposal, Her Majesty's Inspectors (HMIs) and the former Secondary Schools Examination Council.

The distinctive contribution of the English Inspectorate has much to do with the way in which it was created and the manner of its evolution. The current functions, characteristics and ethos of the Inspectorate can only be fully comprehended in historical perspective.

Established in 1839, the year in which the Committee of the Privy Council was formed, the Inspectorate was an attempt to provide a measure of accountability for money spent on education. Inspectors were appointed by the Queen in Council and from the outset asserted a surprising degree of independence of mind and willingness to make detached and, if necessary, unpalatable comment. Kay-Shuttleworth, the first Secretary of the Privy Council Committee, insisted from the start that the main function of Inspectors should be to offer assistance rather than to act as instruments of control over schools. Following the introduction of the Revised Code in 1862, their advisory role was overshadowed by their inspectoral function, souring relationships with teachers. However, the final elimination of 'payment by results', the opening up of recruitment to the Inspectorate and the growing perception by teachers of the Inspectorate as a valuable independent arbiter of educational standards to set against the judgements of their employers, the local education authorities, all helped to rebuild trust between teacher and Inspector and to allay fears of central intervention in the curriculum.

The present statutory powers over the inspection of schools are based upon Section 77 of the 1944 Act, which places a duty on the

Secretary of State to cause inspection, as and when he thinks necessary, of all educational establishments outside the universities. Under the same section of the Act local authorities are empowered to make inspection of their maintained establishments. Part III of the Act requires the registration of independent schools. The implement-ation of this duty has extended to the private sector the inspectoral functions of HMIs, whose recommendations determine whether or not such schools will be either 'registered' or 'recognised'. (See Postscript for changes introduced by 1980 Education Act.)

The Inspectorate operates in England, Wales, Scotland and Northern Ireland. Although working in close association, the regional branches do not operate as a single unified service, nor do they have quite the same traditions. The Inspectorate for England is responsible to the Secretary of State for Education for all parts of its work. The Welsh Inspectorate is at the disposal of the Welsh Office, and it operates as an integrated body with the Chief Inspector and eight Staff Inspectors, who are responsible for giving professional advice to the Secretary of State for Wales on nursery, primary, secondary, special, direct grant and independent schools. It is further responsible to the Secretary of State for Education and Science on other educational functions in Wales. The Northern Ireland Inspectorate comes under the Northern Ireland Education Department for all aspects of education, and it is headed by the Senior Chief Inspector and two Chief Inspectors. The Scottish Inspectorate reports directly to the Scottish Education Department.

In England the head of the Inspectorate is the Senior Chief Inspector, assisted by six Chief Inspectors, who share in formulating general policy for just under five hundred Inspectors. Most Inspectors are deployed in one of ten geographical divisions, each headed by a Divisional Inspector, while there are thirty-seven Staff Inspectors responsible for subject or phases of education throughout the country. Divisions are broken down into districts, with two District Inspectors in each local education authority responsible for schools and for further education. The main function of the District Inspectors is to liaise between the DES and the local education authority. Inspectors have general responsibility for a number of schools or colleges and specialist responsibility for the teaching of subjects or for an aspect of education. Many District Inspectors also combine their district responsibilities with both general and specialist functions. In a sense, one can refer to a basic organisation by geographical division and a separate but overlapping structure of specialisms under the regional Staff Inspectors.

Regional Staff Inspectors are, as it were, senior consultants, who can call on the expertise of the main body of the service through committees, panels and working parties where necessary. The Inspectorate undertakes research or collaborates with bodies such as the National Foundation for Educational Research, gives assistance to government advisory committees (for example, the National Council for Educational Technology or associations concerned with promoting higher standards in teaching a particular subject). Their expertise is also available to other departments of state, such as the Home Office or the Department of Employment. Advice and informative technical knowledge is transmitted through the ranks of the Inspectorate to the DES. There is also a substantial interchange of ideas within the network, through working parties, conferences and meetings. Through these channels an Inspector is given considerable latitude to express personal opinions, and this freedom of action must be combined with work, in small and large groups of colleagues, on various tasks and projects whose purpose is to supply the Department with information. Traditionally, much of the work of Inspectors has involved intermittent visits to individual schools and colleges, followed by a full inspection, undertaken by a group of Inspectors, every five years or so. The full inspection, though much less common, is not extinct, and all Inspectors value the opportunity to maintain contact with schools through fieldwork. The function of inspecting and monitoring standards is currently being re-employed and supplemented (by, for example, the recently created Assessment of Performance Unit). Some Inspectors have been associated with the Department of Planning Organisation in exercises scrutinising the application of resources to particular parts of the educational system. They are thus closely involved in departmental planning and the determination of priority and policy. These new departures do not mean that the Inspectorate has relinquished the task of advising, inspecting and disseminating information as colleague and partner in relation to both schools and local authorities. Despite its influence with teachers, local education authorities and the Department, it has no formal power of decision over educational practice, and its advice can always be ignored. It is very conscious that an effective role as the 'eyes and ears' of the Department has to be coupled with the respect and confidence of teachers and local education authorities.

Evidence submitted to the Select Committee on Education and
Science in 1968 by local authorities, teacher unions and other
interested parties highlighted conflicting opinions about the Inspectorate's role. Sir William Alexander, then Secretary of the Association
of Education Committees, wished to see a smaller elite of Inspectors,
while the Association of Teachers in Technical Institutions wished to
see the Inspectorate expand. Teachers' representatives, in particular,
suggested that full and formal inspection should be discontinued.
Nevertheless, there was a remarkable degree of agreement about the
value and competence of a professional body of men and women
whose role has changed with the education system, has always been
ambiguous and has never fitted neatly into the same category as other
government Inspectorates. While the Inspectorate continues to evoke
a positive response to its work from teachers and local education
authorites, its contributions to educational conferences, its increasing
flow of publications, its selection of in-service courses on offer and,
above all, its continuous informal links with educational practitioners
have forged a powerful weapon for central government to deploy in
pursuit of curriculum change. Crudely used, it would soon be blunted,
but as yet the Inspectorate has succeeded in maintaining some
substantial independence from the government of the day.

ADVICE AND CONSULTATION

The Secretary of State has other statutory sources of advice. The
Central Advisory Councils for England and Wales have performed
the function, traditional to British government, of bringing together
in a committee authoritative and representative persons who can take
evidence, assess it and produce a consensual report signposting some
particular area of policy development.

Official advisory bodies have two separate though related
functions—to provide information on the one hand and to give advice
on the other—although these functions are by no means their
exclusive monopoly. Government has many sources to draw upon
when it seeks to gather information and to obtain guidance. The
Department also has frequent contact with interested parties and
partners: for example, teachers' associations, local authority associations, denominational groups, the Committee of Vice-Chancellors
and Principals, and the Committee of Polytechnic Directors. These

contacts are used for exchanging advice as well as for negotiation. Although other lobby groups may not be within this quasi-official advisory network, bodies such as the Advisory Centre for Education and the Confederation for the Advancement of State Education are sometimes able to impress their advice on the Department directly or at one remove, through official advisory bodies to which they may submit evidence. It has been suggested that Central Advisory Councils 'enhance the progress of social discovery', a comment which might equally apply to some of the non-statutory bodies! Advisory bodies may add political weight to ideas thrown up by research, legitimise particular views by documenting evidence to support recommendations or reinforce attitudes to policies which are already in the process of formation. Reports of various committees and councils may bring into the public arena an understanding of concepts such as 'deprivation', 'equality of opportunity' or 'intelligence', modifying the balance of opinion in the ideological battles which have raged around these themes. The setting up of a committee can also provide government with the opportunity to delay decisions on new policy while appearing to take action, or may provide time in which to create a climate more receptive to initiatives that it wishes to take.

The advisory machinery, although constituted by central government to include interests that are already recognised and regularly consulted, also draws opinion and takes evidence from a much wider spectrum of opinion within education. Advisory bodies transmit voices and translate demands which may be growing in volume but which might otherwise be shut out from the established network of central government and its 'recognised' partners. They are valuable both as instruments of social control and as tools of social development.

The major advisory bodies include a number constituted by statute or statutory instrument. Under Section 4 of the 1944 Act permanent Advisory Councils were established and charged with the duty of advising the Minister 'upon such matters connected with educational theory and practice as they think fit and upon any questions referred to them by him'. The Act enabled the Minister to appoint the chairman and members of the committees for periods of office stipulated in regulations laid down by him, but required him to give an annual report to Parliament on the exercise of powers and duties imposed upon him by the Act and on the composition and proceedings of the Councils. Despite such clear prescription, the Central Councils have taken no initiatives of their own since the publication of their first three reports: *School and Life* (1947), *Out of School* (1948) and *Early Leaving* (1954). The three major reports produced since then by the English Council, *15 — 18* (Crowther Report, 1959), *Half Our Future* (Newsom Report, 1963), *Children and their Primary Schools* (Plowden Report, 1967), were responses to specific request from the Minister. All of these reports were characterised by extensive research in support of their recommendations, which provide data on the subjects covered for all interested in education. Although these major reports have either influenced or foreshadowed and legitimised policy and have contributed significantly towards a consensual understanding of the issues under consideration, since 1967 Secretaries of State have ignored their statutory obligation to reconstitute the Councils. This may be because they have shared Crosland's view that 'the briefs given were too broad and the reports produced were too lengthy.' In recent years Secretaries of State have preferred to constitute *ad hoc* committees and working parties to inquire into more specific aspects of education. The James Report (1972) epitomised the new approach of establishing a separate specialist committee to carry out an investigation within a narrower frame of reference and a limited timespan. This report had no less influence on policy-making than any of the reports of the Central Advisory Councils, although its deliberate failure to act as a commission receiving evidence from all interested parties may have deprived its findings of much general authority. The influence of such a Committee of Inquiry should be compared with that of the Robbins Committee, appointed by the Prime Minister in 1961, whose report has dominated thinking about higher education in many reports ever since.

There are other permanent committees charged with the duty to investigate particular features of the education system, such as the National Advisory Council for Education in Industry and Commerce and the National Council for Educational Technology. Yet others supervise, as well as report on, parts of educational provision; examples are the Technician Education Council and the Business Education Council. All of these bodies issue regular reports, and although members are appointed by the Secretary of State, many of them will effectively be the nominees of bodies acknowledged to have legitimate interests in the particular fields under investigation. In this last category fall the Schools Council for Curriculum and

Examinations, perhaps the most important of standing advisory bodies, and possibly for that reason the focus of considerable controversy.

Although the administration of public examinations for secondary schools has been for many years the historically assumed responsibility of the universities, acting in respect of matriculation requirements, the Minister has also been active since early in the twentieth century co-ordinating what was then (and otherwise might still be) a chaos of examination opportunities. The Secondary Schools Examinations Council was until 1964 the Minister's official creation and his agent for the co-ordination and development of examination policy. The most radical innovation it sponsored, after the introduction of the General Certificate of Education in 1951, was the proposal of the Beloe Committee for a new set of examinations and a new set of examining bodies appropriate to the needs of fifteen-year-olds in the middle 40 per cent of the ability range. By the time these new examinations began to be offered, the Secondary Examinations Council had been replaced by the Schools Council, a move explicitly uniting overall responsibility for curriculum and examinations. The establishment of a Curriculum Study Group in the Department by the then Minister, Sir David Eccles, aroused teachers' suspicions of impending central government control of the curriculum. The political mood favoured extensive teacher involvement in policy-making, and the Schools Council, which succeeded both Study Group and Examinations Council, came to have a majority of teacher members and a remit which ignored the statutory distribution of responsibility under the 1944 Education Act.

The Schools Council became responsible, as the Ministry had intended, for a considerable upsurge in curriculum development. Research projects proliferated, and hardly a single area of the curriculum was left undisturbed. Even so, there have been many who claim, on the basis of substantial evidence, that questions of dissemination and implementation have been largely side-stepped, as have questions of fundamental change inimical to the collectively perceived interests of teachers. From their different perspectives, radicals and government have been suspicious of the teacher majority on the Schools Council and particularly of the influence of the large block of seats occupied by the National Union of Teachers. While the Certificate in Secondary Education has become very widely established and there have been limited experiments with other new leaving examinations for different groups of pupils, successive Secretaries of State have rejected plans for the reform of the Advanced Level of the General Certificate of Education and for the amalgamation of the two existing sets of examination for fifteen/sixteen-year-olds. No such impasse has been reached in Scotland, where tradition has been confirmed by the creation in 1965 of a Consultative Committee on the Curriculum, the nomination of whose members is firmly in the hands of the Secretary of State rather than those of the teachers' associations. Since Mr Callaghan's speech as Prime Minister at Ruskin College, Oxford, in 1976, it has been clear that while the Schools Council can play a useful developmental and promotional role in curricular and examination changes, central government is not prepared to tolerate any rival to itself as final arbiter of national policy for providing a varied and comprehensive educational service in every area.

If there is to be a national source of power other than the appropriate Secretary of State, then it may be the Parliamentary institution of Select Committees, which Governments of both parties have regarded with understandable, if not disinterested, suspicion. In the late 1960s the House of Commons established a Select Committee on Education and Science which produced controversial reports on the Inspectorate and staff—student relations in further and higher education, but the Conservative administration which took office in 1970 replaced it with the Education and Arts Subcommittee. The Subcommittee made a practice of taking evidence from whatever sources it considered appropriate, including officials of the DES, and undertook a major inquiry into planning within the Department in 1976. The Conservative Government elected in 1979 has agreed to the establishment, for the first time, of a comprehensive set of Select Committees in the House of Commons, mirroring the pattern of government Departments. The Select Committee on Education, Science and Arts, nominated in November 1979, is nine strong, under the chairmanship of a Labour Member, Christopher Price; clearly, it is too early to assess the role that the Select Committee may play in the drawing up of future agendas for educational policy-making.

It is difficult to analyse the exact contribution that advisory bodies may make to policy-making. They may act as catalysts for change in education or merely reflect growing pressure which might be recognised in other ways. Yet their significance may be gauged to some degree by relating specific recommendations of a particular report to subsequent action by government. The effect of the Crowther Report on policy may serve to illustrate the possible role of major advisory bodies within the framework of the educational system.

The Crowther Report, *15 — 18* unlike earlier reports of the Central Advisory Council for Education, provided a body of empirical evidence on which its recommendations were based. Consistent with the view of R. A. Butler, President of the Board of Education in 1943, that the Advisory Councils should concern themselves with content rather than administration, many of the recommendations were more relevant to schools and colleges than to Government. The Report emphatically endorsed the 'tripartite system' and did not deny the concept of a 'fixed pool of ability', although it expressed concern about waste of talent, particularly in the second quartile of the ability range. It was critical of premature specialisation, which, it claimed, was largely responsible for the 'two cultures'. It recognised shortcomings in further education and training, such as the failure to create county colleges or to provide continuing education on a part-time basis for young people between fifteen and eighteen, as laid down in the 1944 Education Act; the wastage from part-time courses; the lack of proper induction from school to college. Crowther proposed separate further education colleges for craft, operative and technical students, academic courses in further education parallel to those in school and the further development of practical courses in school. In the event, county colleges were never created, and in 1978 less than 25 per cent of young people aged between sixteen and eighteen in full-time employment received day-release or its equivalent.

The problem of wastage was a major theme of the 1961 White Paper, which proposed reorganisation of courses in further education and the introduction of induction courses. Clearly, the Crowther Report influenced the development of these proposals. The radical restructuring of industrial training in 1964 was influenced more by training developments within the European Economic Community (EEC) and Sweden than the general comments of Crowther concerning the integration of education and training and was sponsored by the Ministry of Labour, not the Ministry of Education. On the other hand, the proposal to develop links between schools and further education colleges was endorsed by Administrative Memorandum 6/62, and the subsequent expansion of link courses in the last fifteen years is a tribute to the influence of both the Crowther Report and the Newsom Report in 1963. Crowther had proposed that the leaving age be raised to sixteen between the school years 1966—7, and 1968—9. As it turned out, although successive Governments were committed to the policy in principle and the date was accepted for action, implementation was deferred until 1972 because of the economic problems of the late 1960s. Other Crowther recommendations seem to have had little or no effect. Bursaries for poorer children staying on at school beyond the statutory leaving age recommended in the Report have not been forthcoming, nor has central government created more technical schools; rather, it has pursued a policy of general secondary reorganisation, although Crowther advocated only limited experiments in comprehensive schooling.

One could continue relating major proposals to subsequent events, but clearly the Report had little immediate impact. The proposal to phase in recommendations over twenty years following the development of a national programme did not materialise, although many recommendations were ultimately implemented, probably as a result of other influences on opinion rather than any deliberate commitment to Crowther. Indeed, one commentator has posed the rhetorical question: 'Was the Report not produced at the wrong time to the wrong Government?'

An analysis of any report of an advisory council or committee may provide some insight but it is usually difficult to demonstrate a direct relation between the advice given and the policy formed. Advisory bodies often serve to reinforce opinions already in existence rather than to stimulate new ideas. Most reports are inevitably less effective when recommending structural change which may involve easily measured extra expenditure than when they propose alterations to, for example, the content of the curriculum. Where they do lead to structural change one might suspect that committees appointed by the government and supported by officials of the Department are meant to furnish government with legitimation on the basis of apparently objective analysis, of restructured or reordered priorities that are already conceived.

While cynics may see this function of major advisory committees as their prime attraction to government, it should be noted that one Permanent Secretary to the Department scorned them as a waste of time and words in evidence to the House of Commons Select

Committee. However convincing his argument, it may well be that in some respects the findings of the Central Advisory Council from time to time have provided Parliamentary Opposition and the wider public of educational pressure groups with points of reference for criticism of government performance and have exposed gaps between political rhetoric and administrative performance. The reports of many advisory bodies are clearly not irrelevant, despite the Permanent Secretary's comments. Their impact may be long-term and often more influential within the profession than within the Department. The accumulation of research evidence and the publicity which follows the issue of a major report can affect professional practice, mould teacher opinion and, in turn, lead to pressure for general educational change.

RELATIONS WITH LOCAL EDUCATION AUTHORITIES

Central government has some choice over those groups that it approaches or listens to on policy matters. It can give favoured organisations ready access to senior officials and even Ministers, only reluctantly receiving others on formal deputations when outright refusal to communicate is impolite. Groups and individuals may find themselves called on for evidence or asked to sit on committees of inquiry; in turn, because they have a reputation for having the ear of the Ministry, they will attract those seeking access to government. In a field of policy such as education, where influence is widely distributed and extensive consultation normal, these practices and opportunities are exploited to the full. The Secretary of State has little option but to consult with the teachers' associations; with the local education authorities, statutory junior partners in the education system and direct providers of the bulk of the service, he has no option at all. Much of the work of Department officials lies in negotiating with individual local education authorities or with the generality through the Association of Metropolitan Authorities and the Association of County Councils.

Griffiths (1966) emphasises three conditions shaping relationships between central government and local authorities: the providers of the service (that is, the local education authorities) have power in their own right and are not mere agents acting under delegated authority; the flow of information and influence is not one-way, and decision-making takes place at both local and national level; there is an acceptance that central government has a responsibility to ensure a general minimum standard for all services. Despite the co-operation which generally characterises these relationships, there are conflicts as local authorities compete for priority in resource allocation, seek to press the special problems of their areas or guard their legal autonomy. Relations can be further complicated when opposed political parties control central government and the majority of local authorities. Their differences may be exploited publicly for party gain; on the other hand, if a political party is in control of both the local authority associations and central government, there will be some attempt to minimise public disunity, although private discussion may be at least as fierce. The radical plans of the Secretary of State for the Environment in the Conservative Government elected in 1979 for a re-casting of both capital and revenue finance arrangements in local government have so alarmed local authorities that regardless of the political persuasion of their spokesmen, the local authority associations have used all persuasive means to achieve modifications.

Nevertheless, local authorities must fulfil legal requirements that are centrally determined and must operate within financial decisions laid down by national government, however reluctantly. In recent years national planning of resource allocation has required increasingly detailed guidelines and restraints on local initiatives. This has affected capital spending most directly but revenue expenditure almost as much. The dependence of local authorities on rates (not a buoyant source of revenue) has made it difficult for them to meet extra demands on their services from local revenue and has pushed them into greater financial dependence on central government, with a corresponding shift in power and control.

Similarly, local authorities can only work within the statutory framework laid down by Parliament on the initiative of the relevant Secretaries of State. There are only very limited opportunities for local authorities to sponsor their own Parliamentary Bills, and such opportunities are irrelevant to educational issues. The facility of establishing local bye-laws has some relevance to education, since matters such as the employment of school-age children may be treated. Generally, however, the constitutional position of local authorities affects relations between central Government authorities and local in two ways. First, local authorities must carry out duties imposed on them by legislation in whatever way is statutorily required. Second, local authorities must conform to the doctrine of *ultra vires*; that is to say, without ascertainable explicit or implicit authority under statute, they may not act. Unlike local authorities in many of the countries of Western Europe, there is no British tradition of general power to act in the interests of the local community. By extension, British local authorities are subject to the jurisdiction of the courts in the interpretation of statutory duties and limitations on the exercise of permissive powers.

The law often provides for the issue by the appropriate Minister of regulations with statutory force. As has been made clear, the Education Act 1944 and subsequent amending legislation provide many opportunities for regulating in detail the educational provision and professional practice of local education authorities. Such regulations are rarely published without prior consultation and the establishment of a broad consensus of agreement about their contents with the local authorities.

Circulars and administrative memoranda may further elaborate on the intention behind particular regulations but cannot be construed as other than recommendations. The Secretary of State has to approve the powers given to school governing bodies, for example, and has issued elaborate guidance to local authorities to help them to submit acceptable proposals; similarly, arrangements for the composition of education committees within the local authorities set up under the Local Government Act 1972 have to be centrally confirmed, and detailed guidance was given by circular as to the criteria that the then Secretary of State would be applying and the areas of discretion that she intended to leave to the local council. Circulars may outline the future intentions of government; they may proffer or request information or co-operation. Central control is further manifest in the exercise of ministerial discretion, which affords central government flexibility in the promotion of new policies and subjects many local initiatives to the overriding sanction of the Secretary of State. The exercise of many discretionary powers under the relevant Education Acts entails a very significant control over the administration of the education service in each local education authority separately. A close relationship must arise from the Minister's authority to approve schemes (for example Section 11 and 13, 1944 Act), to issue orders or give directives (for example, Section 16(1), 17(2), 17(3b), 1944 Act), and to act in cases of default (for example, Section 99, 1944 Act).

Advice and information about the development of new policy is sometimes forthcoming in ministerial speeches; Anthony Crosland's speech at Woolwich outlining a 'binary policy' for higher education gave forewarning of the 1966 White Paper which led to the creation of polytechnics. White Papers often give notice to local education authorities of changes in general policy which may have significant consequences for the planning of educational services at local level. *Technical Education* (1956) and *Education: A Framework for Expansion* (1972) are good examples. Public occasions when the Minister is expected to make a major speech, such as the annual conference of the teachers' associations or the North of England Education Conference, provide regular opportunities to reach a wide and relevant audience with forecasts of change, if not precise policy commitment.

Of course, private discussions take place with individual local education authorities which contribute to the development of a positive collective reaction. The reaction of some of the largest education authorities may be a critical element in the general response to Ministry initiatives; the Inner London Education Authority and its predecessor, the Education Committee of the London County Council, have occupied a special position in both private and public debate between central and local government. The prestige of some Chief Education Officers (Sir Alec Clegg of the West Riding of Yorkshire would be an example) has been sufficient to ensure that the views of their authorities are given special attention in any negotiations between them and the DES; the Education Act 1964, which provided for an age of transfer to secondary education other than at eleven, was a remarkably swift response to sustained pressure from the West Riding, where a number of opportunities for secondary-school reorganisation to include middle schools were being frustrated under the existing legislation.

Two major factors ensure that local education authorities exert significant influence on all central planning and policy-making. On the one hand, there is full appreciation by the Secretary of State and Department officials that the educational system depends upon an effective working partnership; on the other, there exist most powerful associations of local authorities that represent between them the interests and views of all local authorities. The expertise at the disposal of the local authority associations and the collective political power that they represent places them amongst the most formidable pressure groups with which central government has to contend.

In 1956 the then Minister of Housing and Local Government declared: 'The local authority associations have now become a part of the constitution of the country.' Not only have they become part of the accepted but informal process of consultation, but in some areas of policy-making they have been seen as a centre of national negotiating power that rivals the Ministers', and uneasy compromises have had to be struck. Serving teachers are, in fact, employed by local education authorities in the main; it follows that annual salary negotiations take place between teachers' associations and local authority associations as national representatives of the employers. The initial intervention of the then President of the Board of Education had been to encourage such negotiations, which might set national scales of pay; the Education Act 1944 gave legislative sanction for this negotiating machinery (the Burnham Committee) and authorised the Minister to accept or reject, but not to amend, the provisional agreements that might be made from time to time by teachers and local authorities. It is hardly surprising that the Minister should have become frustrated by a decision-making process which determined the total of the largest single element in educational expenditure — teachers' salaries — but excluded him and his officials. One confrontation between Minister and the Burnham Committee in 1960 was resolved when the Committee volunteered to revise its recommendations. In 1963 there was no compromise, and teachers' salaries were determined by a specially enacted statute, discarding the normal machinery. Under the Remuneration of Teachers Act 1965, despite the protest of teachers and local authorities, revised machinery introduced representatives of the Ministry to the Committee and thereby made the Secretary of State party to the salary negotiations from the start.

Subsequent experience has confirmed the role (however much resented) of central government in teachers' salary settlements. Successive national incomes policies with much wider application than to one group of public servants — or, indeed, local government employees as a whole — have forced local authorities to consider teachers' salaries in a broader context of comparison and negotiating machinery; similarly, the moves of teachers' associations towards the trade union movement in general reflect their leaders' recognition that effective negotiation is no longer possible in the isolation of the

Burnham Committee or of any purely departmental machinery.

This discussion of relations between central and local government on questions of teachers' salaries leads naturally to the most critical feature of those relations, resource allocation to and within the education service.

THE ALLOCATION OF RESOURCES
(CURRENT AND CAPITAL)

A most remarkable feature of educational finance in Britain is that of all public money spent on education, only a small proportion comes from the vote of the DES (that is, money approved by Parliament for the Department to spend on education). If one considers that some 11 per cent of expenditure is committed by the Department to the universities through the University Grants Committee, there is only 3 per cent which is directly within the control of the DES. These funds are allocated to research and to various direct-grant institutions, including the Open University, the Cranfield College of Aeronautical Studies and the Royal College of Art. Other Departments also provide money for education, The Home Office, under urban aid programmes, has provided the major proportion of actual expenditure on a range of approved schemes, including some that are educational. The Department of Employment, via the Manpower Services Commission, has funded training programmes and other schemes to relieve unemployment, which substantially fall within or overlap educational provision. The total value of provision by Ministries other than the DES is small; but their grants are specific and earmarked for particular educational activities, while not being subject to any explicit planning or control by the Department which is the central authority responsible for the educational service.

In Britain central government's main financial support for the education service is through Exchequer grants given to local authorities as assistance for the provision and maintenance of all of their recognised services. A few specific grants are given for particular services (the police service, for example) but the RSG, which constitutes more than four fifths of Exchequer grant is the main subsidy for rate-borne services, including education. In England and Wales the RSG is the responsibility of the Department of the Environment; in Scotland, of the Scottish Office. In Northern Ireland a different system obtains; the Department of Education retains direct responsibility for the financial control of the service, paying grants towards the cost of new schools, their equipment and maintenance, alterations and improvements. It also pays grants to colleges of education, awards training scholarships and makes grants for research, youth welfare and adult education. In addition, it has responsibility for the provision of university finance.

As local education authorities have direct responsibility for approximately 86 per cent of all public money spent on education, this raises questions about their sources of income and the degree to which central government should control and direct their expenditure on education. In 1973—4 (in England and Wales) rates were the source of 28 per cent of local authority current expenditure; grants covered a further 45 per cent; and 27 per cent was obtained from miscellaneous fees, income and charges. The comparable figures in 1953—4 were 33 per cent from rates, 36 per cent from grants and 31 per cent from other sources of income. These figures illustrate the trend towards the increased dependence of local authorities on central government for funds and the limited buoyancy of local sources of income. The RSG has grown substantially in the last decade as a proportion of total relevant local government expenditure. Relevant expenditure is the amount of local authority spending which central government is prepared to support. It excludes expenditure financed by fees, charges, rents and so on. In 1967—8, when the RSG was introduced, it constituted 54 per cent of total relevant expenditure, and the percentage, varying over the years, now stands at 61 per cent (1980—1). The amount and form of the grant poses major problems of control and accountability for central government. It has not gone unnoticed that rate income provides only about 8 per cent of national revenues, although local authorities are responsible for about 27 per cent of total public expenditure; nor that a very large proportion of local expenditure financed by rates and grants goes on education. As the RSG is a block grant and its level massively influences educational expenditure by setting the context for local budgeting, Education Ministers are naturally concerned about their inability to channel and earmark funds to the education service or to determine priorities within total education expenditure.

Since the first central government grants of 1833, which were allocated on a percentage basis for building, central government has applied a variety of fiscal tools to influence the growth of the education system and to control public expenditure on the service. Specific grants were extended after 1833 to cover a variety of costs. After 1862 capitation grants became the standard form of central subsidy, but by 1918 there were fifty-seven specific grants available for education, introduced to stimulate particular local initiatives favoured by central government. The Education Act 1918 introduced a complex percentage grant system covering higher and elementary education which was designed to support the provision of minimum standards in all local education authorities and to minimise the differential abilities of authorities to fund their educational services.

The movement from a unit to a percentage grant system reflected the capacity, by then possible, of central government to improve standards rather than merely extend provision. Despite the Geddes Report (Treasury 1922), which recommended a switch from a percentage to a block grant system and the introduction of a block grant for other local services in 1929, the percentage grant system applied to education, with only minor alteration, for forty years. In 1959, in the face of sustained protests from the education public, the block grant system was introduced for all local government services; each authority's grant was to be assigned through a formula which took account of such needs as was implied by the size and age of the population in each area. This was complemented by a rate deficiency grant, a subsidy to enable poorer authorities to reach a national average standard of income. These needs and resources grants, consolidated in 1966, form the basis of the present RSG. No longer does the government automatically share the cost of extra educational provision by a local education authority, as under a service-specific percentage grant. The level of overall local authority expenditure, in money and in real terms, is agreed annually (originally every two years) between central and local government, and it is left to individual authorities to use their various resources to fund education and other services as they think fit. Any further increase in educational expenditure exceeding the nationally agreed projections has to be met entirely from the rates.

Apart from the limited involvement of the DES in the negotiations leading up to the RSG settlement each year, what checks are there on both capital and revenue expenditure, and how effective can they be?

Controls on capital expenditure, particularly relating to the building programme, are the most direct and effective. Procedures for controlling the education building programme in England and Wales are laid down in detail in Circular 13/74. Its salient features are as follows. There is a rolling programme of authorisations for education building (excluding universities), broken down into national allocation for starts in four main areas: schools, nursery schools, special schools and further education establishments. Allocations for primary, secondary and nursery schools are lump-sum authorisations, within which work for each sector must be contained. In other sectors projects are individually authorised. The rolling programme has three stages, with the aim of giving local authorities firmer allocations at regular intervals before the beginning of the financial year in which building is expected to start.

At each stage the national and individual authority allocations may be adjusted in the light of available resources; the Final List for building starts takes inflation into account when announced but is not subsequently adjusted. Authorities have discretion, within their lump-sum authorisations for nursery, primary and secondary building, to undertake major or minor works. Greater freedom from the supervision of the DES is proposed under the present Government's Local Government Bill, which sets out to restructure the whole of local government capital finance. Under existing procedures (and no doubt future alternatives under consideration) the main constraint on local authorities' capital programme is the *level* of funding authorised rather than any dispute over project priorities.

A closely related and equally direct means of central control is that exercised over capital finance generally. Most local authority capital expenditure is financed by loans (approximately 75 per cent), while 5 per cent is obtained from grant, 10 per cent from revenue and another 10 per cent from sales of assets. At present, for capital expenditure throughout local government borrowing approval or loan sanction must be sought from central government, as determined by Circular 2/70. There are two main types of approval; on the one hand, that for the key-sector items; on the other, that for items which fall into the category of locally determined schemes.

Key-sector capital expenditure relates to projects costing more than a given amount, the figure being constantly subject to review. Each project must have the specific approval of the Secretary of State for Education if the local education authority wishes to finance the item by borrowing. Throughout local government key-sector items are those for which Ministers have a special responsibility to ensure standards and to co-ordinate developments on a national basis. As far as education is concerned, the key sector covers buildings and expensive capital equipment (for example, computers, some machine tools, language laboratories).

Locally determined schemes cover all capital expenditure which involves borrowing other than that on key sector projects and some others relating to land acquisition and home improvements. For locally determined schemes an annual fixed-sum block allocation of borrowing power is assigned to each authority. Authorities are notified annually by the Department of the Environment of the total capital borrowing which they may undertake in the ensuing year. The fixed sum includes any specific central government grant, and the amount is usually notified some six months before the beginning of the financial year to which it applies. This procedure means that local authorities are free to determine priorities for borrowing within the set ceiling without needing specific approvals, but it also means that items within the estimates of different local authority departments across the whole range of services are in contention with one another for the limited amount of borrowing power. Furnishing and equipment are typically the kind of educational items likely to be affected by this control exercised by the Department of the Environment.

In Scotland a larger proportion of local authority expenditure is capital, and it is subject to more stringent controls. Capital expenditure is not divided into key-sector and locally determined categories. There is, however, a requirement that local authorities should not incur liability to meet capital expenditure without the consent of the Secretary of State for Scotland. The system is gradually moving towards control of annual programmes, and local authorities are being encouraged to estimate their capital requirements some years ahead. In Northern Ireland the very limited discretion and independent authority of the Education and Library Boards leaves them ever more dependent of the Ministry of Education in Belfast for the authorisation of their capital budgets.

At present the DES cannot control local authority revenue expenditure on education other than through its control of capital expenditure, which usually has revenue implications. It can, however, determine the total supply of teachers, on the advice of the Advisory Committee on the Supply and Training of Teachers. It sets the totals for entry to teacher training; furthermore, between the mid-1950s and 1976 the Department set a quota on the employment of teachers for each local authority in order to spread shortages evenly. The Minister also sits on the Consultative Council on Local Government Finance, which has been formally responsible for negotiating the RSG since 1975. However, the most significant central control over educational expenditure is exercised by the Department of the Environment, in so far as it is possible for allocation of the RSG.

If one excludes fees, charges and other miscellaneous income, some 60 per cent of local authority revenue resources come from central government. The grant is both link and lifeline to local authorities. It is at once the main means of providing support to local authorities and regulator of a major part of public expenditure. Central government is naturally concerned to keep firm control of educational expenditure, which in 1977—8 amounted to £7,055 million (equivalent to 7¼ per cent of Gross National Product). The RSG is allocated to local authorities as the outcome of the following procedure.

Local authorities estimate the future cost of their various services on the basis of the volume of provision in previous years, anticipated increase due to inflation and extra responsibilities placed upon them by new legislation. Their estimates are aggregated, while central government carries out a similar exercise involving Departments with overall responsibility for services administered by the local authorities. Working through the Consultative Council on Local Government Finance and advised by the Treasury, the Department of the Environment negotiates with local authority associations an agreed estimate of overall expenditure, on the basis of such national and local figures with relevant weighting to different services. Such negotiations involve complex arguments about estimating techniques as well as disputes over allocation formulae, rates of inflation and the substance of necessary expenditure on particular services, and this crucial detail is discussed in various working parties and sub-committees of civil servants and local government officers. At a later stage the Cabinet determines what percentage of agreed relevant expenditure will be met by central government. Until 1972 the negotiations took place biannually, with a built-in check to meet inflation (that is, a commitment to meet extra expenditure due to inflation which could not be anticipated in the original settlement and in the same proportions as the original settlement). Now grant negotiations are annual affairs, and government is much more reluctant to meet extra commitment on the same basis. In the 1976—7 negotiations it was laid down that expenditure must be contained within the level forecast. Furthermore, projected expenditure negotiated for the previous year became the starting-point for the following year's negotiations, shifting the argument from volume of service provided to the level of costs of services which was acceptable. Financial limitations of this sort are increasingly being used to control the level and pattern of expenditure. Thus government control over grant is twofold: on the one hand, government determines what it will accept as relevant expenditure; on the other, it controls the proportion of relevant expenditure which it will meet.

It is striking that although the estimate of assistance to local authorities as a whole is worked out very precisely and is related to different service needs, government cannot ensure that the estimate of expenditure agreed with local authority associations will be complied with by individual local authorities, nor can there be a guarantee that the weightings or priority accorded to different services during the negotiations will be consistent with the priorities of individual authorities. The allocation to the local authorities does not involve any direction of money to specific services. It is based on a formula which is neither service-specific nor a simple percentage of what is actually spent, so that what is negotiated corporately cannot be binding in detail. In Scotland the grant settlement is accompanied by indication of where increases may take place in a given service. The settlement of 1976—7 included guidelines for real growth and the implication for staff—pupil ratios. Recent grant circulars in England and Wales have stressed that allowance has been made for growth in particular parts of the education service and the maintenance of others.

The whole business of revenue subsidy and control is lengthy, complex and often inequitable. It is a means by which the ratepayer is subsidised by the taxpayer; it is a poor control mechanism to ensure minimum national standards of services; and it provides no means of ensuring that allocations based on a presumption of priority in and between services that is carefully worked out in national negotiation will be followed by the local authorities, which decide their own priorities within the resources available to them. Control over this major area of education expenditure is not through the DES but through the Department of the Environment and the Treasury. The government has an understandable need to control this major part of public expenditure as part of its responsibility to manage the economy and its duty to be concerned about the provision of adequate services. Block grant has turned out to be a most inadequate tool to combine these purposes. The RSG was not designed as a control mechanism; yet apart from the grant there is no overt control over local authority revenue expenditure. Although capital control is more direct and effective, capital raised from revenue is not at present subject to sanction, and the whole system of control discourages local authorities from assessing the revenue consequences of capital borrowing. The grant controls only a percentage of relevant expenditure and only to the extent of determining the global subsidy. Although the government has recently applied cash limits in negotiations about the grant and minimum standards can be imposed by the Department, persuasion through the Inspectorate and guidance by circulars and memoranda are perhaps the last line of control that can be applied in a service that is essentially locally provided.

Against this backcloth of limited central accountability and ineffective means of planning the allocation of resources between central and local government, it is small wonder that the Layfield Committee, which reported in 1976, was given a brief to examine local government finance with a view to suggesting improvements. The major theme of the Report's recommendations was that there should be more direct accountability for the expenditure of public money at both levels of government and an increased public awareness of the sources from which both central and local government derived their incomes. It was the view of the Committee that if local authorities were to continue to exercise substantial discretion over public expenditure, they must have the power to levy more income directly and thus be more discernibly answerable to electors for the scale and priority of their expenditure. An alternative would be more central direction of resources, with the government continuing to subsidise what local authorities spent and on an increasing scale. If genuine local government were to be kept alive, local authorities would need a wider and more buoyant base for revenue than a property rate alone. The Committee did not favour the transfer of the cost of education to the Exchequer, nor the possible transfer of expenditure on salaries. It argued that central government should pay for the whole cost of a service only if that service were wholly national in character; in the view of the Committee, the education service did not fall into that category. Even in the case of the pooling arrangements among local education authorities designed to distribute the cost of locally provided advanced further education, of which the Committee was very critical, it backed away from any radical suggestions for the restructuring of public control.

The control of higher education expenditure illustrates in other ways the dilemmas and alternatives available to government. In the case of universities direct and relatively tight budgeting procedures are imposed, while totally different indirect and loose constraints operate in the field of advanced further education. The universities receive their support from central government via the machinery of the University Grants Committee (UGC), established in 1919. From then until 1963 the Committee dealt directly with the Treasury. Since its inception the Committee has served as a buffer between government and the universities, but it now negotiates with the DES, which actually provides the money disbursed by the Committee. The UGC is nominally a neutral body and one of the symbols of university autonomy. It makes recommendations to the DES on the financial allocations to be made to all universities in the United Kingdom outside Northern Ireland. Traditionally, each university gives detailed estimates to the Committee of its recurrent expenditure needs to maintain current provision over a five-year period and at the same time bids for further resources for new developments. The Committee, having consulted each university in turn about its estimates, presents a global proposal to the DES, which, prior to negotiations between the UGC and individual universities, will have given an indication of what sums may be available and in what areas expansion may be welcome. Such information clearly conditions the Committee's budget discussions with the universities. Finally, the government determines the total allocation, abiding by UGC decisions on how the money should be allocated to different universities. The same principle applies to the annual settlement of capital expenditure. It is significant that the government retains firm control over total expenditure and substantially influences general priorities within the sums agreed for the quinquennial period, although it does not determine specific allocations to universities and it respects the neutrality and advice given by the UGC. If the system has broken down in any way, it is in response to government's wish to intervene in greater detail in university provision and in the temporary abandonment of quinquennial budgeting in the mid 1970s and again in 1979.

The system of pooling which governs the finance of advanced further education affords the central government (and, for that matter, local authorities) the least direct and most ineffective control of public money spent on education. The pool was devised in an attempt to ensure that expenditure incurred by some local education authorities in providing services which met national and not just local needs should not fall exclusively on them. Thus arrangements were made whereby costs for services specified by the government as being of this character should be met from a pool of resources taken from all local authorities, on the basis of a formula which crudely attempts to measure demands made by each authority on such services. Advanced further education is designated a 'pool-able' service. The pooling system does not encourage providing authorities to monitor and control this kind of expenditure effectively, as they are not directly accountable for it. In fact, there is a positive incentive to expand 'pool-able' services as a source of income for the providing authority; both local authorities and central government find it difficult to judge whether or not such services are providing value for money, and local authority finance committees find it hard to estimate what will have to be contributed to the pool. But the most serious area of concern is the continuing failure to subject such a system to either effective local or central control. For these reasons the whole procedure of 'pool-able' expenditure was recently reviewed by the Oakes Committee (a departmental Committee under the chairmanship of the then Labour Minister of State).

The Report proposed the creation of a national body to advise on the total resources to be made available for all maintained higher education and on their allocation between local authorities and institutions. Pool contributions were to continue, but alternative formulae for determining contributions were to be worked out. The Committee envisaged maintaining authorities meeting up to 15 per cent of the cost of their higher education provision; funding from the national pool would be on a per capita basis to institutions where less than 30 per cent of the work was 'advanced', by approved course in other institutions except those where over 90 per cent of work was advanced, and where the funding of whole 'programmes' might be approved. The national committee, consisting of between twenty-five and twenty-eight members, would bring together representatives of the Secretary of State, the local authorities and the teachers under an independent chairman. New regional advisory councils would be set up to monitor, promote and plan maintained higher education in their areas. Despite scepticism while in Opposition, the present Conservative Government is making legislative provision for new national and regional machinery for the control of advanced further education very much along the lines of the Oakes Report. In the short term, as a restriction on expenditure, it has set an absolute upper limit to disbursements from the pool, which has forced many polytechnics to seek severe economies in their budgets for 1980—1.

Control of resources, whether restrictive or promotional, is a very clumsy method of encouraging the pursuit of national educational objectives, but as the preceding paragraphs have shown, the most elaborate and probably self-defeating mechanisms have been created in the attempt to reconcile local discretion with national account-ability. The most prominent features of existing arrangements for the provision and control of resources for education can be summarised as follows:

1 Control by central government is exercised via different Departments of State.
2 Capital expenditure is regulated by two types of loan sanction.
3 The DES provides very little money for the provision of the service, and its control over educational revenue expenditure is both limited and, for the most part, indirect.
4 Revenue expenditure by local authorities on education is not subject to direction and specific allocation.
5 Expenditure on university higher education is closely controlled, though not directed, by the DES and is operated through an intermediate buffer agency.
6 Current methods of financing advanced further education are not susceptible to effective control and accountability.
7 The major means of controlling resources for education, the RSG and the loan sanction, are not instruments designed to regulate the economy and, in the event, have proved ineffective in doing so; nor can they be used effectively by government to determine priority within and between services provided by the local authorities.

CHAPTER 3

The Local Education Authorities

THE POWERS, RESPONSIBILITIES AND DUTIES OF LOCAL EDUCATION AUTHORITIES

Local education authorities are the main providers of education at all levels and for all ages. Although universities are not under their control, although independent schools exist in substantial numbers, it is the local authorities that have direct responsibility for the vast majority of schools, for a very large part of higher education and for most vocational and non-vocational education at all levels. Apart from the universities, the only other institutions with a sizeable stake in the provision of education for the mass of people are the Churches. Their financial commitment and their independent control is now very limited, although their substantial involvement remains.

The 1944 Education Act made it a responsibility of local education authorities to secure the provision of primary and secondary education for all those between the ages of five and fifteen (now sixteen). The Act also made it a duty to secure the provision of full and part-time further education beyond school age, leisure-time occupation (Section 41) and adequate facilities for recreation and social and physical training (Section 53).

The extent of responsibility and positive commitment imposed on local education authorities under the Act were evidenced by the requirement for the preparation and submission of development plans indicating the ways in which they intended to fulfil their duty to 'contribute towards the spiritual, moral, mental and physical development of the community by securing that efficient education . . . shall be available to meet the needs of the population of their area'

(Section 7). Although development plans were taken with differing degrees of seriousness by different local education authorities (and have now fallen into disuse), the process illustrated also the intended relationship between central Ministry and local education authority. In summary, their duties and responsibilities were divided thus: on the Minister was conferred overall responsibility, a promotional role and a watching, adjudicating brief; to the local education authorities fell a mixture of general and specific duties, much discretionary power to provide over and above minimum standards and every encouragement to expand, within the limits of resources, an education service that was comprehensive in age range, academic levels, welfare concerns and vocational or leisure emphasis.

Control over the opening, modification or closure of county schools (Section 13) and their place in the system of education was placed in the hands of the local education authority, subject only to the adjudication of the Minister when proposals were disputed by local citizens. Control over the curriculum was also in the hands of the local education authority (Section 23), except in the cases of religious instruction—a matter for a local inter-denominational conference in the case of county schools (Section 29)—and the curricula of voluntary aided schools (Section 23). Coupled with the control of the appointment of teachers (Section 24) and the right to inspect (Section 77), the powers of the local education authority were formidable enough to ensure its ultimate constitutional supremacy in the locality.

To facilitate the proper exercise of these sweeping powers, the local education authority was compelled by statute to appoint an education committee, which should include in its membership 'persons of experience in education and persons acquainted with the educational conditions prevailing in the area' (Schedule I, Pt II), and to appoint a chief education officer (Section 88). Before taking any decision (except in emergency) a local education authority must consider a report from its education committee (Schedule I, Pt II). In these ways, the legislators sought to ensure, in the most precise detail, that local educational policy was only made after consideration by an appropriately specialised committee, including experts as well as elected members, which had in turn received the advice of professional officers. Under these conditions it can be no surprise that education officers and education committee members have often thought of themselves as separate from the rest of the affairs of the local authority.

Such a perspective would be reinforced by the statutory provisions for school transport (Section 55), a school health service (Section 48), a school meals service (Section 49) and child welfare, including control of juvenile employment (Sections 37, 40, 59), all of which help to complete the picture of a comprehensive, self-sufficient service only marginally overlapping with other institutions, professions and bureaucracies.

The provisions of the Education (Scotland) Act 1947 are very similar to those covering England and Wales, and the separateness of the government of education has been re-emphasised recently in Northern Ireland by the establishment of the Education and Library Boards.

LOCAL ADMINISTRATION: THE OFFICIALS AND THE DEPARTMENT

Local authorities in Great Britain employed 2,900,000 people (two part-time employees counted as one) in September 1975, an increase of 1,450,000 in the period since 1952. Whereas 6.20 per cent of the working population were employed by local authorities in 1952, in 1957 the figure was 11.3 per cent (Layfield, 1976, Table 22). This expansion in the local government labour force, both absolute and proportional, is not necessarily an indication of any waste of resources, since many services have greatly expanded their scope and improved their quality during the post-war years as a result of local initiatives and central government encouragement or directives. In terms of the numbers of people employed, education ranks as by far the largest service administered by the local authorities. In 1976–77, 541,890 teachers were employed full-time in schools or further education establishments maintained by local education authorities in England and Wales; another 34,000 were employed in substantial part-time teaching in schools; an unspecified (but small) number of occasional teachers and unqualified staff were employed in nursery schools; and an incalculable number were teaching part-time in further education. In Scotland the total number of teachers employed full-time by education authorities was 63,861 in the same year; while in Northern Ireland the figure was 19,811. In 1952 there were 237,000, 33,700 and 8,300 teachers employed by local authorities in England and Wales, Scotland and Northern Ireland respectively; thus a doubling of numbers of full-time teachers occurred during the period in which the number of pupils in schools increased by very nearly 50 per cent and enrolments in further education more than doubled.

In this context the number of education officers remains remarkably small; the Committee on the Staffing of Local Government (Mallaby) which reported to the Minister of Housing and Local Government in December 1966, established from a questionnaire completed by most local education authorities that there were 1,240 education officers in post in England and Wales; that the percentage of posts that remained unfilled after being vacant for six months or more (an indication of the attractions of educational administration to suitable applicants) was the lowest of all the local authority professional and technical staff surveyed; and that the percentage of posts filled by persons possessing less than the desirable qualifications was again among the lowest. Only in the local education service was there no claim that additional posts could not be created because of recruitment difficulties. A similar survey now might produce rather different results. The pay and prospects of teachers with some years of experience who are eligible for recruitment as educational administrators often outstrip those of the common recruitment grade of professional assistant.

It does not follow that the profession of education officer has been stagnating or declining. Between 1951 and 1971, according to Greenhalgh (1974), the numbers of education officers increased from 802 to 1264. The term 'education officer' is used to cover Chief Education Officer, Deputy Education Officer, Assistant Education Officer, Administrative Assistant, Divisional Education Officer and Borough Education Officers and their deputies. A survey of recruitment to such posts (Rendel, 1968) showed that while the average numbers of graduates recruited yearly from 1951—9 inclusive was 26, it was 53 per annum for the years 1960—5. The Mallaby Committee produced some evidence to suggest that this was caused not by a more rapid turnover of education department staff, but by a change in entry standards.

One difficulty in comparing education officers with other professionals employed in local government is that there are no rigid criteria laid down for their selection, as there are for doctors, engineers or health inspectors. Until the implementation of the Local Government Act 1972, a short list of those being considered for appointment as Chief Education Officer had to be submitted to the

Secretary of State for approval before the final selection could be made by the local education authority. A consensus of opinion among teachers would insist upon some teaching experience as a necessary qualification in education officers at all professional levels, although the Inner London Education Authority and its predecessor, the London County Council, did recruit a cadre of young graduates straight from universities. The Association of Chief Education Officers required graduate status, teaching and administrative experience for membership; the Association of Education Officers, any two out of the three criteria. Nevertheless, Rendel (1968) found that 17 per cent of graduate educational administrators had no teaching experience. Again, not all education officers are graduates, but nearly all the senior ones are. One unstated criterion may be masculinity: Greenhalgh (1974) found that only four women had become Chief Education Officers, the first in 1956; Rendel (1968) found that only 15 per cent of graduate administrators in education were women, most of them employed by education authorities in the London area.

In recent years education officers have become more aggressively professional. The Society of Education Officers has sought to create a community of outlook and expertise by holding conference to explore policy issues and options for the medium-term future, and it has sought and received recognition by government as a spokesman for the education service, a role perhaps thrust upon it by the demise of the Association of Education Committees.

The Mallaby Committee were concerned about recruitment to, and the possibility of advancement within, local government service as a whole. In relation to educational administration, they concluded: 'Teaching in schools, colleges and universities may well provide a more attractive career financially than educational administration in those small education authorities where salaries are related to the size of the authorities and to the salary of the Clerk' (Mallaby, 1967, p. 54). They also suggested that previous teaching experience as a criterion for advancement was creating an unnecessary bar to promotion for 'lay administrative' officers. Throughout this century local government has provided opportunity for recruitment at the lowest rung of the ladder, training on or off the job while in employment and the possibility of eventual promotion to the highest posts. In education departments, through custom rather than statutory sanction, the possibilities have been increasingly blocked by the regular recruitment of experienced teachers at senior levels. Additionally, in more recent years the establishment of the post of Chief Executive (distinct from that of Town or County Clerk) has, in many local authorities, opened up the possibility of further promotion for senior education officers beyond the confines of the education department.

The statutory requirement of an education committee and of the appointment of a chief education officer remain; as a consequence, there is no education authority without a specialist education department. Apart from the Chief Education Officer, within each education department there is likely to be a Deputy, two or three third-tier Assistant Education Officers and, below them, two more tiers of officers whose professional background is teaching rather than local government. Most of the employees of the education department, whether employed at clerical or at administrative levels, on line or staff functions, will not come from a teaching background, although long experience may give them a deep appreciation of the problems of educational institutions.

The division of responsibilities within an education department may vary from authority to authority, but all discharge the same central group of functions. A large county authority may delegate many of its administrative duties to area offices, which reproduce, on a less differentiated scale, virtually the same functions as head office. In the past divisional administration schemes have dictated some degree of delegation, making the Divisional Education Officer almost a Chief Education Officer. In other areas (notably London) certain functions (notably staffing) have been devolved to divisions, while other functions, capital programmes, have remained at County Hall. In larger cities geographical compactness has facilitated the retention of one central office. In Leeds, for example, three senior Assistant Education Officers have separate responsibility, under the Director and Deputy Director, for schools, further education, and development, finance and administration. For the Schools Division a prime concern is staffing. In the Further Education Division, where many of the details of academic staffing are delegated to colleges and their governing bodies, the main concerns are back-up, the administration of the system as a whole and responsibility for the operation of the non-institutionalised aspects of further education (adult education, youth work and community development). Future planning and its implications for capital expenditure, the maintenance of existing fabric and financial monitoring fall to the Development and Finance Division.

In addition, in Leeds the largest group of education professionals is to be found in the Advisory Division under the Chief Adviser. Their work takes them into schools, into in-service education, into staffing matters, into school buildings design, into all aspects of the match between total resources available and the resources made available in particular schools. Although their direct power may be strictly limited, their influence over decisions at institutional and authority level may be very considerable. The decision to employ a particular candidate as a teacher may well be in the hands of a head teacher or a committee of lay governors, but the adviser's access to and partial control of information about candidates' background and past performance is an important element in the appointment.

Similarly, questions of new school design and equipment may be solved partly by reference to an adviser whose job is to collect, sift and assess the evidence available from practitioners and theorists locally and more widely. This places great responsibility in the hands of the Advisory Service, although there may be difficulty, not least for the advisers themselves, in detecting the connection between their input of advice and the finally constructed school.

The direct involvement of adviser with the elected members of the education committee varies considerably, according to Bolam, Smith and Canter (1978). Fifty-two per cent of their sample of advisers indicated that they did have some contact, but within that category was the adviser who commented: '[I attend] the schools subcommittee, only attend. I was instructed by the CEO [Chief Education Officer] not to take part in discussions. I have done this for twelve years and often listened where I could have enlightened' (p. 107). The authors found some resentment at what was considered a blocking by the administration of communication between adviser and elected members. A re-examination of their data supported the view that ease of communication was related to administrative style in particular education departments rather than to any other obvious factor, such as size of authority or number of advisers employed.

Very little has been written about the local advisory service. There are clear parallels with Her Majesty's Inspectorate, but most advisory posts are of much more recent origin. Some of the school boards responsible for elementary education before 1902 appointed organisers or inspectors whose job was both to encourage development and to monitor the implementation of board policies. The first thirty years of the new county, county borough, and Part III education authorities saw almost a trebling of the number of advisers, with emphasis on support in practical subjects such as art, domestic subjects and handicraft, but especially in physical education. The period immediately after the Second World War saw a similar scale of expansion in the numbers of advisers concerned with one sector of education — primary, secondary, special or further education — with the emphasis this time on primary school advisers. Only in very recent years have secondary-school subject specialists begun to appear in any number in published lists of local authority advisers. Of 1536 advising staff listed in the Education Authorities Directory for 1973, only 167 (11 per cent) were publicly responsible for subjects such as science, modern languages, English and mathematics. This is not to say that further expertise in these areas is unavailable within the advisory service, nor that some of those otherwise titled do not spend part of their time as subject advisers. Only two years later, after local government reorganisation had allowed or necessitated the redrawing of education department staffing structures, the same group of subject specialists had expanded to 301, 16.1 per cent of the new total of advisers, which stood at 1874 (Swinney, 1980).

The expansion of the advisory service associated with local government reorganisation has not gone unnoticed or uncriticised. Some of the evidence about minimum size of local education authorities was premised on the financing of advisory services on a 'satisfactory' scale. Teacher advisers (that is, practising teacher seconded from schools for a year or more) have begun to appear, increasing the credibility of local advisers as sources of authoritative information and professional competence. Teachers' unions have not been slow to point out that advisers are agents of the teachers' employer rather than disinterested fellow professionals. From a different perspective, head teachers may resent the apparent interference in their schools; in the context of a detailed rejection of influence by advisers on schoolteachers other than through the headteacher, Goodwin (1968) writes:

> it is very easy for a specialist teacher, especially at times of friction with the headmaster, to contact his specialist adviser to seek for comfort, support or advice, generally without the head's knowledge ... But this kind of thing must not be; and all must understand that any direct approach to an outside authority over matters which are

the internal concern of the school is an intolerable and unprofessional practice . . .

Within the education welfare service of many local education authorities is to be found a substantial group of officers, much lower in status than advisers but, like them, tending to have problems of self-definition and of relationships with cognate areas of activity. There is no direct reference to an education welfare service in the 1944 Education Act or subsequent Acts. The existence of some two thousand education welfare officers in the local education authorities of England and Wales is the consequence of the statutory requirement of education for children between the ages of five and sixteen and various mandatory and discretionary provisions for school meals, transport, clothing, child guidance and special education. The enforcement of school attendance in the late nineteenth century could have been carried out on behalf of the education authorities by other agencies such as the police, but in fact a corps of specialist school attendance officers, as permitted under Section 36 of the Education Act 1870, has developed in most local education authorities (with exceptions in Scotland), adding to its basic duties, the distribution of material benefits relevant to the effective availability of education. There is no one pattern of work for the education welfare service; its scope varies from one local authority to another. Its members tend to be recruited after quite wide occupational experience elsewhere, rarely have any general training and are often regarded, by themselves as well as by others, as much lower in status than professional social workers employed in social services departments.

The only survey with any claim to completeness (MacMillan, 1977) indicates the substantial variation in scope of the education welfare service from one authority to another but defines the basic range of responsibilities discharged by the service in 92 per cent of authorities to include court proceedings, child employment, neglect, placement, clothing and free meals. Twenty-four per cent of authorities gave their education welfare officers some additional responsibility for handicapped children, nursery education, maintenance, extra-district pupils and transport. Many of these tasks involve considerable office routine, but it does not follow that the welfare officers themselves thus become little more than clerks; the same survey used Chief Education Welfare Officer estimates to establish that some 70 per cent of officers' time was spent directly on school—home liaison work, whether such work involved visiting schools, children or parents. The 10 per cent of time spent on preparing for or attending court makes it clear that legal action is now used as a last sanction; the bulk of effort is expended on maintaining a vital link between home and school, explaining the family situation to the school, providing moral and material support to the family and acting as a referral point for other social work agencies.

The importance of home/school relationships to success in school has been stressed in numerous research publications on both sides of the Atlantic and was one of the important themes of the Plowden Report (1967). But this same report construed education welfare officers existing role very narrowly and concluded (p. 88) on rather flimsy evidence (MacMillan, 1977, pp. 13—16), that a new type of school social worker was required:

> Teachers are responsible for establishing a good understanding between the school and parents. There will, however, be difficult cases beyond the competence, time or training of the head or class teacher. These should be the responsibility of trained social workers, collaborating closely with the schools, readily available to teachers, and capable of securing help quickly from more specialised social services.

The Seebohm Report (1968), whose recommendations led to the emergence of the generic social worker and the creation of unified social services departments from a multiplicity of local authority welfare agencies and specialised skills, argued for the absorption of the education welfare and child guidance services in the new social services departments. However, as has been recently argued (MacMillan, 1977), it does not follow that the education welfare service is inadequate. Its rationale is, of course, based on the premise that compulsion in education is worthwhile, even if contrary to the wishes of the parent or the child. This view is now less fashionable, but it is still very widely held by a public whose children do not, on the whole, have a problem of unjustified absence from school. The education welfare officer sees himself as being devoted to preventative and remedial action.

Those few local authorities who acted on the Seebohm Report's recommendation and transferred educational welfare from the education department to social services, took the opportunity to restore the *status quo* with the reorganisation of local government structure. The more recent Pack Report (1977), an official investigation into truancy in Scotland, recognised the importance and distinct role of the education welfare officer, argued for more training, but rejected any suggestion that these officers should become professional social workers.

Whatever his specialist teams (and the list could be extended to include school catering services and architectural and building services), the main responsibility for stimulating and implementing education committee policy rests with the Chief Education Officer and perhaps a dozen of his immediate subordinates. The expectation among teachers, many parents and possibly central government administrators is that he will act as a focus for professional standards, alternately restraining and encouraging elected lay members as appropriate. While Ministers of Education Forster, Fisher, Boyle, Crosland may be famous for their policy initiatives, at local level it is very often Chief Education Officers whose names are associated with worthwhile developments. Fairbairn is seen as the author of the Leicestershire scheme of junior and upper comprehensive schools begun in the 1950s; Sir Alec Clegg is associated with the middle school, among other innovations and priorities; of an earlier generation James Graham, rather than his committee chairman, is remembered for the establishment of a very substantial teacher training college at Becketts Park in Leeds; and Morris is remembered as having fought his committee over many years to establish successfully the village colleges of Cambridgeshire.

This stereotype can be challenged, however, on grounds of historical accuracy and of an inadequate conceptualisation of the current role of the Chief Education Officer. By no means all school boards or their successor local education authorities appointed Chief Education Officers or selected men with the qualifications or background experience to carry through the role of intellectual and administrative pioneer. The elected membership of the West Riding Education Committee was so dominated by well-born and determined educationists that, after an unsuccessful initial experiment in 1904, it did not countenance a further appointment of a Chief Education Officer until 1929. The work of Sidney Webb in education in the 1890s, was a member of the London County Council Technical Instruction Committee, not as an employee.

There are at least two administrative styles appropriate to and successfully practised by Chief Education Officers. One emphasises the policy leadership role of the chief and conforms to the expected stereotype; the other puts the stress on administrative skills which facilitate the work and initiatives of departmental staff but which may not be so easily glamorised. Pioneering instincts and serendipity may well have served the education service well, whether originating in the chief officer or committee members, in the days when a comprehensive public education service, its range and institutional forms, had still to be developed and when other local government services were still largely concerned with physical infrastructure or were very small in scale. In the post-war period and, more certainly, in the 1970s and 1980s, with educational resources under great pressure and educational aims questioned on all sides, a Chief Education Officer with all the tactical skills for survival has perhaps proved more appropriate.

Even so, the over-simple implication of such a judgement is that the Chief Education Officer is the one essential ingredient in the local educational structure. In fact, few officers would disagree that it is the combination of chief and education committee chairman that can make or break the case for education within an authority. All the chief officers interviewed by Kogan and Van der Eyken (1973) laid great stress on the closeness of their relationship with their chairman. To understand this relationship and its importance, it is necessary to look at the role of elected members in local government, at the growth of overt organised party politics and at the theories of local government management which have been increasingly applied in recent years.

ELECTED MEMBERS: THEIR PARTIES, FUNCTIONS AND ROLES

The Maud Committee on the Management of Local Government (1967) undertook a survey of the local councillor, his workload and his priorities. Although there were differences of emphasis among councillors in different areas and of different persuasions, the common pattern that emerged was of committed, conscientious public representatives working long hours, often in difficult conditions, for no more reward than personal satisfaction or increased self-esteem.

Although elected by the general public, councillors are less than

representative of the community in their backgrounds:
(Maud, 1967, p. 135)

> members do not reflect the community in terms of age, sex,
> occupation or education. Members tend to be drawn from the older
> sections of the population; their average age is 55, and that of
> women members is somewhat higher. Over a quarter of the adult
> male population are in the 21 — 34 age group, but only a twentieth
> of men members are of this age . . . only about 12 per cent of
> members are women . . . employers and managers, and farmers and
> professional workers, occupy a larger proportion of seats in the
> councils than their proportion in the general adult male population.
> But the converse is true of skilled and unskilled manual workers . . .
> Members of local authorities are, on the average, better qualified
> than the electors whether in terms of GCE passes, teacher's
> certificates, professional qualifications or degrees. The younger the
> member the higher on the average is the level of qualification held.

Summarised in these ways, the contemporary locally elected
representative is not the social, commercial or industrial leader found
in county or city government in the nineteenth and even early
twentieth century, as documented by Birch (1959), Lee (1963) or
Hennock (1973). Rather, a class of public persons has come into
existence that is characterised by the extent and range of its members'
public service. While the reduction in number of councillors effected
in the course of local government reorganisation (there were over
40,000, excluding parish councillors, in 1967) may have excluded
some of the oldest and least formally educated, there is no evidence to
suggest any radical change in the characteristics of members over the
last few years, with one exception. The redrawing of local government
boundaries so as to mix old county areas with old county boroughs
has certainly been accompanied by the extension of overt, organised
party politics in local authorities. Although the Conservative Party
has long been organised at local level in urban areas, it has sometimes
been content to avoid party labels in rural areas, where local elections
have often been contested by no more than one candidate. The *soi-
disant* independent has also survived in such areas but is increasingly
likely to be challenged by candidates wearing the party label.

Parties may serve to communicate the bias and political
temperament of candidates at elections, while remaining dormant
between times. In large counties like the old West Riding candidates
were elected on a Labour ticket, subscribed in general to the policies

of a County Council Labour group, but were in very loose association with each other over policy matters, partly as a result of the scattered and varied nature of the county, partly because of the fragmentary way in which the Council conducted its business and partly because no party organisation of activists existed at County Council level to act as ginger group or ideology-bearing structure.

By contrast, in the big cities Labour has often been very tightly organised in party and Council groups for local politics. The London Labour Party, which gained a majority on the London County Council in 1934, was said to be closely controlled by its leading Council members, most outstandingly Herbert Morrison. In Leeds elaborate constitutional arrangements characterise the relationship between the City Council Labour Party (concerned only with local government matters) and the Labour group of councillors. The City Party is responsible for the election manifesto, the policy sections of which are drawn up by specialist groups of party activists and the councillors sitting on the appropriate Council committee. Each month councillors may be challenged on decisions taken or statements made by the Labour group or (when in a minority on the Council) on their reactions to the policies of the majority party.

Each Labour candidate for Council is drawn from a panel made up of those who have been interviewed and approved by the City Party. Each candidate in turn affirms his loyalty, if elected, to the standing orders of the Labour group, which require members' unswerving support for Labour group decisions; similar sorts of pressure, perhaps less legalistically elaborate, are brought to bear on Conservative councillors. Liberal Party groups usually wear a lighter yoke but are rarely in the position where the consistency and coherence of majority party policy-making are at a premium.

Within the party group on Council procedures may be established to allow every member the possibility, in principle, of monitoring the decisions taken in his and his party's name. Wiseman (1967) has outlined the procedures of the Leeds City Council Labour group. Each group of members representing Labour on a particular committee has to meet to consider the agenda and supporting papers before following a common line at the subsequent public committee meeting. In each cycle of committee and Council meetings the full Labour group meets to discuss major policy issues that are coming forward for decision. Immediately prior to the Council meeting at which minutes of service committees are to be confirmed the full

Labour group meets to consider any queries and agrees (if necessary and if in power on the Council) to withdraw the committee minute, or (if in opposition) which committee decisions of the majority party to contest at the full Council meeting. In addition, of course, there are many informal meetings of Labour members, and an executive committee of senior Labour councillors known as the Advisory Committee) will be the first to be consulted when urgent decisions need to be taken.

It does not follow from these very elaborate arrangements that there is any automatic difference in the quality of decisions taken by the Council under the leadership of the different parties. If it did, an observer would expect to see much more uniformity of policy among Labour-controlled local authorities than is apparent from an examination of party policy as clear as the introduction of comprehensive secondary education. In some cases school reorganisation may have been resisted on ideological grounds by Labour leaders nurtured in the pre-war period of expansion of grammar schools (Fenwick and Woodthorpe, 1980); in other cases party control appears to have amounted to little more than 'boss politics'—that is to say, the politics of position and minor patronage over honorary public office (such as school governorships) untinged by ideological considerations which might have consequences for substantive policy. Indeed, a case can be made to show much greater ideological commitment on the part of more flexibly organised local Conservative groups. Homogeneity of political purpose may not be a very clear function of the elaboration of party organisation.

Nevertheless, party group organisation provides a forum for debate and the determination of policy if the opportunity is taken by councillors. In this political world, as in the Council as a whole, there emerge councillors with differing strengths and priorities. Newton (1976) looked at the self-image of councillors in Birmingham in a number of different dimensions and sketched, in a series of cameos, councillor types discharging a variety of functions recognisable as part of a complex political process. He asked councillors about their relationships with their constituents, as conscience-bound representatives or as mandated delegates of the voters. He measured their loyalty to the party group when faced with conflicting pressures and their identification with the ward that they represented or the larger area of the whole city on whose council they sat. Again, Newton found distinctions between councillors in their orientation towards broad policy issues or the problems of individual citizens.

From his evidence Newton pinpointed five different stereotypes of the councillor: parochials, people's agents, policy advocates, policy brokers, policy spokesmen. The first two categories include those who place great emphasis on dealing with individual problems and on the problems of the ward that they represent, in the first case rather like unpaid welfare workers, in the second as tribunes of the people 'protecting the population against governmental injustice' (Newton, 1976, p. 138). For policy advocates, as the name suggests,

> political activity consists not in solving individual problems, but in working on policy matters both in the party group and in committee . . . Policy advocates typically enter the Council at a fairly early age and stay on for a long time. The average age of entry is thirty-eight and the average length of experience, fourteen years. This suggests a greater commitment to politics than either the parochial or the agent, and it is not surprising, therefore, that three-quarters of the advocates were, or had been chairmen or vice-chairmen. (*ibid.,* p. 140).

By contrast, policy brokers, rather than following a commitment to some substantive policy, 'are rather more likely to see themselves as moderates who perform the classical political brokerage role of mediator and reconciler of different interests' (*ibid.,* p. 141). Finally, the policy spokesman sees himself as reconciling his responsibilities towards his ward constituent and general policy by speaking directly on their behalf on policy issues.

Newton's analysis of the different roles and combinations of roles that councillors see themselves playing is given in this detail not because it is definitive or unquestionable but because it illustrates the complexity of political life in local government. With analytical tools such as Newton provides it is possible to look at overtly political inputs to the local education service, to make some sense of their motivation and their function and not to dismiss local politicians naively as inteferers in the smooth running of an administrative machine. It is to be expected that local political intervention will be resented by some; however, it must not be assumed that councillors see their work on behalf of their individual constituents simply as a challenge to educational bureaucracy, as a questioning of 'professional' decisions in the case of particular children, students or communities. Such councillors may be on or off the education committee, but they are not necessarily without rationale for their interventions. At the same time, education committees have in the past attracted their fair share of policy advocates and have consequently sometimes needed their share of policy brokers. It may be the case, as has often been claimed, that policy advocates in education, regardless of political party, have sometimes had more in common with each other than with their political colleagues on other committees. The sharper ideological edge of the policy spokesman may have redressed that balance more recently, as major policy issues have clearly divided political parties.

Individuals may not fit the models with any precision, but the characteristics detailed may be recognised and admired or scorned, especially in discussions of the role and importance of education committee chairmen. For it is he (or she) who has to carry his party committee group with him and, if possible, the opposition; similarly, he has to convince his leader and his political colleagues generally that the necessary resources for a policy initiative should be made available, that the public controversy which a particular decision may arouse should be outfaced or that the protests of a minority within the party group should be overborne. In all this he may receive invaluable assistance from his Chief Education Officer, who will be carrying on parallel negotiations as necessary with his fellow chief officers; but in the privacy of the party caucus, where professional officers penetrate only very rarely, it is the chairman who must carry the day by argument, by cajolery or by threats.

The Maud Committee (1967) concluded its deliberation on party politics with the very weak declaration: 'all we can say is that in some places party government is preferred while in others it is considered to be detrimental' (p. 8). There can be no doubt that the thirteen years that have followed have extended the influence of party government, reinforced by changes in local authority structure and combining in particular with changes in management processes. The Maud Committee's summary (p. 8) of the potential of party politics in local government is no less telling now than in 1967:

> it is clear that party government has the same advantages overseas as it has here: ideological drive, greater coherence, clearer responsibility and more consistency. The same disadvantages are also apparent: restrictions of choice of candidates to the politically minded, tendency to a doctrinaire approach, the making of decisions behind the scenes, appointment to chairmanships and other offices on the strength of service to the party, and partisan treatment of neutral business.

THE INTERNAL ORGANISATION OF LOCAL AUTHORITIES: ITS EFFECT ON DECISION-MAKING PROCESSES

A relatively simple financial process and set of negotiations has been transformed over the last fifteen years by innovations in local authority management structure and by processes which have made it even more important for education committee chairmen and Chief Education Officers to co-ordinate their respective activities.

In the late 1960s more and more local authorities experimented with the appointment of Chief Executives and with the establishment of a central Policy and Finance Committee. Traditionally, finance committees had been concerned, as their title suggests, with all matters financial and with the controversial question of the annual rate to be set, but they had not intervened directly in determining the policies or priorities of service committees, least of all the education committee. Similarly, the senior position among chief officers had gone to the Town or County Clerk, who headed the Council's legal services but did not in any way interfere with the policy content of committee deliberation unless there were legal implications to be considered. The two initiatives reflected the growing discontent with the lack of political and administrative co-ordination in the affairs of local authorities.

The predominant theoretical rationale for internal change lay in 'corporate management', which attracted national approval in the Report of the Maud Committee on Management of Local Government (1967). Figure 3.1 shows the radical transformation of committee structure and function and officer accountability which the Maud Committee proposed. The Committee argued that the delegation of powers to individual service committees frustrated the creation of a managing body for the local authority. 'Service or function, committee, principal officer and department tend to be interlocked and self-contained' (p. 28). With rigid fragmentation, it was difficult 'to identify the major issues which confront a local authority and to isolate them from the mass of routine matters. It is essential that major issues are identified, and that staff work and planning are done and presented in such a way that decisions can be taken on these issues' (p. 37).

FIG. 3.1 Maud Committee proposals for local authority management organisation. Source: Ministry of Housing and Local Government *Report of the Committee on the Management of Local Government,* HMSO, 1967, p. 50.

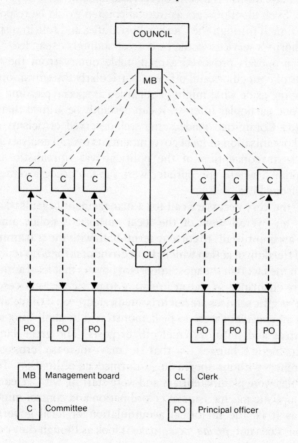

The Maud Committee's solution was to attempt, despite denial (p. 38), to reassert the crude traditional distinction between policy and administration. It asserted the supremacy of the Council, many of whose decisions would be delegated to a small management committee of five to nine councillors, while service committees would become 'deliberative and representative bodies' (p. 43). The management committee would resemble a Cabinet in many ways; members would speak for particular spheres of interest but would not be responsible for them, nor would they be drawn solely from the majority political party. Statutory requirements for the establishment of certain committees, including an education committee, would be abolished, as would any ministerial control over the appointment of particular officers. Such chief officers as were appointed would be responsible to the Council through the Clerk, whose duties and role in respect of the authority's services would be correspondingly expanded.

Such proposals provoked a predictable outcry from the vested interests of councillors and officers, particularly the educationalists. Yet, leaving aside what might be regarded as special pleading on the part of one particular interest, it can certainly be argued that while the Maud Committee made some well-deserved criticisms of the internal organisation of local government, its overall analysis was ill-founded, its conception of the political was unrealistic and its prescriptions, where appropriate, were far too crude a remedy for acknowledged ills.

First, the very necessary call for a management organisation that permits an overall view of the local authority's policy aims and options apparently fails to come to terms both with the real limitations on local freedom of action which the doctrine of *ultra vires* represents and with the fact that the most important powers that local authorities enjoy are enshrined in statutes relating to particular services; these roots in specific services are not to be eradicated, even if the desirability of such an expedient were to be demonstrated by abolishing service committees and statutory chief officer posts. The great danger of such cosmetic changes is that it may increase cross-service interference without increasing informed co-ordination. If local authorities were plenipotentiary and were starting with a clean slate, such simplistic mechanisms of co-ordination and control might just work; as it is, the historical accumulation of local government functions does not, *prima facie,* make it look as though they could or should be co-ordinated.

Finally, it may not be surprising, although it is disappointing, that an official committee made up largely of academics and administrators should be unable to cope with the incidence of party political activity in local government. Having recognised its value as well as its dangers, the committee fails completely to exploit and control as appropriate; rather, it seeks to emasculate by proposing a Cabinet system denuded of all its potential coherence and thus pushes all politically controversial decisions back into unofficial caucuses and informal gatherings.

While the Maud Committee Report did not receive universal assent (indeed, one of its members appended a note of dissent to the critical recommendations to abolish decision-taking functional committees), its approach, its analysis and its priorities are, not surprisingly, to be found influencing the succeeding Royal Commission on Local Government in England, which was also chaired by Sir John (later Lord Redcliffe) Maud and which reported in 1969. The necessity for a comprehensive, coherent and consistent set of policies in each local authority, an ideal to be achieved at least in part by internal administrative structure, has remained an important element in central and local government thinking among politicians and officers ever since, and this change of perspective may be the most significant outcome of more than a decade of debate about many different aspects of local government. To those outside local government, however, the most striking changes must be in the structure of authorities, areas and functions which followed on, though not from, the Royal Commissions in England, Wales and Scotland.

THE EVOLUTION OF UNITS FOR THE LOCAL PROVISION OF EDUCATION

The tendency of reform in the structure of local authorities and, in particular, of those responsible for education has been towards progressively larger units of administration. Government's first intervention in the provision of education was to offer financial assistance to the sponsors of individual schools. The school boards of the second half of the nineteenth century predated the creation of the County Councils; intended by statute to supplement and complete voluntary provision, their foundation often dependent on local initiatives, many of the boards covered very small areas and catered for very limited populations in only one or two schools.

The major change for the rural school boards came in England and Wales with the passing of the 1902 Education Act. Controversial at the time for its abolition of a system of *ad hoc* authorities and for the contribution to the running of Church schools from local public income that it made possible, the Act may have been more significant in uniting the control of the education service with that of other developing local services in most-purpose authorities. Even so, the attraction of the small local authority as the means by which the interests of the immediate community surrounding the school could be articulated was such that within the new county education authorities responsibility for elementary education very often remained with the second-tier authority, the municipal authority or urban district council.

In Scotland some 984 elementary school boards had been established, one in every parish and burgh. These school boards continued to exist until 1918, despite the view of government (expressed as early as 1892) that they were too small to undertake responsibility for the development of secondary education. This responsibility was given instead to the county councils and the four (later six) largest burghs. By 1918 the established view was that parishes were too small to retain sole educational responsibility, and the multitudes of school boards gave way to thirty-eight *ad hoc* education authorities, mirroring the counties and the largest burghs. Area management committees at the parish level were retained, but it was not long before the education service was, as in England, taken over by the most-purpose county authorities. A very substantial reduction in the number of education authorities had been achieved and many of the smallest school boards eliminated, yet Scottish local education authorities in the 1960s varied enormously in size. 'The number of pupils for which an education authority is responsible ranges from 180,000 in Glasgow, to just over 2000 in Peebleshire and just under 2000 in Bute, and 16, nearly half, of the authorities have under 10,000 in their areas' (Scottish Education Department, 1968).

The range of size among local education authorities in England with equal statutory responsibilities was just as great. At one extreme the smallest county borough, Canterbury, had a total population of 32,000; at the other, Lancashire comprised nearly two and a half million people.

Northern Ireland presents a somewhat different picture because of its system of provincial government; from 1921 to 1972 the Northern Ireland Parliament discharged all responsibilities for education that are, for the rest of Britain, under the control of Westminster. Within Northern Ireland some seventy-three directly elected local authorities (twenty-seven of them with populations of less than 10,000) administered various services. Until 1923 local control of education had been almost entirely in the hands of the providers of individual voluntary schools, subject to regulation from Dublin. Thereafter it became the responsibility of eight local education authorities, each empowered to set up one or more education committees for their area. Eighteen education committees were established, but the number was restricted to one for each local education authority in 1947. Since the suspension of Stormont in 1972, the Northern Ireland Parliament's responsibilities have been discharged by the Secretary of State for Northern Ireland, a member of the British Cabinet. Even so, in 1970 just under one-third of primary schools were sponsored by a religious denomination and were under the control of an individual manager, usually the parish priest.

Clearly, over the past century of local authority involvement in the provision of education each restructuring has been motivated by, or has afforded the opportunity for, a reduction in the number of independent sources of political and administrative power in the education system, whether by bringing previously separate responsibilities under the control of one authority, by eliminating a class of authority or simply by reducing the numbers within a particular class of authority. This is not to say that there has been no resistance to the consolidation of responsibility for education in the hands of fewer authorities, nor that the direction of reform has always seemed straightforward.

The Royal Commission on the Government of Greater London (1960) found itself with the unenviable task of devising a system of government for the capital which would take account of present-day rather than nineteenth-century social geography and yet maintain some intelligible connection between the providers of services and those provided for. A council covering a much larger area and population than the former London County Council was proposed, with a second tier of borough authorities discharging responsibility for most services, including education. And yet in order to preserve the continuity of educational provision in the area of central London which had previously been the responsibility of the London County Council, an *ad hoc* body, the Inner London Education Authority, was set up, consisting of county councillors for the area and one representative of each of the twelve Inner London boroughs.

The 1944 Education Act quite clearly made the counties and county boroughs the local education authority for their areas. Yet contrary to the original intentions of those who framed the Act, the legislation provided for the delegation of some responsibility for primary and secondary education to second-tier local authorities, municipal borough or urban district, or to *ad hoc* bodies to be known as divisional executive. Some second-tier authorities, if they were large enough, could require delegation of responsibilities for schools and were known as 'excepted districts'. Forty-four excepted districts were established under the 1944 Education Act, along with some 169 divisional executives: through piecemeal reform of local government, they had been reduced in number by 1974 to thirty and 142 respectively. About a third of the counties had no divisional executives; ten contained a single excepted district; and the rest had schemes of divisional administration to cover all or part of their area. Lancashire set up thirty-seven divisional executives, paralleling the areas of second-tier authorities, but by 1949 was reducing the numbers, with ministerial approval, to twenty-seven. On the other hand, Surrey managed to persuade four potential excepted districts to withdraw their applications for education powers and to co-operate in a scheme for nine divisions covering the whole county.

In analysing what was thought to be wrong with local government, the Royal Commission on Local Government in England (1969) commented: 'Perhaps the most frequently voiced criticism of the present structure is that many local authorities, whether county, county borough or county district councils, are too small in terms of area, population and resources, including highly qualified manpower and technical equipment.' The Commission was referring to the evidence submitted to it by government Departments, local authority associations and professional organisations. Pre-eminent among those calling for structural changes that would radically increase the size of local authorities were the representatives of the education interest. Not surprisingly, the County Councils Association, among whose members were those authorities with the largest areas and populations, submitted that a minimum population size of 500,000 was necessary for any authority with responsibilities similar to those of counties. The Ministry of Housing and Local Government implicitly set a minimum of 300,000. The DES thought local education authorities should administer a minimum population of 500,000. 'The Association of Education Committees put the minimum population at 400,000 though some of its members thought this was too high.' (Royal Commission, England, 1969, p. 37). (This was an understatement of the disagreement within the Association of Education

Committees. The Association's executive had acted under delegated powers to submit evidence to the Commission, pre-empting a special meeting of the full membership, which agreed to delete any reference to a minimum size for local education authorities.) The Commission noted that at least three-quarters of present education authorities failed to meet this minimum-size criterion.

Not all those giving evidence accorded the same priority to size; the Association of Municipal Corporations, representing many of the smallest education authorities, doubted the positive correlation between efficiency and size, and the Commission carried out its own research in an attempt to secure more objective evidence. However, a highly technical comparison of size and performance of local education authorities produced very little evidence one way or another; a systematic but subjective assessment of local education authorities by the Inspectorate gave positive support to those who advocated larger authorities, but not without some qualification: 'one of the best authorities had a population below 200,000. One of the worst had a large population.' (Royal Commission, England, 1969, Vol. III, App. 11, p. 223). The Royal Commission's majority recommendation was for unitary local authorities with a minimum size of 250,000, its conclusions clearly influenced very much by the weight if not the soundness of the education lobby's arguments.

Even then, one of the members of the Royal Commission dissented from this finding. Mr J. Longland, then Director of Education for Derbyshire, thought that some twenty of the local authorities recommended as a result of the application of this principle of minimum size were too small to provide an efficient education service. Another member, Mr Senior, had very different grounds for dissent; he thought that the majority had given priority to the question of size to the exclusion of other equally important criteria.

> They have adopted a principle of organisation—the unitary principle—and determined a range of population size for unitary authorities by analysing the theoretical requirements of functional efficiency and democratic viability in isolation from the geographical context in which local government must operate—though with a tender regard for the need to 'maintain the momentum' of the existing administrative pattern. (Senior, 1969)

The Commissioners and many of those who gave evidence did seem to identify size with population and only indirectly with resources or area, much as past legislation had used population figures to justify the exercise of functions by particular local authorities. If the notion of size is ambiguous, how much more so is the notion of 'quality of performance'—and yet the case for change was largely made in terms of the positive correlation between size and efficiency. But what are the outputs of education or social work? Which of them can be measured? If higher outputs are associated sometimes with larger authorities, sometimes with smaller, which should have priority? What level of output is satisfactory? The Royal Commission's research examined twenty-seven measures of educational provision; only five measures correlated significantly with size, and two of them indicated that smaller authorities did better. Critics might claim that this was hardly an adequate basis for determining the size of local education authorities (cf. Wood, 1976).

During the same period the Wheatley Commission (1969) examined local government in Scotland and seems also to have accepted that size was synonymous with efficiency, although they rejected the strait-jacket of unitary authorities. As in England (but in more acute form), the problem for the Commission was to reconcile a uniform system of authorities with the facts of social geography. The Highlands Region which came into existence in 1975 is bigger in area than the next two largest sister regions, Strathclyde and Grampian, put together; within the Strathclyde Region the Glasgow District Council area contains a larger population than the whole of any other region. Again, echoing its English counterpart, the Wheatley Commission accepted the evidence of the education lobby and concluded: 'the appropriate size of authority for education is best expressed in terms of population. 200,000 population is about the minimum required for an authority to provide an acceptable standard of service. It is not possible to identify a maximum size which should not be exceeded' (Royal Commission, Scotland, 1969, p. 11). The Wheatley Commission had an additional reason for attempting to create large regional authorities that were to be responsible for major services such as education; it affirmed its commitment to a strong local democracy and saw the need, particularly perhaps in education, to create units of local strength which might challenge successfully the too easily enjoyed authority of the Scottish Education Department.

The combination of bitter religious and parallel political division and an even smaller but similarly unevenly distributed population has hindered the maintenance of a successful system of local government in the province of Northern Ireland. Mr Brian Faulkner, Unionist Minister of National Development in the Northern Ireland Parliament, instituted a review of local government in 1969, no doubt stimulated by the much more elaborate investigations then just completed in England and Scotland. In evidence to the review body, the Northern Ireland Ministry of Education expressed satisfaction with the arrangements for local education authorities that had existed since 1923, but then, in somewhat stark contrast, took the opportunity of a general local government review to suggest the creation of up to five Area Boards for education and library services:

> A reasonable proportion of the membership of the Boards should be representative of the local electorate and there should also be representatives of the transferrors of schools, the maintained school authorities, the teachers and other persons interested in education or the public library service. (Ministry of Development, 1970, p. 18)

The Ministry argued that such boards would improve on existing arrangements

> in that Boards would be responsible for viable administrative areas of broadly comparable size and importance from the point of population and financial resources. They would have a broadly based membership drawn from sections of the community most capable of making a worthwhile contribution to educational administration. A system such as this would facilitate the creation of well-balanced Boards consisting of responsible and public-spirited persons, who on the one hand would owe their loyalty primarily to the Boards and on the other, because they would be in a position to interpret the views of the main sectional interests, might be expected to induce a spirit of confidence, cooperation and goodwill amongst those interests. (Quoted in Ministry of Development, 1970, pp. 18—19)

It is difficult to avoid drawing the conclusion that the Northern Ireland Ministry of Education was looking for a way of introducing proportional representation through its power to nominate members of the proposed Boards and then of beginning to break down the barriers between the Protestant ethos of state provision and the grant-aided Catholic schools. Certainly, when Stormont was suspended the new Secretary of State, ruling directly from Westminster, went ahead with the removal of education from the control of elected local authorities and confirmed the Area Boards as his agents in the localities.

Recent experience of local educational administration in Northern Ireland, in Inner London and, earlier, under the school boards of England and Scotland demonstrates the capacity of the education system to survive apart from the rest of local government. Northern Ireland might be thought to confirm the view that there are at least some social, political and administrative circumstances in which education is clearly best served by being organised in isolation. Nevertheless, those pressing education's case at the time of the Royal Commission often argued rather that local government should be adapted to suit education; that related services should be kept in step with the school system; and that local government finance should meet the needs, first and foremost, of an expanding education service. It was this theme, sometimes explicit, sometimes muted, in evidence to the Redcliffe-Maud Commission that, along with the insistence on size as a critical factor in efficiency, stimulated Commissioner Senior to make his most astringent comments on education.

> Education is, indeed, the cuckoo in the local government nest. In origin extraneous, in appetite voracious, it requites its foster-parents' tireless devotion with a less than filial display of family feeling. Yet even the cuckoo does not demand that the nest in which it chooses to lay its egg shall be designed to suit its offspring rather than the hedge-sparrow's, solely on the ground that its offspring will be consuming most of their food.

> 323. Education, however, is less accommodating. It insists upon unquestioning acceptance of the doctrine of the 'seamless robe'—that responsibility for all non-university education, from play-school to polytechnic, should be carried in each area by one unit of local government . . . (Royal Commission, England, 1969, Vol. II, pp. 75—76)

The view that Senior captures and slightly caricatures in the above passage can hardly stem from any long-standing educational principle, since educational institutions in Britain have sought to thrive by stressing their uniqueness, and universities for one have never been part of local educational government. Rather, the view is based on the historical experience of the educational administrator and local politician in coping with divided responsibilities in county areas under the Education Acts 1902 and 1944. As Senior would agree, artificial and unnecessary distinctions in local government that separate one part of the education service from another are unwelcome; but the argument could be used to undermine any local government of education, dividing as it does the control of the education service by geographical area, and even if the 'seamless robe' argument is accepted in principle, it does not follow that every other consideration and every other local government service should be sacrificed to it.

Between the end of the Second World War and the middle of the 1970s the control of education at local levels had been in the hands of over 160 authorities, counties and county boroughs, in England and Wales and thirty-five education authorities in Scotland (twenty-nine county authorities, two joint county councils and the four cities of Aberdeen, Dundee, Edinburgh and Glasgow); while in Northern Ireland eight local authorities had responsibility for education, subject to the Province's own Parliament and Minister of Education.

In the area of the Greater London Council, which came into existence in 1965 and which contains one-sixth of the population of England, education is controlled by twenty of the thirty-two London boroughs. In the area of the twelve boroughs of Central London which had previously been governed by the defunct London County Council, an *ad hoc* board known as the Inner London Education Authority was set up, composed of one borough councillor for each of the Inner London Borough Councils and the Greater London councillors for the same area. Before the reform of 1965, which attempted to take account of the facts of social geography in the London area, responsibility for education had fallen on five county education authorities, apart from the London County Council; of these Middlesex was abolished, and the others, Essex, Hertfordshire, Kent and Surrey, had their areas slightly or substantially reduced.

The Redcliffe-Maud Commission in England recommended the establishment, in all areas except three outside Greater London, of fifty-eight unitary authorities responsible for all existing local authority services. In three specific conurbations two tiers of authority, one county and a number of districts in each case, should be established. The consequence of these recommendations for the education service would be that in nearly all cases it would be the responsibility of large authorities; the unitary district would not have its functions divided in any way, and it would always find related services under the control of the same authority. The then Labour

Government altered the number and location of the metropolitan counties and decided that education should be a county responsibility in the metropolitan areas; otherwise it accepted the Royal Commission's commitment to a single tier of local authorities based largely on the extension of the boundaries of the larger cities and towns. Such a view may have been encouraged by the strength of Labour's tradition in the county boroughs. Conversely, the Conservative Party was familiar with the two- or three-tier county system, in which it had overwhelming political strength; and the Conservative Government elected in 1970, before Labour had been able to put through its reforms, was committed to a universal two-tier system, with education the exclusive responsibility of thirty-nine non-metropolitan counties and some thirty-six districts within six metropolitan counties covering the West Midlands, South Yorkshire, West Yorkshire, the Manchester area, Merseyside and Tyneside. With the 1972 Local Government Act, which came fully into force in April 1974 and was paralleled in Wales and Scotland, where two-tier systems were more readily accepted, the education service became the responsibility of far fewer authorities, whose control was undivided and whose relationships with cognate services was intact.

A further success for the local education service was the retention of the two statutory requirements of an education committee and a Chief Education Officer. In other respects, however, structural reform provided the opportunity for a change of management ethos in local authorities and for the implementation of many of the ideas of the Maud Committee, as reinterpreted and modified by the Bains Committee, which had been jointly appointed by the Secretary of State and the local authority associations to explore the details of management structures which might be appropriate to the new authorities. The Bains Report re-emphasised the need for corporate objectives and planning and for the subordination of service perspectives and priorities to the overall aims of the authority. Parallel to any central committee of councillors, it proposed a management team of chief officers under the chairmanship of the Chief Executive. Put into effect by most local authorities, the management team sometimes included only the central-function chief officers (those for legal affairs, finance and perhaps personnel), while in other authorities a larger team almost always included the Chief Education Officer. At best, such arrangements gave the Chief Education Officer the opportunity to see what was happening elsewhere in the authority that was relevant to proper educational provision and to defend the interests of education; at worst, his own service, with its numerous staff, large capital commitment and overwhelming budget, might attract a great deal of attention from Treasury finance officers, from newly appointed personnel officers, and from management specialists demanding unequivocal and objective measures of output or success in attaining objectives.

The six years since reorganisation have seen an outcry from many education committees and education officers (Winter, 1977) which has dwarfed the willingness and success of others in experimenting with new management techniques within and across departments and has masked some of the other causes of difficulty associated with educational provision and outside intervention.

First, the introduction of legislation designed to regulate employment and to protect the position of the employee faced with disciplinary action or dismissal (most recently, the Sex Discrimination Act and the Employment Protection Act 1975) has made it impossible for any education department to maintain within its ranks the necessary detailed expertise. It does not follow that personnel departments supply the need adequately, but the education department's dependence on outside sources of help has increased.

Second, local government reform and the introduction of many aspects of corporate planning techniques has coincided with more severe economic difficulties for the country and consequent constraints on public expenditure, nationally and locally, than have been known since the 1930s. In a period of restraint or of a reduction in services a corporate process of evaluation of alternatives, however painful, may be thought even more desirable than in a period of expansion. It challenges education committees, chairmen and Chief Education Officers to present their case and to defend their interests in new and sometimes unfamiliar ways. But in most respects those involved in the local government of education are simply engaging more fiercely (and with more at stake) in the traditional battle for resources which has always been at the centre of local government.

THE FINANCING OF EDUCATION BY LOCAL EDUCATION AUTHORITIES

In the financial year 1978—9 local authorities' expenditure in Britain totalled some £15,000,000,000 and another £120,000,000 was spent by Northern Ireland local authorities. Capital expenditure in the same year was well over £4000 million. Capital and current expenditure together represented 11.3 per cent of Gross Domestic Product (Layfield, 1976, Table 29). Across all local authority expenditure some 40 per cent was on educational services, but since only non-metropolitan counties and metropolitan districts had responsibility for education, the proportion of their expenditure that was devoted to education was considerably higher. As Table 1 makes clear, the education service has been by far the largest consumer of local government resources since the post-war creation of nationalised industries removed from municipal control several major trading enterprises and caused a decline in other municipal trading.

TABLE 3.1
Revenue Expenditure of Local Authorities Analysed by Service

	1947—8		1966—7	
	£m	%	£m	%
Education	209	21.8	1,386	38.3
Housing	59	6.1	558	15.4
Trading	279	29.0	302	8.3
Police and fire	44	4.6	271	7.5
Highways	70	7.3	260	7.2
Public Health	62	6.5	252	7.0
Individual health	19	2.0	129	3.5
Welfare	—	—	119	3.3
Other	218	22.7	345	9.6
Totals	960	100.0	3,622	100.0

Source: N. P. Hepworth, *The Finance of Local Government,* Allen & Unwin, 1971, p. 36

At the same time, much of education expenditure is mandatory. Of total recurrent educational expenditure, most is on statutory provision of school education and related ancillary services. From the Figure 3.2 it can be seen that such provision as is discretionary (in scope, if not in principle), such as the youth service or the non-vocational element of further education provision, forms only a very small proportion of expenditure. The main thrust of educational expenditure in the post-war years has been to cope with rising numbers within the statutorily required framework of schools and with accelerating demand for post-compulsory education, whether in school fifth and sixth forms or in further and higher education. Figure 3.3 shows the very close connection between the rate of increase in total local education authority expenditure and expenditure on primary and secondary education, despite the much faster rate of increase from a very low base of expenditure on further education and

FIG. 3.2 Analysis of education expenditure by sector. (1) Including expenditure on training of teachers; adult education; and polytechnic expenditure amounting to 3.1 per cent. (2) University expenditure is for Great Britain; other expenditure relates to England and Wales only.
Source: Department of Education and Science, *Statistics of Education, England and Wales* vol. 5: *Finance and Awards, 1977,*
HMSO, 1979, Chart 2

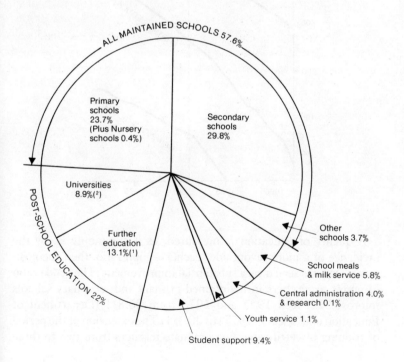

the training of teachers. While the relationship still holds, Figure 3.3 also illustrates the over-optimism of predictions for educational expenditure in the 1970's.

FIG. 3.3 Local education authority revenue expenditure — England and Wales. Source: K. Ollerenshaw, *Education and Finance,* Institute of Municipal Treasurers and Accountants, 1969.

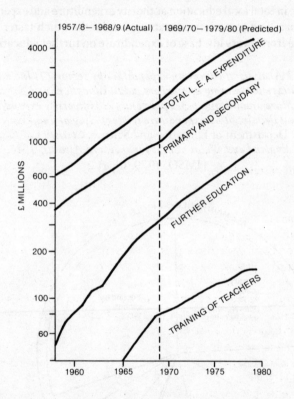

If quality of education is measured, as it commonly is, by the incidence of a more favourable teacher — pupil ratio, then the post-war period has seen a very substantial improvement. The crude ratio of pupils to teachers in maintained primary and secondary schools improved between 1955 and 1976 from 26.8/1 (Department of Education and Science, 1977) to 20.3/1. The extension of the period of training of certificated non-graduate teachers from two to three years with the 1960 training entry, and the more recent introduction of compulsory training for all new graduate teachers except those with degrees in science or mathematics, may also be said to have improved the quality of educational provision. Improvements in teachers' salaries, as documented in Greenhalgh (1968), in concert with the factors noted above and with their corollary that education remains, like much of local government, a labour intensive service, make teachers' salaries the largest element in local education authorities' budgets and a virtually inescapable commitment. In parallel, capital expenditure on new schools and subsequent expenditure on the servicing of debt and the maintenance of fabric has grown to cope with geographical shifts and increases in child population, with the replacement of old buildings, especially primary schools, and with the specialist accommodation required by developments in the curriculum of both primary and secondary schools. Again, there is little discretion for the local education authority, although short-term financial expediency has often found its victim in school maintenance budgets. In this context, and where measures of output are very difficult to determine in principle and in practice, the search for efficiency, though varying from one authority to another, is now generally intense.

Educational expenditure has not always had such priority for either central or local government. It is extremely difficult to calculate satisfactorily the proportion of public expenditure devoted to education; does a school health service incur education or health expenditure? Where does education end and leisure activities begin? In addition, published statistics are not always conveniently or consistently presented for precise estimates over time to be made. Even so, studies such as Vaizey (1958) do indicate that the proportion of national income devoted to education grew slowly during the inter-war period, fell during the Second World War and only recovered to its pre-war peak in the middle of the 1950s. From then on, according to Vaizey, the rise in real expenditure on education has gathered momentum and has taken an increasing share of national income. It would seem clear that although much of this increase can be explained in functional terms (that is, by the expansion of the school-age population and a greatly increased demand for post-compulsory education), most apparent to the local authorities who provide education, there has been a political response at national as well as local level which goes beyond these in giving greater priority to public expenditure on education than to that on other services. It is no wonder, then, that the contemporary political culture of education associates increases in the absolute level of educational expenditure with only one possible corollary, that of an improved service, despite the sustained, if not permanent, downward trend in the birth rate and the apparent, but more questionable, levelling off of demand for traditional post-school education. The financial policies of the Conservative Government elected in 1979 have gone a stage further in reversing established commitments to educational expenditure not merely by taking full account of changing demographic factors but also by removing statutory obligations on local education authorities in respect of such para-educational services as school meals.

Local authorities have two main sources of revenue that are independent of central government: the rates and direct charges to consumers of services. Both are politically sensitive issues, if only because of the immediacy of their impact on the citizen in the form of the annual rate demand or the fee for an adult education course. For the education service charges are significant only for pre-school and post-school provision, since maintained primary and secondary schools are prevented by law from charging fees; textbooks are provided free, unlike in some European countries; and school funds raised by parents are usually administered quite independently of the authority, although they may have a substantial impact on a particular school's total discretionary resources. In further education the situation is very different; a range of fees are charged, varying according to the length, mode and institutional level of the course. Fees for advanced further education courses are set nationally; fees for non-advanced courses are, in theory, determined by each local education authority but may well emerge from regional and national consultative machinery. (For an individual college before the Second World War, very often grant-aided and semi-independent, the income from fees might amount to less than 1 per cent of total income or as much as 40 per cent.) Since further education college budgets are now commonly set without direct reference to fee income (except in the case of students from overseas or those on 'economic' courses), they are affected by the variation in student demand for courses that different fee levels may stimulate. As further education institutions very often attract students from outside the area of the local authority providing the institution, an elaborate system of recoupment between local education authorities has evolved, which means, in effect, that much of the income from fees in one local authority's accounts may appear in those of another authority as expenditure. For courses of advanced further education provided particularly in polytechnics but also in many other colleges of further education the even more elaborate pooling system operates, whereby every local education authority contributes a sum calculated roughly according to the size of the appropriate age group in its population, and the pool is disbursed to local education authorities in proportion to their contribution to the provision of advanced courses. The obvious incentive to cost-inflation here, since there is no direct connection between those who have to pay for provision and those with discretion to spend, has been the subject of the Oakes Report (1978) and the Conservative Government's more recent legislation in 1980.

About a third of local authority revenue is raised from the rates. The total rate fund expenditure of the Leeds District Council in 1976–7 was £159,528,822, of which £101,151,630 was attributed to the provision of education. Net of income from fees, recoupment, pooling and other miscellaneous sources, some £80,666,107 of educational expenditure had to be financed from rates and RSG. A substantial increase in expenditure on education is almost bound to have an effect on the rate levied: similarly, a policy designed to keep down the rate is very unlikely to be able to avoid substantial restrictions on educational expenditure.

Central government has always acknowledged in principle its obligation to support local authorities financially in their provision of services required or recommended under national statute. Assigned revenues and tax windfalls were originally recognised ways of discharging this obligation while keeping expenditure within bounds; in education 'whisky money', the financial surplus on a scheme for compensating displaced licencees, stimulated the first major involvement in educational provision of the new most-purpose local authorities in the 1890s. The system of 'payment by results' which distributed central finances to the elementary schools in the second half of the nineteenth century illustrates another means of controlled subsidy. The grant giver calculates an appropriate unit of cost and pays out only up to the maximum of eligible units. The present Conservative Government is looking for ways of introducing unit grants in education and other locally provided services in an attempt to combine necessary central subsidy with maximum local economy. Any expenditure over and above standardised unit costs falls on the local provider, who is in turn constitutionally answerable to a rate-paying electorate. Nevertheless, a unit grant may serve to encourage its potential recipients to provide a service, if only to reap the benefit of some income. Where minimum universal provision is secured, a percentage subsidy to recognised expenditure is one sure way to encourage expansion and the raising of standards of provision.

From 1918 until 1959 a large part of education expenditure was funded by specific percentage grant from the then Ministry of Education. Clearly, this encouraged local education authorities to expand their education service and to innovate, since the local authority would create twice the value of any revenue raised by local taxation. When the Local Government Act 1958 introduced the general grant for nearly all local government services, including education, there was an outcry from teachers, educational administrators and members of education committees. Government's explicit intention was to reduce the extent of its intervention in the specific objects of individual local authority expenditure. Thus a block grant, negotiated bienially between the Ministry of Local Government (now part of the Department of the Environment) and representatives of the local authorities, would take account of estimated future expenditure on most local services throughout the country. The negotiators would agree on a percentage to be met from national sources of revenue and would distribute the global sum to individual local authorities according to formulae based on criteria of local resources and needs, while leaving these same individual authorities to decide their particular priorities for themselves. The statutory requirements imposed on authorities for the provision of particular services (such as education) would remain, but much greater discretion would lie with individual authorities, and expansion beyond that envisaged in the agreed global figures would have to be met from local sources of revenue, thus placing responsibility for raising money as well as spending it more fairly on local government's shoulders. In reply to these proposals leading spokesmen for education, the Secretary of the Association of Education Committees and the General Secretary of the National Union of Teachers, argued that block grant would lead to reductions in expenditure, inevitably in education, and to an inequitable distribution of central government funds among local authorities; that it would force local authorities to feel the full effects of any economic inflation; that it would not increase the discretion over educational policy of local authorities; that it would work against the necessary expansion of education in the coming years; and that it would destroy the delicate balance of responsibilities between central government, local government and the teachers in the schools built up over nearly a hundred years.

Clearly, behind these points lay the sectional fear of educationalists, confirmed now, as then, by some elected members serving on education committees, that elected members and local authority officers as a whole have little sympathy with the provision of education beyond a statutory minimum. The experience of the 1960s, when educational expenditure continued to increase substantially under the new financing arrangements, may have reassured some, but recent financial stringency across all services, along with other changes, has produced a new crop of arguments and special pleading.

Since 1966 the Rate Support Grant, as the general grant from central government is now known, has comprised three separate elements — needs, resources and domestic. The last has been a device intended to reduce the impact of rates on the householder by subsidising the domestic rate payable by a specific amount in the pound. 'The resources element seeks to enable authorities who receive it to spend a similar amount per head for the same local rate poundage' (Layfield, 1976, p. 454). Central government acts, in effect, as an additional ratepayer, making up the deficiency between the total rateable value of the particular authority and a set figure somewhat above the average for all local authorities. The resources element for eligible local authorities is then determined by the rate poundage that a local authority charges. As that charge goes up, so does the resources element grant from the government as additional payer, just as it does for other ratepayers of the local authority.

Even more vital to the local determination of service provision and annual rate charges is the needs element, for which the distribution formula takes account of various geographical and demographic factors. The figures quoted and negotiated nationally refer to national aggregates of local authority expenditure and central government subsidy. What a particular local authority receives by way of subsidy may vary from the average on a number of grounds. In the last financial year before local government reorganisation the proportion of local authority expenditure funded by central government ranged in county boroughs from 45.7 per cent to 77.6 per cent and in county councils from 54.8 per cent to 81.4 per cent. Even a year later, after structural reform which was aimed in part at the standardisation of local authorities, metropolitan district funding varied on the same basis between 43 per cent and 74.3 per cent.

The resources formula seeks to give most to the poorest authorities and least (perhaps nothing at all) to a few of the richest. The proportion of the total national subsidy distributed according to resources may weaken or reinforce the redistribution of public funds from rich to poor. Within the needs element the various factors taken into account, such as proportions of young children or old people, the implications of a scattered or declining population, may vary in weight from one year to the next, with great significance for the finances of particular local authorities. Table 3.2 shows that the importance of one part of the needs element formula may be reinforced by the proportion of the funds available that is attributed to it; out of five factors, the 'population' formula was thus responsible for distributing among local authorities some £1191 million and the 'education units' some £833 million from a total needs element value of £2297 million. It is not surprising that long and detailed negotiations take place between the Department of the Environment and the local authorities at political and official levels to settle both the broad policy issues and the problems of their implementation through agreed distributive formulae. For these reasons, if for no other, a 'damping' mechanism has been introduced to spread over two or three years the effects of any substantial changes in formulae introduced as part of the annual bargaining.

Mention has already been made of the lack of discretion that local education authorities have over much of their expenditure which is, as Byrne (1974) says, 'intractable'. The traditional process of local authority budget-making reduces options even further, though without perceived cost as long as finance expands more or less in step with demand. In effect, local education authorities have estimated the cost of maintaining existing policies and have then explored the possibility of the expansion of provision in negotiations between education committee and finance committee. Proposed expenditure in any one year is largely the continuation of previous expenditure (however originally justified), its implied further commitments and an increment for new policy initiatives.

In detail, the elements of a traditional budget may be seen as follows. The previous year's expenditure, including the costs of new initiatives taken at various stages in the year, may be calculated with some precision, although the budgeting process takes place while this

TABLE 3.2 *Rate Support Grant: Formula for the Calculation of
Needs Element, 1973—4*

Type of grant	Amount to be distributed (£ million)	Relative importance (%)
Basic grant		
1 Population: £24.30 per head	1.191.4	51.82
2 Children under 15: £1.89 per head	22.1	0.97
Supplementary grants		
3 Children under 5: £1.69 per head	6.6	0.29
4 Persons over 65: £1.69 per head	10.8	0.47
5 Education units: £0.152 per head of population multiplied by the number of units per 1000 population in excess of 200	833.6	36.26
6 High density: a percentage of the basic grant, being one half of the amount by which the number of persons per acre exceeds 18	9.3	0.40
7 Low density: a percentage of the basic grant payable where road mileage exceeds two per 1000 population	81.1	3.53
8 Roads: £430 per mile for all roads other than trunk roads. £2.101 per mile for principal—an adjustment to take account of density of population	99.9	4.35
9 Declining population: a percentage of the basic grant, being the amount by which the decline in population over the past 10 years exceeds 0.5%	29.6	1.29
10 Metropolitan authorities: 5% of the basic grant to authorities wholly or partly within the metropolitan district	13.0	0.57
	2.297.4	
Adjustment to ensure that total amount distributed corresponds with amount fixed for needs element	1.6	0.07
	2.299.0	100.00

Source: Derived from Rate Support Grant Order, 1973.

base year is still in progress. The cost of implementation over a full year of the base year's initiatives is added on (extra teachers, for example, may be recruited first for September, a third of the way through the base financial year). Extra resources may be necessary to maintain existing policies because of changes in demand, such as an increase in the number of pupils of compulsory school age; similarly, demand may have eased in some areas of the education service, putting less pressure on resources to maintain the *status quo*. At some stage, in respect of all these calculations, an allowance has to be made for inflation, the change over the year in the price of the resources that education uses. These include buildings (heating, lighting and maintenance, as well as the initial provision and the servicing of loan debt), furniture, stationery, books, equipment and, most obviously, teaching and non-teaching staff. Only then can calculations be made of the extra resources that might be available for new policy and in lean years there has often been little room for manoeuvre beyond the contingent changes in demand that the varying sizes of age group produce. By the standards of the last quarter-century, the 1980s are likely to be very lean years indeed, with a medium-term fall in educational demand, close and critical scrutiny of educational expenditure and a reduction in the real resources available to local government as a whole.

The call for greater efficiency in education is easier made than answered; it would suggest moves towards greater capital investment at the expense of professional labour, in direct contradiction of the traditional measure of improved educational quality, the teacher pupil ratio. Alternatively or in addition, it would suggest a different mix between professional and other labour in schools and colleges. This has been the steady trend in post-war school spending (Vaizey, 1968), but it raises some awkward questions of professional differentiation and accountability (see Duthie, 1975, for an account of the introduction of auxiliaries in Scottish primary schools).

Potentially even more disruptive of previous expectations is the redeployment of resources on a substantial scale from one educational use to another. Within limits this has always happened, but at local system level, often in an unplanned way; opportunities have been seized as they have occurred rather than being made. Pressure on resources is now such that the redeployment of teachers, the closure of schools and their reuse for other purposes, rationalisation of the overlap between colleges and the upper levels of secondary schools are all strategies beginning to be pursued, with more or less grudging acceptance of their inevitability, by teachers' associations and other interests. It does not automatically follow that all resources released will be used to pursue other educational objectives, nor that government will necessarily always see the education service as the appropriate agency through which to seek educational improvements. The emphasis on home conditions as a factor in educational achievement can prompt the view that greater spending outside the education service might, paradoxically, have substantial benefits within it. From a different perspective, central government, especially under the Labour Governments of 1974—9, has put large funds into post-school industrial training through the Training Services Agencies of the Manpower Services Commission. Some of those funds have found their way into colleges of further education which have provided courses for the Training Services Agency. Much to the chagrin of local education authorities, these funds have been available only at the discretion of a para-governmental organisation strong enough to impose its own demands on the education service and with a clear sense of its priorities, right or wrong.

The next decade is likely to see considerable changes in the shape of educational budgets. The question of what, if anything, will have been achieved is problematic, since the outcomes of educational provision are conditioned by the external societal context, and many important outcomes are not susceptible to easy quantitative measurement, if they are measurable at all. Undoubtedly, the largest single pressure on the local authority's budget is central government, through its manipulation of the RSG. Under Governments of both parties, restrictions have been increased, but the Conservative Government elected in May 1979 has been the first to set out, explicitly and without regret, to curb local authority expenditure. In many respects its actions mirror those of its Labour predecessor, but they go further in their determination and manipulation of the terms of settlement of grant to remove the local authority's room for manoeuvre.

The Labour Government which fell from office in 1979 had negotiated a settlement with the local authorities in November 1978; this set total relevant expenditure in the financial year 1979—80 at £14,959 million, including a cash-limited amount for inflation during the year of £850 million. Consequent on this national settlement, each local authority made its budget; not surprisingly, pressures for service expenditure within local authorities led to budgets which in aggregate exceeded the previously agreed national totals. Deducting the sum for inflation and the sum for other items such as loan charges, the Labour Government had negotiated a total for current expenditure at November 1978 prices of £12,038 million; the aggregate of local authority budgets in April 1979 on the same price basis, turned out to be £12,489 million, a discrepancy of £451 million.

In Circular 21/79 the new Conservative Government, in calling for reductions in local authority expenditure, chose to ignore the discrepancy and demanded a 3 per cent cut (£361 million) in the figure agreed the previous November, in fact requiring a 6.5 per cent cut in agreed budgets one-third of the way through the financial year in which they were to be effected. In demanding a 3 per cent cut, government was able to enforce its will by deducting the appropriate amount from the RSG, leaving the local authorities with little alternative but to make corresponding economies. The over-budgeting of £451 million could not be dealt with in the same way, as it had never been part of the grant settlement. Instead, government made it clear that when negotiating the grant settlement for the following year (1980—1) it would assume that the £451 million had not been spent and was therefore available in local authority balances to be used before any demands were made on central government subsidy. Finally, government announced that it would be looking for further substantial cuts in local government expenditure in 1980—1. Resistance by individual local authorities to immediate economies would only defer the problem and would increase its scale when the need for economy was finally addressed.

From this account there can be no doubt that the structure and strategy of a local authority budget may lie largely in the hands of a really determined central government, despite the apparent crudity of the block grant mechanism, since so much of local authority expenditure is otherwise conditioned by statute or national agreement. It might be argued that the Northern Ireland Education and Library Boards—unequivocal agents of the Ministry, to which budgets have to be submitted and which approves every major item of expenditure—would be a more straightforward and no more cumbersome system of financial control. But this is not to say that the scale and objects of educational expenditure do not vary substantially from one education authority to another. Taylor and Ayres (1969) illustrate again and again regional variations in expenditure which are not to be explained by variations in demand. Byrne (1974) shows, with evidence gathered from three very different education authorities, the influence that personality and preconceptions can have on the bias of expenditure over a long period of time. The differences in other local authority services may be even more startling, but they should not be allowed to mask the subjective nature of many educational expenditure decisions, nor the question-able assumptions on which such decisions are often based.

This may also be evidence of the differential success of education committees, their chairmen and chief officers, in fighting the demands of other local services for resources. There can be little doubt of the scepticism of the non-educationalist, political and administrative, of some of the pretensions of the educationists. Whether right or wrong, the local authorities as a whole have demonstrated their unwillingness to accord any special place to the education service through their concerted campaign, in the first few years of the new local government structure, to kill off the Association of Education Committees (AEC). The AEC had brought together members and officers in a special cause and spoke for the service, both to government and to teachers, as the management side of Burnham salary negotiations under the leadership of its secretary.

Prior to 1974 the Association of Municipal Corporations (AMC), the County Councils Association (CCA) and the AEC (founded 1904) were the major local authority associations concerned with education. Although the Municipal and County Associations had their own subcommittees to consider education, the county boroughs and county councils, whose corporate interests they represented, were willing to allow the AEC to take the main initiatives and responsibility for promoting the views of local education authorities and for protecting their interests. The AEC was in a uniquely powerful position; it was the voice of one service in local government representing all local education authorities except the Inner London Education Authority but including the Northern Ireland education committees and the education authorities of the Isle of Man and the Channel Isles. The AEC represented all these local education authorities on the Burnham Committee until 1974 and, through its influential weekly journal *Education,* provided information about education which covered every facet of local authority responsibility. The Association was concerned with the promotion and defence of the education service and played a prime role in informing and advising central government. It was consulted on every major issue affecting local authority provision of education and, according to both Sir Edward (now Lord) Boyle and Anthony Crosland, the AEC had a major influence on policy-making. Sir William (now Lord) Alexander, secretary to the AEC for most of the post-war era, was a powerful force in his own right, respected for his grasp of the main issues by Ministers of different parties, by central government, by local officials and no less by representatives of the teachers' unions, who often regarded him as their most formidable adversary in salary negotiations. The scope of AEC interest was wide and its concern with detail meticulous. It provided a service to the local authorities which helps to explain their willingness to see their interests represented by an association concerned with only one of their functions.

Since 1974 we have seen the demise of the AEC, the AMC and the CCA and the emergence of the Association of Metropolitan Authorities (AMA) and the Association of County Councils (ACC). The new associations reflect the restructuring of local government units and the adoption of 'corporate management' by most councils after reorganisation. Soon after reorganisation the new metropolitan and county associations which represent the interests of the local education authorities formed a Council of Local Education Authorities (CLEA), which now includes every local education authority in England and Wales. This body reflects a widespread feeling in local government since reorganisation that services should be integrally related and resources corporately managed, and that traditionally separate, 'departmentalised' provision of services should be discouraged. The CLEA now speaks for the local education authorities on the Burnham Committee and puts forward their joint view elsewhere, but the AMA and the ACC both retain their own education spokesmen, and it is not always clear how authoritative the CLEA's statements are. It is not without irony that one of the stated aims of the reforms of local government that have taken place was the establishment of a single voice to speak for the local authorities in their dealings with central government. In education that has ceased to be possible, while central government's pressure on the local education authorities has substantially increased.

CHAPTER 4

The School

There were nearly ten and a half million pupils in maintained schools in Britain and Northern Ireland in 1975, the great majority in the compulsory school-age range of five to sixteen years. A very small proportion of the child population, another 500,000, are educated outside the state system, and some of these are boarding pupils in independent schools, whose fees are paid by the state because of the domestic circumstances of their family. For most young people and their parents and for teachers the common experience is the local primary and secondary school. In many ways germane to this chapter, the aims, scope and organisation of individual schools are similar, if not the same, for nearly all children. Even so, there is great diversity of experience from place to place and over time during the school life of individual children.

THE VARIETY OF SIZE AND TYPE OF SCHOOLS

First of all, schools vary greatly in size. In 1947 the mean average size of primary schools in England and Wales was just over 180 pupils; in Scotland, less than 130 pupils; and in Northern Ireland, 115. By 1975 the average size of primary schools had increased to over 200 pupils per school in England and Wales and 240 in Scotland; while in Northern Ireland it was 190. These simple averages conceal a wide range of sizes from the one-form-entry infant school with a capacity of under 100 places, to the six English primary schools with over 800 pupils. The Report of the Northern Ireland Department of Education in 1975 notes:

> The total number of primary schools was further reduced during 1974: from January 1974 to January 1975 the total fell from 1138 to 1123. At the latter date the number of schools with an enrolment

of fewer than 50 was 281 as compared with 298 the year before. During the same period there was also a decrease in the number of schools with an enrolment of greater than 500; in January 1974 there were 104 such schools and one year later the number had fallen to 100. (Northern Ireland, 1976a)

In the province very small schools result in part from denominational segregation in education, but they also reflect (as in Scotland, Wales and parts of England) the necessity for providing education for younger children in rural areas within reasonable distance of their homes. Again, the decline in the birth rate since the mid 1960s, with its inevitable consequence, falling enrolment, makes its first impact on some primary schools, whether in rural or urban areas.

Many of the same trends are affecting secondary schools, but, in addition, the changeover to comprehensive secondary schools, the extensive broadening of the secondary school curriculum and the increased rate of staying on beyond the minimum leaving age have made for larger schools. Average enrolment just after the Second World War in England, Wales and Scotland was around 350, in Northern Ireland about 250; only eight maintained secondary schools in England out of a total around 4500 had enrolments of over 1000 pupils. By 1977 there were 1451 (32.8 per cent) in that category. The mean average size of secondary schools had more than doubled during the same period throughout the country.

Very nearly all children of secondary-school age in Scotland attend comprehensive schools; the tradition of the common school having a much longer history in Scotland than elsewhere in Britain, the implementation of the secondary education policy of successive Labour Governments in the 1960s and 1970s has been relatively easy, and the small number of grant-aided schools which retain selection are gradually being eliminated from the public system.

By contrast, the structure of secondary schooling in Northern Ireland — 184 secondary intermediate schools (Northern Ireland, 1976b) and eighty secondary grammar schools, most of them sponsored by mutually suspicious religious denominations responsible for capital expenditure and jealous of their remaining independence of government — has made any move toward common secondary schooling a matter for extensive but wary debate rather than systematic action. By 1976, despite government affirmation of policy, in only five cases had an intermediate school merged with the local grammar school, and only two intermediate schools, remote from the nearest grammar school, had come to provide for the educational needs at secondary level of all the children in their catchment area. In England and Wales the same policy has seen 81 per cent of secondary-age children in comprehensive schools and sixty-one English authorities who have in 1980 a complete system of comprehensive schools.

However, it is not possible to claim anything approaching uniformity of school provision across the country. The exigencies of building stock and available capital finance have demanded ingenuity of local education authorities seeking to eliminate selective allocation of pupils to secondary schools. While many authorities maintain comprehensives for pupils of eleven to eighteen years, many also changed to a three-tier system (five—nine, nine—thirteen, thirteen—eighteen; or five—eight, eight—twelve, twelve—eighteen), while others have brought together resources for the education of students between the ages of sixteen and nineteen in sixth-form colleges, tertiary colleges or further education institutions, fed by secondary schools covering the eleven—sixteen age range. One of the earliest applications of comprehensive principles was in Leicestershire, where pupils entering secondary schools at eleven either stay until their course is finished at sixteen or transfer at fourteen to an upper school whose courses range up to GCE Advanced Level.

With such varied histories and with such a plethora of new tasks and new terms of reference before them, it is no wonder that schools differ. Their ethos may have a great deal to do with their location and their pupil catchment area—a single school in a small country village or town differs from a high school in one of the richer suburbs of a large city, or a high school serving an area of transient population in the inner city — and while none of these factors fully determines the character of a school, each may well condition and reinforce the attitudes, aspirations and practices of both staff and pupils. Despite variety, however, there are many aspects of schools which are common or which may vary only by degree, lessening as the uniformity of legislation, regulation, administration and human and physical resources increases.

The 1944 Education Act denoted two types of schools maintained by local education authorities in England and Wales—county and voluntary. County schools form a large majority and are established and wholly funded by the local education authority. Voluntary schools are those established by such sponsors as the Church of England and the Roman Catholic Church. Many of these predate the Education Act, but some have been established or redeveloped since 1944 as voluntary schools, since the Act provided for government grant towards a large part of the capital costs of the maintenance and renewal of the physical fabric of Church schools, as well as for local authority funding of normal running costs. Whereas running costs of Church schools have been met by local education authorities since 1902, the principle of aid towards capital expenditure was re-established only in 1936; it was restricted to secondary schools and aimed at the easing of problems of reorganisation in all-age schools and the raising of the school-leaving age to fifteen. Schools planned under this legislation before the outbreak of war still exist, 131 in all, and are known as 'special-agreement' schools. More common are 'aided' schools, a category of voluntary school created by the 1944 Education Act. The category includes, subject to the agreement of the Secretary of State, those Church schools already in existence and some established in the post-war period under the increasingly generous provisions for capital grant. An aided school remains the property of its governors, although 85 per cent (in 1980) of the costs of new building, external repair and maintenance is reimbursed by the Secretary of State and although the local authority pays for such items as internal repairs, playing fields and the running of the school. By the standards of available Church resources and the multiplicity of calls upon these resources, the substantial power retained by the governors of an aided school are justified by the financial commitment that they enter into. The local education authority and the Secretary of State bear by far the larger part of the cost of Church schools in return for the contribution they make to the provision of education in an area and in recognition of the contemporary and historic connection between religious belief, practice and education.

Nevertheless, a third category of voluntary school, the 'controlled' school, was created by the 1944 Education Act, which relieved the Churches of financial responsibility for many of their schools, while retaining a residual Church interest in them. The governors of a controlled school are not usually responsible for any expenditure in connection with the school, and only a minority of the members of the governing body represent the voluntary interest.

In Scotland the question of creating different legal and adminis-trative categories of school in order to maintain the Church interest, did not arise, since a radically different solution had been arrived at much earlier. In Northern Ireland, on the other hand, the force of religious division and mutual suspicion made neither the English nor the Scottish solution practicable. After the Education Act (Northern Ireland) 1930, which provided, in transferred and provided schools, for non-denominational Bible instruction to be given by teachers appointed by school management committees (not less than half of whose numbers would represent the previously existing voluntary interest), many Protestant managers transferred their primary schools to the Local education authorities; Roman Catholic schools, of which the parish priest was often the sole manager, failed to accept transfer on these terms. Even today only a small minority of the recognised grammar schools are managed by the education authorities; most are grant-aided in a variety of ways but remain under the control of either Roman Catholic or Protestant boards of governors.

Governors and managers of schools do not usually exist in Scotland. In Northern Ireland their existence and government approval of their composition and terms of reference is a condition of eligibility for recognition and grant. In England and Wales the 1944 Education Act (sections 17—20) requires the establishment of governing or managing bodies (for the first time, in the case of maintained county secondary schools) for every type of county school. For primary schools a managing body of not less than six persons is required. In the case of a voluntary aided or special-agreement school, two-thirds of the managers are nominated by the sponsoring body and one-third by the local education authority; in the case of a voluntary controlled school, the sponsoring body nominates one-third of the members, the local education authority two-thirds. Rules of management (that is, the specification of the power of the managers) are drawn up by the local education authority; within limits related to questions of religious instruction, the local authority can choose whether to restrict or enlarge by delegation from itself managers' powers over the activity of the school. Additional safeguards for the voluntary interest and the Minister are built into the provisions for the establishment of governing bodies for secondary schools. The Articles of Government, equivalent to the primary school Rules of Management, have to be approved in the case of county schools, and drawn up in the case of voluntary schools, by the Secretary of State. To avoid unnecessary conflict between local education authorities and the Minister and to make its intentions plain, the Government published a White Paper (1944) on the principles of government in maintained secondary schools.

It is quite clear that the Minister intended the governors of secondary schools to exercise considerable powers over the curriculum, finance and the appointment and dismissal of teachers. The realism of such proposals continues to be a matter of dispute and is further discussed later in this chapter in the context of the recent Taylor Report (1977). What is certain is that some local authorities welcomed the principles proposed and claimed that they reflected their current practice and future intentions; other authorities, with or without extensive experience of governing bodies, were determined to minimise what they regarded as the disruption and fragmentation of policy and administration which would follow from full implementation of the Minister's advice. Such authorities took full advantage of Section 20 of the 1944 Education Act, which provided that in the case of county secondary schools a governing body might be responsible for more than one school. Taken to its extreme, the provision would allow one governing body, virtually synonymous in membership with the local authority's education committee, to be responsible for every county secondary school in the authority's area. Among the county education authorities existing until local government reorganisation in 1974, although advantage was commonly taken of Section 20 to group schools, the extreme solution was never adopted. However, it has been found that a quarter of the pre-reorganisation county boroughs had one governing body for all their schools (Baron and Howell, 1972). It must follow from this that, in the minds of locally elected representatives and education officers at least, the existence and role of governing bodies is a matter of some importance, whether to the advantage or the detriment of the local authority and its schools.

The 1944 Education Act was particularly concerned to establish the distinction between primary and secondary education and finally to reconcile state and Church interest in education. The detailed categories and arrangements for participation in the control of the schools outlined above went some way towards meeting those aims. Section 13 of the Act also restrains the freedom of the local education authority to open, close or change the character of a school. Formal publication of its intentions is required; an opportunity for the registering of objections is provided; and power of final approval is reserved to the Secretary of State. To those administering the schools such procedures may sometimes seem an unnecessary complication. To those who wish to object to any proposed change they may seem only to meet minimum requirements. They certainly give some protection to the school against sudden, arbitrary alteration of its terms of reference from outside; they provide no protection against other sorts of change initiated inside the school. (See Postscript for changes introduced by 1980 Education Act.)

Local education authorities (and the Secretary of State) are required to have regard to the general principle that children are to be educated 'in accordance with their parents' wishes'. This requirement is rarely used to argue a case for specific provision within a school for an individual child; rather, it is used to establish some parental influence over the choice of school to which his child is allocated. Even then, the parent's wishes are to be judged against other criteria, such as unreasonable expenditure. Indeed, the Act is more concerned to delineate the duties of a parent to secure efficient education for his child and, if that is to be through a maintained school, to secure regular attendance. Recently, the statutory procedures designed to secure school attendance, which provide for appeals to the Secretary of State by aggrieved parents, have been exploited to enable sufficiently determined parents to obtain places for their children at the schools of their choice rather than at the ones offered by local education authorities. While intended to deal with this anomaly, the Education Act 1980 in fact extends parental freedom of choice (for some) very substantially. Children will be able to attend schools outside their home local authority area if parent and receiving school so agree, and the receiving local education authority will be reimbursed automatically.

STAFFING STRUCTURES AND INTERNAL ORGANISATION

So far we have examined some of the legal provisions for public participation in the running and development of the school. The law also specifies to some degree directly—and, in addition, through regulations which it empowers the Minister to make—the role and influence of the essential ingredient of schools, the teachers.

Under the Schools Regulations (1959) every school must have a head teacher 'who shall take part in the teaching' and a staff of assistant teachers as necessary 'to provide full-time education appropriate to the age, abilities and aptitudes of the pupils'. Although instructors and student teachers can still be employed in schools, only those with an educational background and training specified by the

Minister count as qualified teachers. Until 1969 the Schools Regulations also prescribed the maximum number of pupils on the register for a class, which varied according to the age of the pupils, and this had implications for the minimum staffing of schools. The revocation of the Regulations was a response to the increasing practice of varying teaching-group sizes according to short-term educational needs within schools and the move away from rigid class-based teaching.

A great deal more is implied about the structure of administration and responsibility for teaching in the details of salary agreements published in conjunction with the Statutory Instruments authorised from time to time under the Remuneration of Teachers Act 1965. At present, salary agreements negotiated between the teachers unions, the local authority associations and the Minister provide a number of scales for head teachers and deputy head teachers, a category of senior teacher and four scales for other assistant teachers. The principle accepted for many years in negotiating teacher salaries is the recognition of educational and training qualifications and of experience in teaching or equivalent occupations.

More recent is the recognition and elaboration in the salary scales of the varying administrative responsibilities carried by different members of staff. In the small primary school the distinction between head teacher and assistant teacher may still be all that is necessary, the one recognised as having responsibility for the internal organisation of the school, the other as discharging the task; in broad measure, the relationship is comparable with that of colleagues as class teachers, whether of five-year-olds or of ten-year-olds. The larger the primary school, the more complex become the administrative tasks of the head teacher and the greater the need for delegation to assistants, which is recognised in pay schemes.

In the early years after the Second World War the shortage of teachers in general and of academically well-qualified secondary school teachers in particular reinforced the tendency to use such salary differentials as then existed among assistant teachers in secondary schools (mainly in grammar schools) to recognise academic seniority. Thus an experienced and well-qualified assistant might be rewarded as much for his commitment to sixth-form teaching as for his assumption of administrative responsibilities. Extension and change in the curriculum, the expansion of examination provision in secondary modern schools, the development of differential arrangements for pastoral care, the introduction of comprehensive schools and, above all, the increase in the size of the average secondary school combined to create a need and a demand for recognition of the numerous responsibilities that assistant teachers were shouldering.

The system of scales for assistant teachers introduced in 1971 and subsequently modified from time to time attempted to rationalise the structure of salaries on a national basis, while leaving to the school—most probably to its head teacher but sometimes to its governing body—the flexibility necessary to produce a staff structure which matched talents, rewards and the needs of the pupils as they changed over time. Each pupil in a school, weighted according to age, counts towards a total for the school (the more pupils and the older the pupils, the higher the score), and that total determines the number of points available to the school and thus the number of posts above basic scale, apart from head and deputy heads (whose numbers and salaries are calculated separately but in similar ways). An appointment on Scale 2 absorbs a certain number of points from the total; an appointment on Scale 3, a larger number. Discretion is left at school level as to the mix of posts which best fits the needs of the school, subject to their availability against the total point score. No system would give head or governors all the opportunities they might like to create posts of responsibility or to recognise the work of staff within the school, but at least the present arrangements, designed for an expanding school system, have combined comprehensiveness with a fairly high degree of flexibility. Their danger may be, rather, that they put a great deal of patronage in the hands of a few. They have created a range of career and promotion possibilities for the secondary school teacher which he can follow up step by step within one school or across several. In the small secondary schools, especially those middle schools counted as secondary which take the age range nine or ten to thirteen or fourteen, the opportunities may be limited by the school size and by a lower weighting for younger pupils in the points score. The main problem in such schools is not for the individual teacher, who may be able to further his career elsewhere, but for the school, which finds it more difficult to attract or retain good staff because of the insufficiency of posts above basic scale. Falling rolls (which are discussed below) may alter fundamentally any judgement of the appropriateness or success of the system of scale posts.

An indication of a school's approach to its task and of some of its priorities may be provided, other things being equal, by an examination of the structure of posts to which it adheres. At one extreme might be the school which recognises responsibility only in respect of academic subject departments, awarding Scale 4 posts to those leading such departments as English, maths and science, Scale 3 posts to other heads of departments and Scale 2 posts to some of those who act as deputies in departments. At the other extreme, academic departments may be depreciated in favour of heads of year or of house and an elaborate system of rewards for associated pastoral responsibilities. More likely is a range of structures between these two extremes which nevertheless reflects significantly different assessments of the needs and priorities of a particular school. Individuals may enjoy 'above-scale' posts on the basis of a job specification made out on one set of criteria or, more likely, may be expected to discharge a combination of academic, pastoral and extra-curricular duties in return for eventual recognition. Since the Burnham agreement of 1971 the restriction of promotion to those undertaking greater administrative responsibilities has been officially rescinded, and it has become possible again to reward a teacher for classroom commitment itself.

Conditions of service for schoolteachers in general are very vague. As far as the detailed teaching and ancillary tasks that the teacher must perform are concerned, a great deal depends upon custom and practice, modified from school to school by local tradition and by the increasing professional assertiveness of teachers that is expressed through their unions. Apart from direct subject instruction, teachers in secondary schools very often find themselves engaged in a variety of clerical tasks, from the statutory registration of pupil attendance to the collection of dinner money. Some, without specific relevant qualifications, may be concerned with school sport inside and outside school hours, with arranging educational and other group holidays, with sponsoring clubs, projects and social activities, with attending evening meetings with parents of pupils, whether to discuss academic matters or to organise the social and fund-raising events of a Parent—Teacher Association. None of these activities is prescribed for teachers, but some of them at least will be expected of all secondary school teachers; such demands on the primary school teacher's time and energy outside school hours are usually less. Clearly, assistant teachers are motivated to undertake these activities both by a professional sense of the potential contribution to their main educational task and by the expectation of career advancement which engagement in such activities may promote.

Those already holding promoted posts may have a clear idea of the responsibilities that accompany their enhanced role, whether by maintaining previous inexplicit assumptions within the school or through a precise job specification. Even in the latter case, reality of practice may well differ from the theoretical formulation because the holder of the post offers a different interpretation, because the authority he is stated to have is not accepted by those junior to him or because the head teacher from whom power is formally delegated in fact allows little discretion. Such gaps between constitution and reality are found in all organisations but are particularly striking within schools, where the teacher inevitably has a great deal of discretion within the classroom, where notions of professional equality are strong and where the tradition of formal, hierarchical order (other than in its simplest manifestation between head and assistants) is still weak.

National negotiations determine the supply of status levels in schools, which form a sequence of steps up the promotion ladder. The number of actual appointments at each status level is a function of the same national negotiations and the exercise of discretion at local authority and school level on the basis of financial and educational policy. The local authority may make available the maximum number of points that the national scheme for weighted pupil totals allows or it may take a mid-point in the available range. The authority may insist on each school conforming to one pattern of responsibility posts, with only minor variations allowed, or it may give very substantial discretion to the head (and, by implication, to the school governors). Within those constraints promotion is a function of demand from teachers and the criteria and processes of selection applied by those responsible for appointments to posts above the basic scale. Hilsum and Start (1974) have carried out the only large-scale and contemporary investigation of careers and promotion in English schools, on which the following paragraphs are based.

Among a sample of teachers in primary and secondary schools taken in 1971 it was found that 57 per cent held a promotion post of some kind (71 per cent in secondary schools, only 44 per cent in primary schools); 11 per cent were heads, 8 per cent were deputy heads and 38 per cent held posts at other promoted levels (at that time, Scales 2 to 5). There were three times as many promoted posts below head and deputy head level in secondary schools as in primary schools, but as a result of the small average size of primary schools there were many more posts of head and deputy head held by primary school teachers. Men occupied a disproportionate number of promoted posts (even more in secondary than in primary schools), a bias reflected in, and perhaps explained by, the very much larger number of applications for promotion received from men teachers than from women teachers. Graduates and non-graduates fared equally well in promotion in primary schools, but in secondary schools graduates fared better. Some kind of promotion was possible for all subject teachers in secondary schools within their specialism; a specialism in a minority, shortage subject enhanced the prospects of a small-sized departmental headship, but physics, chemistry, English and mathematics were the subject areas offering most prospects of promotion. As a subject specialist group, historians appeared to have the best chance of becoming heads of secondary schools. Thus subject specialism is a very important factor in promotion prospects in secondary schools.

Rapidity of promotion increased over the decade preceding the Hilsum and Start survey. The first promotion of primary teachers came after about seven years teaching; of secondary teachers, after about three years: 'first and second promotions . . . were being awarded about three and six years earlier respectively than during a decade previously' (Hilsum and Start, 1974, p. 289). Promotion was nevertheless associated with length of teaching experience, as expected, and service in two or three schools, rather than just one or four or more schools, appeared advantageous.

While these were some of the factors that were objectively operating, the subjective perceptions of teachers about the factors that did operate and should operate displayed some marked contrasts:

> the ten factors most frequently selected by teachers as those which *ought* to favour promotion were—in order of size of 'vote'—flexibility in teaching methods, familiarity with new ideas, ability to control pupils, concern for pupil welfare, variety of schools, length of experience, good relations with staff, subject specialism, administrative ability and extra-curricular work. Of these ten, those that appeared among the ten most frequently selected by teachers as actually favouring promotion were: length of teaching experience (sixth), variety of schools (eighth), extra-curricula work (ninth) and familiarity with new ideas (tenth) . . . Among the ten most frequently 'thought' factors which were not placed on the 'ought' list were:

being a graduate, specialism in a shortage subject, social contacts, conformity with advisers and good relations with the head (Hilsum and Start, 1974, p. 293).

Quite clearly, teachers think qualities associated in their minds with successful classroom experience should count most in promotion, but they are more sceptical in their expectations of the promotion race where they see seniority, conformity and social familiarity playing an important part. Neither their hopes nor their expectations are completely out of line with the reality as discerned by Hilsum and Start, whose research was not of a kind which could have stilled or confirmed teachers' cynicism about promotion. Perhaps more surprisingly, neither the reality nor the ideal give great prominence to any direct test of teaching success in the form of measured pupil learning. There are many procedural and methodological objections to be made to the use of such a criterion, and yet teachers would be the first to acknowledge, on a common-sense basis, that some teachers are more competent than others; and the qualities that teachers do rank highly as promotion criteria—flexibility of teaching methods, familiarity with new ideas, concern for pupil welfare, ability to control pupils—implicitly recognise the relevance of teaching competence—and are yet no easier to measure.

Whatever promotion may bring for most teachers, the central experience lies in classroom teaching. Only recently have there been attempts to look at what teachers actually do in the classroom, how their time is distributed over tasks which contribute directly to instruction and over other tasks which may follow simply from being in charge of a group of dependent children. In this short chapter there is no time to consider the detailed findings of Hilsum and Cane (1971) and Hilsum and Strong (1978), to which the reader is referred. Such accounts give a limited but hitherto missing picture of the job that teachers do, its variety and intensity, its extension beyond apparent working hours and its inherent lack of definition.

New to most schools is the array of non-teaching ancillary staff now common, especially in the large secondary schools. Dinner ladies and teaching auxiliaries in primary schools, laboratory technicians, audio-visual aids technicians, clerks, librarians are now found in many (though by no means all) secondary schools. Such staff are employed on local authority conditions of service, are clearly differentiated in status from the teaching staff but may be regarded as playing a critical part in the success of the educational endeavour of the school. The temporary absence of clerical staff or technicians may throw such an additional burden on to teachers that they can no longer carry out their main tasks efficiently. The combination of individual personality and specific responsibilities of a school caretaker may make him a formidable influence on the policy and practice of the school. Often the great difficulty there is in distinguishing categorically the tasks undertaken by a teaching auxiliary and the qualified primary school teacher with whom he or, more likely, she is working, except by reference to formal hierarchy, which may create status tension within the classroom or school or substantially increase the teaching facility (Duthie and Kennedy, 1975). The reorganisation of secondary schools has often presented an opportunity to re-examine assumptions about the distribution of non-teaching tasks between teachers and other staff. In one case (London Borough of Croydon, 1971) a combination of direct observation of the performance of clerical tasks by workstudy specialists and senior teaching staff estimates of the present and future clerical workload of teachers was used to devise a new formula for clerical assistance which might optimise professional staff commitment to teaching. Similar direct observation was used to produce formulae for the allocation of laboratory staff in place of the previous simple measure (of laboratory space in use) which took account neither of changes in teaching methods nor of expansion in the range of specialist rooms and technical demands to include metal workshops, for example, in addition to pure science laboratories. Using teacher estimates of the use that would be made of the facility, it was proposed that one audio-visual aid technician be employed in each reorganised high school. Most ambitiously, it was proposed, using Library Association recommendations as a basis, that even in the smallest high school at least part-time professional library staff should be available.

While most educational issues are equally relevant to primary and secondary schools, the limited numbers of teachers in most primary schools often makes possible much less complex systems of delegation and co-ordination of responsibilities. Within his classroom the primary schoolteacher may have wide discretionary powers; he may be absolute king in choice of subject material, pedagogical approach and disciplinary methods. In the staffroom at break or lunchtime the teacher can consult his colleagues in informal ways about individual pupils, reassert common approaches and take part in the conscious development of policy for the school in conjunction with the head. Much of this potential ease of communication will depend on personality, especially that of the head teacher. Even more important is the effect of practical and theoretical experiences in trainee teaching, which will have established for most teachers definite expectations about the variety of consideration and practice accepted as relevant to teaching success. The temptation to stray beyond the bounds of these expectations may be restrained as much by group feeling as by explicit action by the head teacher. Staff solidarity may also protect individuals against the differing views of parents. The breakdown and perversion of these unifying factors can, it would appear, be seen in the case of the William Tyndale Junior School in London. There experimental practices split the staff into two groups, one supported by at least some of the parents, and the head played an ambiguous and ineffectual role in attempting to hold the various parties together.

In the secondary school the head of a large department may have under him assistants more numerous than a whole primary school staff. Significantly different aims and practices may be manifest from one department to another. Inter-subject relationships may require conscious co-ordination if any subject is to be successfully taught. Standards of discipline (school dress, homework and so on) and policy for examinations or for the care of individual pupils will have to be established across the whole school, if not uniformly at least coherently. With a teaching staff which may total more than a hundred, the necessary administration and policy-formulation organisation is a much more complicated matter for the secondary school and, in particular, for the head teacher, on whom, according to British tradition, the main responsibility will fall. Staff meetings with formal agendas and minutes, standing committees of senior staff, working parties on particular topics, discussion documents are some of the more structured responses employed, which add to rather than replace informal discussion in staffroom and department and one-to-one communication between head and assistant teacher. Figure 4.1 gives one illustration of the sort of organisational structure which may define formal roles and relationships within a school, and the requisition procedure outlined on page 135 illustrates one time-consuming area of administration.

It may be said that not many years ago the present elaborate administrative practices of secondary schools would have been difficult to find, and yet the basic tasks of educational institutions remain the

The School

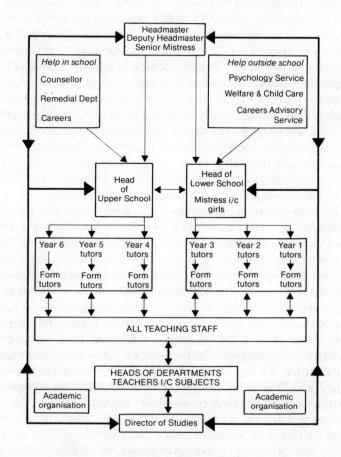

same—which lends weight to the claim that the numerical size of schools in recent years has brought in its train an ever-expanding school bureaucracy, with few concomitant educational benefits. But the larger secondary schools can be seen as a response to other changes in education and in the social environment rather than as the prime cause of change.

In stereotype, the small grammar school of the 1950s and before had a clearly defined task before it: to educate a proportion of the most able boys and girls within the context of a single set of stable examinations and a prospect of entry to higher education or the professions. In its practices and standards the grammar school could draw on a long tradition upheld in grant-aided and independent schools of similar mould. Nearly all its staff would have had a common university background and, very likely, a community of values which would endorse those of the school.

The secondary modern school, developed in many cases out of pre-war senior elementary schools, provided for the vast majority of children, excluding those detected at eleven years of age as being of considerably more than average ability. These schools provided a five-year course to the age of sixteen, although many of their pupils might leave for employment at the earliest possible date after their fifteenth birthday (until the raising of the school-leaving age to sixteen in 1972). National policy, supported by the teachers' unions, deterred these schools at first from offering formal public examinations at the end of the course, in the hope of encouraging the freer development of an appropriate curriculum. Most of their teachers were qualified through two years (later three) in a teacher training college.

The introduction of comprehensive schools, often involving the amalgamation of the pupils, staff and buildings of neighbouring grammar and secondary modern schools, and certainly requiring for the first time a school policy appropriate to all abilities within the school, was a major incentive to new educational initiatives and new methods of controlling and directing such initiatives. But it must be remembered that the organisational trauma of secondary reorganisation has itself occurred within a context of other developments bearing on, but independent of, such institutional change.

CATERING FOR THE CLIENTS

From employers, parents and pupils themselves have come increasing demands for a secondary school experience that is more relevant to the future lives of pupils. A particular aspect of this concern has been the demand for formal qualifications at the end of a secondary school career. Secondary modern schools responded in varying degrees, at first with the provision of opportunities to sit GCE Ordinary Level examinations and other reputable examinations such as those of the Royal Society of Arts. In 1965 a whole new additional set of examinations was established as a result of the Report of the Beloe Committee (1963), aimed at children of middle-range ability. The new Certificate of Secondary Education offered teachers greater opportunities than did the GCE to devise their own syllabuses and examination methods. New subjects of study were also introduced or old ones revised for the abler pupil sitting for GCE in grammar or comprehensive school. Government took the initiative in 1964 in creating a national institution, the Schools Council, intended to stimulate, explore and assess curricular innovation in both primary and secondary schools. New approaches and new content had always been options open to teachers in principle under the regulations of the examination boards, but at a time of reassessment of school aims these institutional developments, along with independent curricular initiatives in such fields as science and mathematics, created a still continuing ferment of activity and a plethora of choice. The very substantial expansion of the teaching force in the 1960s also ensured that there were many teachers fresh to their task and receptive, for good or ill, to new ideas.

The tradition, however informal, of care for the individual pupil and his personal development in British schools was often transformed by the emergence of larger schools at the same time as the transfer from the United States of the tradition of specialist training in personal guidance and counselling. While few schools employ full-time counsellors, the vast majority have devised systems of pastoral care that involve members of their teaching staff in the roles of form tutor, year tutor or head of house. The role of the form tutor may amount to little more than that of the old form teacher, but it is likely that he or she will at least have to relate and co-ordinate his activities with other form tutors, with other members of staff formally discharging wider responsibility for a whole year group (or section of the school in a house system) and with a deputy head taking overall responsibility for pastoral care throughout the school.

The bureaucratisation of pastoral care has brought certain issues of policy and practice to the fore. On the one hand, the assumed competence of teachers to engage in personal counselling can be questioned; on the other, the disjuncture of pastoral and teaching responsibility can present the pupil (and his parent) with two distinct and sometimes contradictory pictures of the school's interest in him. The co-ordination of pastoral and academic responsibilities must be a matter of constant management monitoring in large schools, since there can be no final resolution of the dual task. The confidentiality of school records presents another dilemma—who among the staff should have full access? And access on what terms? Informal arrangements, possible in a small school where personal trust can be based on intimate personal acquaintance between head and assistant and among assistant teachers, cannot apply in the large campus school, where some teachers may rarely meet and where head teachers delegate a great deal of personal contact to their deputies and other senior members of staff.

Specialist systems of pastoral care are in part a response to emphasis in research findings on the importance of home—school relations, and parental interest in particular, to the relative success of a child in school. In both primary and secondary schools, though by no means universally, teachers have instituted Parent or Parent—Teacher Associations, either on their own initiative or in response to parental pressure. A long tradition in some schools of parental fund-raising has been supplemented by educational concern, whether for the individual child or the school in general. Open days or evenings, formal meetings between a child's parents and his teachers, variations on the school report, school prospectuses, opportunities for parents to take an active part in the work of the school are all extra burdens on the teacher, justified in terms of the positive relationship between parental involvement and educational success. Where grammar schools might previously have presumed that parents who chose attendance at such schools for their children understood or accepted the ends and means of the grammar school, no such assumption can be made about the parent of a child at a neighbourhood comprehensive school, who is without effective choice or influence.

CONSTRAINTS AND CONTROLS: HIERARCHY AND AUTHORITY

We have made much of the variety of practice in schools and the discretion left to head teachers and their staff. But it would be wrong to suggest that there were no limitations to discretion and environmental influences other than those that are self-imposed. The local education authority, through directive and through its advisory service, and backed up by its superior control of resources, can

exercise a decisive influence on the strategy and the opportunities of
the school.

The largest single resource of any school is its staff, teaching and
non-teaching, and when there is no general shortage of teachers
school establishments are determined by the local authority. With a
stable or expanding school population, the maintenance of existing
standards such as the teacher—pupil ratio may leave much discretion
to the head in shaping the pattern of staff resources; with falling
enrolments, each time a member of staff leaves the head is obliged to
fight to maintain a balance of strengths among his staff and to
economise to the satisfaction of the local authority. In periods of
general economy non-teaching staff may be seen from the outside as
the most expendable resource, and yet the effective deployment of
teaching staff may depend on suitable support from technicians or
clerks. The indefinable quality of many educational outputs may
make argument on these lines difficult to sustain in convincing
detail, yet it is presumably, the premise on which support staff were
first appointed.

Buildings new or old, space for specialist subjects and facilities for
physical education and sport are matters largely beyond the control of
the school, although one of the acquired skills of head teachers is the
ability to attract physical resources through pressure on the local
authority.

Most schools do not have a budget covering all their revenue
expenditure, although experiments with financial management on
this scale within schools have been undertaken by some authorities.
But nearly all schools have a budget to cover consumables like
stationery, library books, textbooks, science equipment, audio-visual
equipment, travelling expenses, cleaning materials and the like. These
are often determined by local authorities according to formulae
relating unit sums to pupil enrolment—they are, in other words,
capitation allowances. It is very difficult to compare these allowances
from school to school, authority to authority or year to year, since so
much depends on what is meant to be covered by the allowance, from
what base of resources the school starts and how the school chooses
to spend its funds. Within the school decisions about the distribution
of funds may be retained in every detail in the hands of the head
teacher, who ultimately sanctions expenditure, or funds may be
distributed in varying amounts to senior colleagues, such as heads of
academic departments, for use as they see fit. In the cases of either of

these alternatives or the many possible variants negotiations take place among the staff over priorities for expenditure. Lyons (1976, p. 127) has compiled a list of steps to be taken in the requisition procedure of one large comprehensive school.

1 Staff informed of requisition procedure.
2 Head teacher produces draft allocation list.
3 Consultation between and within departments.
4 Consultation between head teacher and heads of departments.
5 Cases made out for special allowances.
6 Head teacher seeks local education authority approval for special allowances.
7 Local education authority informs head teacher of capitation allowance and any special allowances.
8 Head teacher produces final allocation list and informs heads of departments.
9 After 1 April placing and receipt of orders for new financial year, ensuring that 70 per cent of the allowance is spent by the end of July.
10 Staff review new textbooks and order specimen copies.
11 Departments spend remainder of allowance mainly on replacement stock, stationery and materials for practical work.
12 Near the end of financial year heads of departments inform head teacher of any outstanding balance.
13 Head teacher confirms remaining balances with local education authority.
14 Local education authority informs school current year's expenditure is to end.
15 Expedite or cancel outstanding orders or, exceptionally, carry balance forward to next year.
16 Close current year's accounts.

Although the school may present a united front to the outside world, the above account will make it clear that there are many opportunities for conflict within a school. In the first place, in a large secondary school there will be multiple hierarchies of authority. A teacher may be a member of the English department for part of his time, attending its departmental meetings and taking part in its discussions about curricular development, but he also has a similar role within, say, the history department, where a rather different consensus of opinion may be arrived at on pedagogical matters common to both departments, such as mixed-ability teaching or homework. At the same time the teacher may be a year tutor, with special responsibility both for a large group of pupils and for a number of staff, to one or more of whom he may be subordinate in other roles. One teacher may identify himself with those of his colleagues who have the same academic interests, whether in that school or beyond, and may accept their authority rather than that of a different subject specialist who happens to be head of faculty or head teacher; another may see himself primarily as a teacher rather than a subject specialist, emphasising, in discussion and in his classroom practice, his perception of the pupils' needs rather than the institutionalised boundaries of academic disciplines. Yet another may find it easier to identify with the school, its system of offices and corporate identity than with any one section of it. The management of these sorts of conflict—the bases of which lie in the multiplicity and ambiguity of aims of the schools and their extension in recent years, as well as in the nature of all organisations—is the difficult job of senior staff and particularly of the head teacher.

While the secondary school head may traditionally have been the symbol of authority and stability in the school, and usually the intermediary between the school and the outside world, whether of parents or local authority, he has now a much more complex task—that of continuously managing acceptable change. He is still responsible for the conduct of the school, and is still seen as bearing such responsibility, but it is impractical for him to intervene in every activity in the school. He is unlikely any longer to know every pupil personally. He must concede greater authority to his subordinates over the detail of many curricular matters, while still maintaining strategic control. He must make use of his senior assistants, whether as trouble-shooters, supervisors of daily routine administration or s chairmen of working parties and committees. Many head teachers resist the language of management theory as irrelevant to educational institutions, but few fail completely to act on some of the theory's more commonplace precepts. Nothing is, in principle, more bureaucratic than a school timetable, yet no school is without one. Its function is rationally to distribute time, space and human resources in pursuit of the educational goals of the school. Such too may be the function of other bureaucratic practices, such as formal meetings, agendas, minutes, consultation. Like the timetable, these practices may be abused for private ends, sectional dispute or the defeat of prime objectives, but without them overall lines of communication within a large institution will hardly exist and the head's authority may be more charade than reality.

There are those who question the authority of the head. While the tradition of head teacher as undisputed decision-maker within his school, jealously guarding his independence from outside interference, is strong, it does not have a very long history in British education; the tradition stems from the victory of headmasters of nineteenth-century independent schools over their ushers (or second masters) and, to a substantial degree, over their governing bodies. While the tradition has blossomed within the maintained schools as more and more of the smaller independent schools have been absorbed and as secondary provision has expanded, there is a parallel tradition of subordination to the local education department and to local authority members that is based on the experience of the elementary schools (Burnham, 1968; Bernbaum, 1976).

Whatever the tradition, it may be argued that the role of head is misconceived or inappropriate to the practical and professional of contemporary schools. Barrow (1976) argues that the distinguishing criterion of the head is his capacity to promote rational consideration of alternative courses of action and to make appropriate judgements on policy. It would be difficult to dispute that if sufficient persons of substantially superior judgement existed and could be picked out accurately, then his conception could and should be the only adequate reality. But in fact, as Barrow concedes, the supply of superior judges is limited and erratic. Judgements may best be made collectively, structured by committee and chairmanship, rather than through consultation followed by hierarchical fiat. Teachers and head teachers sensitive to the extensive demands made on contemporary schools for both considered viewpoints and instant decisions may well see the need for a variety of decision-making processes within the school that are appropriate to the different issues that arise. Many teachers would see discussion and consensual decision as the method of dealing with major long-term policy options, although some may be less than realistic about the commitment of time, energy and thought that such processes entail. Few head teachers are prepared to go as far as Watts of Countesthorpe College in eliminating their constitutional superiority and relying solely on their access to information (for example, from the local authority) and their capacity to convince by argument; most use the word 'consultation' to cover a process of discussion which is as limited or extensive in content and participation as they choose it to be. Few can specify as clearly as Spooner (1977, p. 30) the carefully organised pattern of meetings and decisions that characterise (if they do not guarantee) shared policy-making:

> There is a certain beauty, I think, when the machinery that breaks a large unit down into its separate parts and makes it work is the same machinery that diagnoses problems, promotes solutions and builds up broad policy, particularly as the whole process also serves as a vehicle for the communication of those things that are most difficult to communicate to teachers—the things they don't want to know, such as the implications of policy decisions.
>
> By attending at least once a term the meetings of the separate units, departmental, school (or house), the head has a ready-made sounding board both for the projection of his own ideas and the receipt of others. This is vital both for him and his deputies. They need the frequent chilling touch of reality to temper their enthusiasms, just as they also need to stand aloof from each day's conflict with its confusing detail so that they may set some guidelines, unify broad policy and pace the school's endeavours. The head's alternative, which is to trust his own judgement based on his chance observations, is surely a poor substitute for the combined expertise of his staff.

THE GOVERNMENT AND MANAGEMENT OF SCHOOLS

We have emphasised the discretion, the variety of practice, the latent or manifest conflict within the contemporary secondary school, and the means commonly used to analyse and co-ordinate the energies of large groups of teachers. In all this we may seem to have lost sight of governing and managing bodies, those charged, in the words of the Government White Paper, with the 'general direction of the conduct and curriculum of the school'. Our emphasis has been correct, since not all governing bodies have, in fact, been given such constitutional powers by local education authorities, and many have, through grouping practices mentioned earlier, been unable to act in any effective way; many more have chosen or have been led to adopt a much more modest estimate of their functions than the literal

However, recent years have seen not only an upsurge of parental interest in the school and public concern over educational standards but also their common expression as a demand for a greater public say in the relative detail of educational policy. Ministers have had much comment to make about curriculum but exercise little direct statutory power. Local education authorities are legally charged with control of 'secular instruction' but, at committee level, have rarely ventured to pronounce. One focus of attention for those dissatisfied with current administrative and political practices has been the potential of governing bodies. In 1976 the government set up a committee, under the chairmanship of Councillor Tom Taylor, to look at the past history of governing bodies and to make recommendations for the future. The Taylor Report (1977) was met with enthusiasm by some, scepticism by others and outright hostility from the organised representatives of many of the teachers.

The Taylor Committee's starting-point was the variety of past practice and ambiguity in the definitions of the role of local education authorities, governors and managers and head teachers of individual schools. The 1944 Education Act clearly makes the local education authority responsible in general for the schools that it maintains. The Minister's model Articles, followed subsequently in many local authorities, suggest that 'the Headmaster shall control the internal organisation, management and discipline of the school'. On this basis a clear line of responsibility can be seen between any one school, its head and the local authority. But the model Articles also suggest that the 'Governors shall have the general direction of the conduct and curriculum of the school' (Ministry of Education, 1945). The clear line of responsibility between employee and employer is broken by the insertion of a third body, which is usually neither and whose composition tends to bring an independent judgement to bear on the affairs of the school and the policy of the local authority. To whom is the head responsible, and for what? Where does the discretion of the governors begin and end? How is the distinction between 'general direction' and control of the 'internal organisation, management and discipline' to be specified in detail?

The Taylor Committee cut this Gordian knot by inserting the governing body firmly into the hierarchy of decision-making. The local education authority retains ultimate control but delegates the interpretation of their Articles of Government or Rules of Management would suggest.

closer supervision, regulation and promotion of the individual school to the governors, who in turn, it is confidently anticipated, delegate day-to-day discretion to the head but require much more involvement in policy-making and resource allocation within the school. One option open to the Committee was to try to define substantive areas of policy in which the head, governors and local authority would each have unfettered responsibility, such distinctions to be justified in terms of legitimate professional and lay community interests. But they concluded (Department of Education and Science 1977b, p. 52):

> there is no aspect of the school's activities from which the governing body should be excluded nor any aspect for which the headteacher and his colleagues should be accountable only to themselves or to the local education authority. It follows that the responsibility for deciding the school's curriculum, in every sense of that word, must be shared between all levels and between all those concerned at every level.

It is difficult to see how a rational inquiry into the relationship between schools and society could come to any other general conclusion, but at the same time, it could not be expected that existing interests would accept such a radical redefinition of their long-practised discretion without protest. It has been argued that the relationship is correctly defined but is sufficiently discharged by the combination of local authority and teachers, rendering an intermediary body redundant. Equally, it has been suggested that the professional status and responsibility of teachers are at stake and that the interference of lay governors—ignorant, prejudiced and at one remove from the intricacies of administration and educational practice within the school—can only produce disruption, delay and irrelevance.

Such charges are difficult to refute, since their accuracy or inaccuracy depends on the details of future behaviour of governing bodies. If the model examples of behaviour put forward by the Taylor Committee are followed, there would seem to be little ground for anxiety, since initiatives for new policy are often expected to come from the teachers, would always be subject to scrutiny by them and by the local authority's professional advisers and would be ratified or rejected by a governing body representative in equal parts of local authority, community, parents and staff. It would be possible for some of the more bizarre predictions, (such as that the governors would want to write the timetable) to come true, but highly unlikely.

Given the past deference of governors to teachers, especially head teachers, in matters of internal organisation and curriculum, it would seem much more likely that the teacher representatives on the governing body would have far greater influence than their numerical strength would suggest. The more telling criticism of the Taylor Committee proposals might be that despite considerable additional expense of time, money and effort, few of Taylor's aims will be achieved to any substantial degree. In any case, the Labour Government that received the Taylor Report shirked its implementation while endorsing its spirit, and its Conservative successor has hardly gone any further in seeking to channel public concern constructively through governing bodies.

We can see now that far from being an organisation with a clearly defined single goal, pursued unanimously by the participants, the school is a complex of interests, seeking multiple and necessarily ambiguous goals in uneasy compromise with its changing environment. The management and legitimation of consensus necessary to every organisation is of particular importance in the school and is particularly demanding of its members. Without some degree of consensus within the school and between the school and its social and political environment, without some reduction in the areas of overt conflict, whether negotiated or imposed, the school would be unlikely to survive. The current danger may be that in fear of an imposed redefinition, schoolteachers may fail to take the opportunity to negotiate a new compromise with their clients.

CHAPTER 5

The Further Education College

It has never been easy to define further education. Alternative titles
are all more restrictive, more misleading or more ambiguous; 'adult
education', 'technical education', 'vocational education', 'science
education', 'continuing education', 'leisure education', 'training' have
all been, and are still used for reference to the field, but all fail to
convey, at the very least, the excitement of variety that is a cornerstone
of further education.

THE CHARACTER AND VARIETY OF FURTHER EDUCATION COLLEGES

Like schooling, and often indistinguishable from it, further education
has its origins in voluntary initiatives by individuals and groups of
citizens throughout the country. Early pioneers may have been
motivated by charity or by a concern for the wider spread of science
education; in particular localities the initiatives may have come from
employers or from workers perceiving an economic return in
education. Quite commonly, the intentions of the promoters of classes,
colleges and other institutions led to quite unforeseen consequences:
the students attracted were different from those at whom the
institutions were aimed; relatively advanced scientific or technical
education could not be offered successfully until more basic
educational standards had been achieved for the majority; classes
intended for the liberal education of working men degenerated into
middle-class literary coteries. Nevertheless, initiatives did not cease,
nor enthusiasms wane, and with the setting up of local government
authorities and the availability of public financial subsidy, the stage

142

was set, towards the end of the nineteenth century, for a more structured promotion and monitoring of further education.

If there is an underlying theme in further education provision, it is the rejection of the 'exclusive association of learning with book-learning'. A. N. Whitehead (1923, p. 45) argues:

> The peculiar merit of a scientific education should be that it follows our deep natural instinct to translate thought into manual skill and manual activity into thought . . . The essential source of reasoning is to generalise what is particular and then particularise what is general. Without generality there is no reasoning, without concreteness there is no importance. Concreteness is the strength of technical education. In order to obtain its full realisation of truths as applying and not as empty formulae there is no alternative to technical education.

It is no surprise that such a rationale should be widely endorsed by further education teachers often qualified for their professional duties as much by practical experience as by formal educational certification, and by students very often combining course work with employment and motivated by quite specific vocational aims.

It should not be assumed, however, that the provision of further education was on any very large scale or was represented by any extensive commitment of public resources until quite recently nor that the ethos outlined above is even now all-pervasive. Variety of aim, of client group, of mode of study, of institutional arrangement remains the keynote of further education, implicit in the generality of the statutory requirements under the 1944 Education Act. Section 41 lays upon local education authorities the duty of securing

> the provision for their areas of adequate facilities for further education, that is to say,
>
> (a) full-time and part-time education of persons over compulsory school age; and
> (b) leisure-time occupation, in such organised cultural training and recreative activities as are suited to their requirements, for any persons over compulsory school age who are able and willing to profit by the facilities provided for that purpose.

To many people, including many of their students, further education colleges are still just 'night schools'; those working in the system know how incomplete that description now is. Further education has an impressive entrepreneurial record, responding in all sorts of different ways to new demands. It has met deficiencies in other parts of the education system, from primary to higher education, with, for example, adult literacy courses, full-time and part-time courses at GCE Ordinary and Advanced levels and the development of degree-level courses through the Council for National Academic Awards.

It will be clear by now that no one unit of further education provision can claim to be fully representative. The variety of activity outlined above is paralleled by the variety of institutions sketched in the following paragraphs. However, all post-school education outside the universities now operates under one national set of Further Education Regulations. This chapter therefore attempts, within its limited confines, to convey the flavour of life in institutions of further education, the opportunities and the constraints on staff and students, while acknowledging that in any one college, institute or adult education centre the balance of experience may be substantially different.

One barrier to the provision of a picture of the typical institutions of further education is the rapid rate of change, and the change of direction, in further education since the 1944 Education Act. For example, in addition to its general provisions, the 1944 Education Act provided, in Sections 43−6, for the establishment of county colleges, to be attended compulsorily on a part-time basis by all young workers between the ages of fifteen and eighteen as from a date to be determined by the Minister of Education. These provisions have never been put into effect, and it would seem unlikely that they ever will be, although the motivations behind the provision still inspire some present-day educational policies and policy suggestions.

Immediately after the Second World War there were 681 major institutions of further education maintained by local education authorities. Each had at least some full-time students, and there were some 5000 evening institutes. In addition, public financial support was given to the provision of liberal education for adults by university extra-mural departments and the Workers' Educational Association, a voluntary body employing full-time tutor-organisers and part-time tutors throughout the country. Under 5000 full-time teachers were employed in maintained institutions, the bulk of teaching being undertaken by part-time tutors and lecturers recruited from industry, commerce, the professions and other parts of the education system, as appropriate. The dominance of part-time over full-time teachers was paralleled by the ratio of part-time to full-time students. Of 1,600,000 students, 1,350,000 attended only evening classes; 200,000 had some day-time education; and only 45,000 were full-time students. Implicit in these figures is the fact that most further education provision served a small geographical catchment area and related to local employment opportunities, although some specialist colleges drew students from the region or even the whole country.

Government priorities for post-school education in the immediate post-war period, as indicated by the Percy (1945) and Barlow (1946) Reports, were for the expansion of the supply of high-level scientists (mainly to be undertaken in the universities) and of technicians (the assumed prerogative of the further education colleges). However, until the mid-1950s expansion of further education was limited. The 1956 White Paper on Technical Education marks the beginning of an expansion in further education motivated, as on earlier occasions, by the desire to compete effectively in international technology and trade.

Circular 305/56, which followed the White Paper, recognised a hierarchy of vocational further education institutions, regardless of the plethora of titles that the institutions themselves had. (Technical College, College of Further Education, College of Technology, Institute of Technology, College of Art, College of Commerce are all titles in common use, but they are rarely accurate guides to the scope of activities inside the institution.) A 'local' college, as the term suggests, was intended to serve a local community, providing relatively low-level courses, such as Ordinary National Certificate, for students mainly in the sixteen—nineteen age range, although often older. 'Area' colleges, serving a wider hinterland, engaged in this kind of work but, in addition, ran courses up to Higher National Certificate or perhaps diploma or comparable standards. The 'regional' colleges were to concentrate their activities on higher-level work, including degree-level courses, preparing students for entry to a variety of professions. They would cater to regional and, to a lesser extent, national demand.

While many institutions of further education are multi-disciplinary, especially those providing low-level courses, there have been, and still are, specialist colleges of music or art in most large centres of population. The largest single group of specialist colleges maintained by local education authorities have been the colleges of education, formerly called training colleges. Until the issue of the Further

Education Regulations 1975, these colleges were run under entirely separate arrangements. Their special place is the result of both history and the particular role they play in supplying the school system with its basic resource, teachers. Monotechnics all, many of them sponsored by the various religious denominations, they provided a two-year course of teacher training until 1960, when it was lengthened to three years. Until the 1960s the maintained colleges in this group represented the main contribution of local education authorities to the provision of full-time higher education.

The 1956 White Paper also outlined proposals to create a number of colleges of advanced technology out of those further education institutions that were already concentrating on degree-level courses. Since 1952 the Ministry of Education had given grants towards the running costs of twenty-five specified locally maintained institutions. By 1957 eight of them were to become fully direct-grant funded and were to focus their attention even more on graduate and postgraduate full-time and sandwich courses. (One other, the Manchester College of Technology, was granted a Royal Charter and transferred to the university sector.)

Scotland had not evolved a system of further education through erratic and uneven local initiatives, as had England; since 1901 seven central institutions—that is, institutions sponsored directly by the Scottish Education Department—had functioned on a regional basis with outposts (the local further education centres) in support. With the expansion of demand, especially at lower levels, some fifty local institutions developed, mainly in the post-war period. In Scotland's case, according to the 1956 White Paper, it was the base of the two-tier system rather than the apex that needed strengthening.

The categorisation of institutions has led to the transfer of courses and the creation of a hierarchy of colleges, but the policy has not been totally or inflexibly implemented. It was not until the Pilkington Report (1966) that the full manifestation of the policy established in 1956 was widely felt. The greatest cleavage in the structure of further education colleges followed the 1966 White Paper *A Plan for Polytechnics and Other Colleges,* which led to the designation of thirty polytechnics from amalgamations of existing institutions concentrating almost exclusively on undergraduate and graduate courses or professionally comparable courses but remaining outside the universities. The colleges of advanced technology had by then been translated into universities as a consequence of the Robbins

Report (1963). A ladder of institutions with universities at the top, which allowed each college in an expanding system to have hopes, if it so wished, of rising one rung higher, was replaced by a 'binary' system, within which universities were to be separate but equal; as a consequence, polytechnics were to be the main repositories of advanced courses in the local authority sector. It was the express intention of government that polytechnics should retain part-time study opportunities and some lower-level courses but, as in the colleges of advanced technology, the trend has often (though not always) been to move towards the almost exclusively full-time, degree-level-only pattern of the universities. Again, the rhetoric of the polytechnics suggests that they are pre-eminently vocational institutions, in contrast to the universities; in fact, some polytechnics have been only too eager to develop new courses in the arts, which are hardly to be distinguished from those offered in the universities; it goes without saying that universities, which train among others doctors, lawyers, architects, engineers, can hardly be called non-vocational institutions.

With the decline in the birth rate, government has reduced and redesigned the scope of the colleges of education. Few are now monotechnic; many are preparing students for a variety of degrees and professional qualifications; others have amalgamated with, or have been absorbed into, other institutions, often polytechnics; and some have closed. At the present time there are over 600 major establishments of further education, including the former colleges of education, whose range of courses covers the whole spectrum of professional qualifications, in scope as various as the technical and professional skills required throughout industry, commerce and public service. There are specialist colleges of art, music, agriculture, building, domestic science and so on, but the majority of colleges cover a variety of vocational needs most relevant to the locality in which they are situated. Most colleges have major departments of commerce, general studies, engineering and building, and perhaps a department representing the specialist needs of an area (for example marine engineering at South Shields; mining at Whitwood College, West Yorkshire).

Even so, by far the commonest experience of further education is attendance at an evening institute or adult education centre, of which there are over 5000. Consisting exclusively of part-time students, very often housed in school buildings, the establishment consisting of part-time teachers with perhaps a full-time principal or head of centre, much of the provision of recreational education and some low-level vocational education goes on in circumstances radically different from those of the purpose-built further education colleges.

STUDENTS AND COURSES

Students are not restricted from entry into further education by age after completion of the statutory period of school attendance, although the majority of students on day courses are between the ages of sixteen and twenty-one, covering the traditional span of apprenticeship, preparation for higher education and the period of study for a graduate or comparable qualification. Mature people over twenty-one make up the vast majority of evening students on non-vocational courses. Courses are taken in various forms—full-time, sandwich, day- and block-release and evenings only.

No other sector of education is as dependent upon external factors to determine academic and professional validation, recruitment, syllabuses and examinations. In addition, all course provision is subject to some degree to the approval of the local education authority, the regional Advisory Council and the DES.

Some colleges prepare students for their own college diplomas and certificates, relying upon their standing with employers and others locally, sometimes even nationally, to give currency to the qualifications obtained. But the vast majority of students follow courses leading to recognised qualifications validated to some extent beyond the confines of the colleges. In 1975 some 433,000 students out of a total of 962,000 on non-advanced courses were following City and Guilds courses, a vast programme of craft and technical qualifications with national currency. With a Royal Charter from 1878, the City and Guilds of London Institute is still the major examining body for non-advanced courses. City and Guilds courses cover over 300 subjects in areas of study as diverse as agriculture, catering, mechanical engineering and textiles. The top City and Guild award is the Insignia, conferred on the most experienced and successful candidates on craft and technician courses on completion of a thesis. Most of the general induction courses developed since the 1961 White Paper, *Better Opportunities in Technical Education,* have been under the auspices of the City and Guilds, as have many of the courses providing the educational complement to industrial training programmes.

Since the Second World War the emphasis has shifted from study in a student's own time to daytime study in varying amounts. Increasingly, courses are being designed as modules or blocks to be built upon or replaced as the nature of skill demand changes. Courses are being developed in relation to each other, allowing more points of entry or fruitful departure leading to further courses or terminal qualifications. This has included the development of more direct and organic links between part-time and full-time routes to various qualifications. *Better Opportunities in Technical Education* was government's first attempt to systematise non-advanced craft and technician qualifications; paradoxically, it led at first to the stigmatisation of some courses as appropriate only for specific levels of industrial operation. However, the narrow interpretation of the 1961 White Paper has been substantially offset by the implementation of the Haslegrave Report (1969), as courses for technicians have developed to allow cross-linkages, to defer premature specialisation and to open up what were becoming blind alleys. It is now common for major courses to be prefaced by induction and diagnostic periods to allow students opportunities to adjust the line of their academic development before committing themselves to study routes which might lead to drop-out or failure.

Following the Haslegrave Report, the Technician Education Council (TEC) and Business Education Council (BEC) have been created to replace City and Guilds and other validating bodies and to plan, administer and review the development of a unified pattern of technician courses. While the Councils will prescribe maximum contents of courses and standards of awards, the colleges will be free to devise their own syllabuses and examinations for students, between craftsmen and technologists, and their counterparts in the field of commerce.

It is intended that the two Councils should also replace the system of National certificates and diplomas, at ordinary and higher level, which have evolved since the end of the First World War. This system brought together the Ministry of Education, the appropriate professional bodies and individual colleges to develop courses. The 'National' courses provided employers with a system of qualifications at technician and technologist level which they could comprehend,

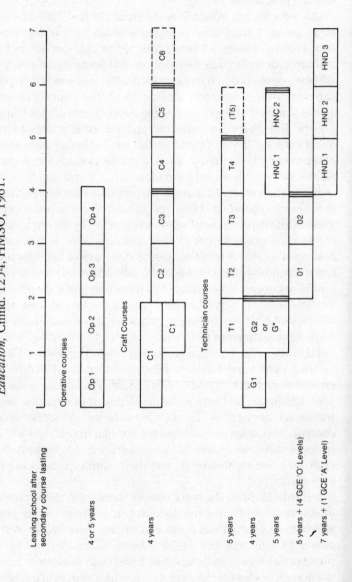

FIG. 5.1 Outline of pattern of further education courses.
Source: Ministry of Education, Better Opportunities in Technical Education, Cmnd. 1254, HMSO, 1961.

while allowing students to obtain qualifications of national academic standing. They also allowed teachers substantial participation in the planning and examination of courses. At the same time industry was supplied with more technicians and professionally qualified personnel than the universities could then produce. The National courses established the part-time route to professional qualifications. They provided exemption from at least part of the examinations of many professional institutions, although in recent years this facility has gradually diminished. In 1975 just under 20,000 students were following Higher National Diploma (HND) and over 25,000 Ordinary National Diploma (OND) courses, the full-time route; while nearly 36,000 and over 63,000 were following the part-time route to Higher National Certificate (HNC) and Ordinary National Certificate (ONC) respectively.

In the short term, the reorganisation of courses under the BEC and the TEC is substantially increasing the workload (and perhaps the confusion) of colleges and students. The working methods of the Councils may inhibit or extend discretion and initiative in curricular matters at college level, but in the longer term a more flexible and integrated system of technical qualifications should be created for the student, allowing him or her to step on and off the escalator of qualifications at the most appropriate time and level. But there will still be many students following vocational courses validated in other ways, with currency in the locality or among practitioners in specialist fields.

The growth of General Certificate of Education courses in further education colleges, which has led to the enrolment of more than 250,000 students for such courses in every year since 1971−2, is representative of a fundamental extension of further education provision which has been gathering momentum since the early 1960s. A significant and increasing percentage of Advanced Level passes each year is obtained through further education institutions, and both Ordinary and Advanced Level courses are offered to students by day or evening. This whole phenomenon, together with the growth of 'link courses' between schools and colleges, has led to an overlap of provision and interchange of resources between secondary and further education on a very large scale. It has also led to competition between the two sectors for the opportunity to educate the sixteen−nineteen age group. With reorganisation of selective secondary education into a comprehensive system, an increasing number of education authorities have taken the opportunity to separate provision for this age group in sixth form colleges, under either Schools or Further Education Regulations. In other cases the weight of voluntary enrolment, whether by those seeking a second chance after examination failure at school or by those preferring the ethos of further education for the pursuit of traditional sixth-form studies, has effectively turned some further education institutions (or, more commonly, general studies departments within them) into something akin to sixth form colleges. Lord Alexander, former Secretary of the Association of Education Committees, has called for the creation of a tertiary sector to cater for the sixteen—nineteen age group under common regulations wherever their course of study happens to be located. Within the last decade thirteen tertiary colleges have opened to meet the needs of academic full-time students, along with the traditional vocational part-time and full-time requirements of young people in this age group. There are now over seventy sixth form colleges, some linked or loosely federated with local further education establishments. The overlap, the new demand and the small size of many sixth forms in comprehensive schools clearly concentrated the mind of the Labour Secretary of State on the question of the education of students between sixteen and nineteen, and proposals from the McFarlane Committee are currently awaited. Falling secondary-school rolls over the next few years will focus attention further on the economies of scale that may be achieved through separate education for this group.

The other major new group of participants in further education are the full-time higher education students. Some of these are following Higher National Diploma courses; many more are following three- or four-year teacher-training courses leading to degrees validated by universities or the Council for National Academic Awards (CNAA); and still more are following degree courses across the whole range of subjects validated by the CNAA. The CNAA is gradually emerging, since receiving its Charter in 1964, as the body validating nearly all advanced study at degree level in further education establishments. It is true that external degrees of London University still operate in further education, and the reorganisation of teacher training has led a number of universities to validate new degrees in education and other subjects in the former colleges of education; however, as these institutions become more firmly embedded in the further education system, increasingly their higher-level work is likely to be validated by the CNAA. By 1979—80 over 1000 CNAA validated courses were being followed by approximately 114,000 students, and the great majority of these courses operated within polytechnics.

The CNAA can trace its ancestry to the recommendations of Percy Report (1945) that a National Council of Technology should validate high-level courses; and, in so far as the polytechnics fulfil the role of major centres for the study of applied science, technology and management outside universities, they echo a further Percy proposal, the creation of 'colleges of technology', the British counterparts to German, Russian and American institutes of technology. The CNAA has allowed further education colleges, particularly polytechnics, to develop their own characteristic higher education courses with national and international currency, while remaining in the public sector of education. Colleges submit syllabus and examination structure for scrutiny and approval by the Council, which applies the traditional standards of the universities. Many CNAA degrees are in subject areas not offered by the universities and provide for the development of integrated studies which cross traditional academic demarcations. Some polytechnics place greater emphasis than others on the direct vocational relevance of their degrees, in line with the rationale of the original 'binary' policy. With more than 150,000 students on degree courses, further education colleges are now making a very substantial contribution to total provision of higher education opportunities.

Over the last decade or more the impact of strengthened institutions for the promotion of industrial training has been felt increasingly in the colleges. The Industrial Training Act 1964 first provided the institutional and financial means and incentives for employers individually and collectively to extend training facilities and to use colleges of further education as agents. The engineering industry and the public services had always set a good example in providing on-the-job training and day-release for further education, but the establishment of Industrial Training Boards (ITBs), industry by industry, each with the power to levy funds from individual firms and to make grants in respect of training provided or secured, heralded a much more systematic and comprehensive approach to training. These initiatives were taken not by Education Ministers but through the Ministry of Labour, and while there were many administrative teething problems and success was by no means uniform, the main complaint of the colleges was their lack of involvement in decision-making and the pressure put on them to conform to the ITB's narrowly defined requirements. The legislative amendments brought in by the Conservative Government of 1970—4 under the impetus of growing employer criticism of the ITBs in fact created the institutional mechanisms for even greater expansion of labour-training schemes under the Labour Government of 1974—9, which were particularly concerned to minimise youth unemployment. The Employment and Training Act 1973 established, on the model of a nationalised industry in many respects, the Manpower Services Commission, which eventually took over the traditional Ministry of Labour responsibilities for employment services and training.

With very substantial administrative discretion and funds, the Training Services Division, as executive arm of the Manpower Services Commission, has promoted many large-scale schemes for taking unemployed school-leavers off the dole and into a combination of work experience and training. Training opportunities have also been offered to older people, especially women, which have drawn them into colleges of further education for commercial courses. The Job Creation Scheme, the Training Opportunities Scheme and the Youth Opportunities Scheme are all examples of the large-scale and imaginative responses of the Training Services Division to the major problem of unemployment and retraining facing Britain.

The major implications for colleges have been threefold: first, there has been an access of students without previous qualifications and often without sustained motivation whom, for the first time, colleges have had to try and help; second, a new source of substantial funds outside the education system has been created, which can provide staff salaries and fund equipment and can cover the costs of physical plant; third, the colleges have had to learn to cope, to negotiate and to compromise with an agency which does not always share in the educationists' presuppositions or endorse their priorities. There can be no doubt that developments in industrial training have had as substantial an effect on the colleges as any other change in the post-war period.

It should be clear from the above account that it would be unwise to conclude that further education students on vocational courses form a homogeneous body with a common consciousness or many common experiences. Tables 5.1 and 5.2 illustrate fully the variety of qualifications students may be taking.

TABLE 5.1 *Advanced-Level Courses Leading to Recognised Qualifications, November 1975*

| | Polytechnics | | Other major establishments | | | | Evening institutes | | Number of students All establishments | | |
| | | | Maintained and assisted | | Direct grant | | | | | | |
	Men	Women	Men	Women	Men	Women	Men	Women	Men	Women	Total
Full-time courses											
University first degree	694	374	445	449	37	17	—	—	1,176	840	2,016
CNAA first degree [a]	19,826	11,411	3,224	3,144	—	—	—	—	23,050	14,555	37,605
University higher degree	55	10	7	—	1,037	188	—	—	1,099	198	1,297
CNAA higher degree [b]	385	102	46	28	1	—	—	—	432	130	562
Postgraduate and research	1,381	735	162	111	57	4	—	—	1,600	850	2,450
HND	3,461	1,180	2,345	711	—	—	—	—	5,806	1,891	7,697
HNC	—	1	13	24	—	—	—	—	13	1	14
Art Teacher's Diploma	236	262	32	24	—	—	—	—	268	286	554
Professional qualifications	5,727	2,780	5,094	2,604	5	—	—	—	10,826	5,384	16,210
College diplomas and certificates	3,046	2,167	1,584	1,351	905	776	—	—	5,535	4,294	9,829
Other courses	2,444	6,004	608	1,467	55	50	—	—	3,107	7,521	10,628
Total	37,255	25,026	13,560	9,889	2,097	1,035	—	—	52,912	35,950	88,862

continued overleaf

| | Polytechnics | | Other major establishments | | | | Evening institutes | | Number of students All establishments | | |
| | | | Maintained and assisted | | Direct grant | | | | | | |
	Men	Women	Men	Women	Men	Women	Men	Women	Men	Women	Total
Sandwich courses											
University first degree	109	14	–	–	–	–	–	–	109	14	123
CNAA first degree [a]	17,896	3,036	265	51	–	–	–	–	18,161	3,087	21,248
CNAA higher degree [b]	55	8	–	–	–	–	–	–	55	8	63
Postgraduate and research	17	1	–	–	–	–	–	–	17	1	18
HND	5,906	932	3,679	1,007	515	97	–	–	10,100	2,036	12,136
HNC	3	–	34	8	–	–	–	–	37	8	45
Professional qualifications	812	137	1,197	392	–	–	–	–	2,009	529	2,538
College diplomas and certificates	719	146	743	91	–	–	–	–	1,462	237	1,699
Other courses	17	8	14	1	–	–	–	–	31	9	40
Total	25,534	4,282	5,932	1,550	515	97	–	–	31,981	5,929	37,910
Part-time day courses											
University first degree	40	11	49	16	–	–	–	–	89	27	116
CNAA first degree [a]	2,344	559	162	28	–	–	–	–	2,506	587	3,093
University higher degree	138	21	19	–	–	–	–	–	157	21	178
CNAA higher degree [b]	685	89	5	5	–	–	–	–	690	94	784
Postgraduate and research	2,778	307	1,608	85	–	–	–	–	4,386	392	4,778
HND	2	–	1	–	–	–	–	–	3	–	3
HNC	9,146	2,108	17,814	2,578	–	–	–	–	26,960	4,686	31,646
Professional qualifications	12,538	2,088	17,090	2,978	–	–	18	4	29,646	5,070	34,716
College diplomas and certificates	1,684	238	320	159	4	37	–	–	2,008	434	2,442
Other courses	1,564	942	3,296	1,628	–	–	–	–	4,860	2,570	7,430
Total	30,919	6,363	40,364	7,477	4	37	18	4	71,305	13,881	85,186

Evening-only courses											
University first degree [a]	624	189	405	207	—	—	—	—	1,029	396	1,425
CNAA first degree [a]	563	176	136	62	—	—	—	—	699	238	937
University higher degree	46	5	12	7	—	—	—	—	58	12	70
CNAA higher degree [b]	320	51	—	2	—	—	—	—	320	53	373
Postgraduate and research	1,151	113	465	31	—	—	—	—	1,616	144	1,760
HND	10	—	4	1	—	—	—	—	14	1	15
HNC	1,376	145	2,258	257	—	—	—	—	3,634	402	4,036
Professional qualifications	8,667	1,512	12,535	1,551	—	—	16	4	21,218	3,067	24,285
College diplomas and certificates	318	105	65	44	—	—	—	—	383	149	532
Other courses	798	143	2,329	764	4	45	79	136	3,210	1,088	4,298
Total	13,873	2,439	18,209	2,926	4	45	95	140	32,181	5,550	37,731
All advanced courses											
University first degree [a]	1,467	588	899	672	37	17	—	—	2,403	1,277	3,680
CNAA first degree [a]	40,629	15,182	3,787	3,285	—	—	—	—	44,416	18,467	62,883
University higher degree	239	36	38	7	1,037	188	—	—	1,314	231	1,545
CNAA higher degree [b]	1,445	250	51	35	1	—	—	—	1,497	285	1,782
Postgraduate and research	5,327	1,156	2,235	227	57	4	—	—	7,619	1,387	9,006
HND	9,379	2,112	6,029	1,719	515	97	—	—	15,923	3,928	19,851
HNC	10,525	2,254	20,119	2,843	—	—	—	—	30,644	5,097	35,741
Art Teacher's Diploma	236	262	32	24	—	—	—	—	268	286	554
Professional qualifications	27,744	6,517	35,916	7,525	5	—	34	8	63,699	14,050	77,749
College diplomas and certificates	5,767	2,656	2,712	1,645	909	813	—	—	9,388	5,114	14,502
Other courses	4,823	7,097	6,247	3,860	59	95	79	136	11,208	11,188	22,396
Total	107,581	38,110	78,065	21,842	2,620	1,214	113	144	188,379	61,310	249,689

[a] From 1974 onwards includes the former Diploma in Art and Design courses.
[b] From 1974 onwards includes the former Higher Diploma in Art and Design, which was previously shown under Postgraduate and research.

Source: *Statistics of Education 1976, England and Wales*, HMSO, 1977, vol. 3, Further Education. Table 12

TABLE 5.2 *Non-Advanced-Level Courses Leading to Recognised Qualifications, November 1975*

| | Polytechnics | | Other major establishments | | | | | | Number of students All establishments | | |
| | | | Maintained and assisted | | Direct grant | | Evening institutes | | | | |
	Men	Women	Men	Women	Men	Women	Men	Women	Men	Women	Total
Full-time courses											
Ordinary National Diploma	27	16	14,597	7,784	—	—	—	—	14,624	7,800	22,424
Ordinary National Certificate	—	—	304	10	—	—	—	—	304	10	314
City and Guilds	133	13	32,198	16,462	7	2	16	—	32,354	16,477	48,831
GCE	5	12	45,818	40,719	—	—	8	—	45,831	40,731	86,562
Other non-advanced	1,689	1,870	16,516	35,203	656	220	—	—	18,861	37,293	56,154
Total	1,854	1,911	109,433	100,178	663	222	24	—	111,974	102,311	214,285
Sandwich courses											
Ordinary National Diploma	12	30	2,667	381	192	20	—	—	2,871	431	3,302
Ordinary National Certificate	11	—	1,287	3	—	—	—	—	1,298	3	1,301
City and Guilds	6	—	1,490	194	—	—	—	—	1,496	194	1,690
GCE	—	—	5	37	—	—	—	—	5	37	42
Other non-advanced	83	20	509	1,221	32	—	—	—	624	1,241	1,865
Total	112	50	5,958	1,836	224	20	—	—	6,294	1,906	8,200

Part-time day courses											
Ordinary National Certificate	93	3	42,065	13,847	35	—	—	—	42,193	13,850	56,043
City and Guilds	5,649	271	296,060	36,822	524	106	5	—	302,238	37,199	339,437
GCE	3	2	12,704	24,860	—	653	141	—	12,848	25,515	38,363
Other non-advanced	2,178	572	19,422	13,415	—	—	—	—	21,600	13,987	35,587
Total	7,923	848	370,251	88,944	559	759	146	—	378,879	90,551	469,430
Evening-only courses											
Ordinary National Diploma	—	—	2	2	—	—	—	—	2	2	4
Ordinary National Certificate	—	—	4,598	1,171	—	—	—	—	4,598	1,171	5,769
City and Guilds	836	131	31,093	10,018	—	—	722	636	32,651	10,785	43,436
GCE	78	130	68,821	79,959	—	—	18,431	26,038	87,330	106,127	193,457
Other non-advanced	2,733	705	16,069	7,553	—	—	793	459	19,595	8,717	28,312
Total	3,647	966	120,583	98,703	—	—	19,946	27,133	144,176	126,802	270,978
All courses											
Ordinary National Diploma	39	46	17,266	8,167	192	20	—	—	17,497	8,233	25,730
Ordinary National Certificate	104	3	48,254	15,031	35	—	—	—	48,393	15,034	63,427
City and Guilds	6,624	415	360,841	63,496	531	2	743	742	368,739	64,655	433,394
GCE	86	144	127,348	145,575	—	—	18,580	26,691	146,014	172,410	318,424
Other non-advanced	6,683	3,167	52,516	57,392	688	220	793	459	60,680	61,238	121,918
Total	13,536	3,775	606,225	289,661	1,446	242	20,116	27,892	641,323	321,570	962,893

Source: Statistics of Education, 1976, England and Wales, HMSO, 1977, vol. 3, Further Education, Table 13.

THE GOVERNMENT OF COLLEGES

Some homogeneity is introduced by the constitutional structure of colleges developed over the last twenty years. All institutions of further education with full-time students have had governing bodies since the implementation of the Further Education (Local Education Authority) Regulations 1959. Many establishments, including some of those without full-time students, had governors before then, either because they were grant-aided foundations or because the education authority in which they were located thought it appropriate; in other cases a subcommittee of the education committee may have acted as governing body. Mandatory establishment of the present structure of governing bodies resulted indirectly from the recommendations of the Robbins Committee. This committee, reporting in 1963 on the future development of higher education, was responsive to the wishes of the teacher training colleges for greater institutional autonomy, in line with that of the universities; they recommended the introduction of degrees in education for intending teachers and the gradual assimilation of the colleges to the university sector. While government accepted the first of these two recommendations, it rejected the second, partly at least because of the desire of local education authorities to retain control of the maintained training colleges. A Departmental committee was set up under the chairmanship of a civil servant, Mr (now Sir) Toby Weaver, to inquire into college government and to recommend ways in which university-style academic freedom could be reconciled with public control and local authority responsibility.

During the same period government's rejection of a perpetually shifting hierarchy of further and higher education institutions, with universities at the apex of the pyramid, in favour of two distinct systems, with polytechnics at the head of the public sector and equal in status to universities, necessitated detailed discussion of appropriate forms of institutional government for the polytechnics. There can be little doubt that the increased political consciousness of students during the late 1960s also had its influence on the drafting of the Education (No. 2) Act 1968 and the subsequent explanatory Circular 7/70.

The new Act was concerned with all maintained institutions of further education—not just the colleges of education—that had full-time students. It required the controlling local education authorities to set up governing bodies, under Articles of Government subject to the approval of the Secretary of State that delineated the functions of 'Governors, the Principal and the Academic Board, if any', and Instruments of Government that defined the membership of the governing body, subject to approval by the Secretary of State in the case of colleges of education but not in other cases.

While the terms of the Act might seem to leave a great deal of discretion in the hand of the local education authority, Circular 7/70 went into much greater detail on the questions of appropriate membership for and functions of different sorts of college. The Weaver Report (1966) had conceptualised governing bodies as a buffer and a link between local education authorities and colleges; it is not surprising, therefore, that a number of years passed in negotiations between local education authorities, colleges and the DES before acceptable arrangements were made throughout the country.

Now in all colleges governors are responsible for the 'general direction of the college', and they, together with the maintaining local education authority, control individual colleges. The governing bodies are legal entities with executive powers and functions of their own, all of which are specified in the Articles of Government. Details of decision-making powers over finance, staff appointments and student discipline will vary between colleges, according to the Articles, which broadly follow the patterns laid down in Circular 7/70. The governors consist of nominees of the local education authority, senior staff of the college *ex officio*, including the principal, elected academic staff and student members and co-opted representatives of appropriate commercial, industrial and other interests. Circular 7/70 recommends that local education authority representatives should form less than half of the governing body and that in most cases a proportion as small as a quarter should be acceptable. It was expected that industry and commerce might take about one-third of places and that other education interests such as secondary schools, universities and professional institutions would have representatives.

In its negotiations with local education authorities over the approval of Articles of Government for colleges government was clearly in favour of the maximum autonomy for each college compatible with the overall efficiency of the system of further education in the locality and the region. Circular 7/70 distinguishes three classes of college, according to the proportion of advanced work that is, teaching at degree or equivalent level) and the age of the majority of students. The higher the proportion of advanced work and of students over eighteen years of age, the greater the degree of autonomy and the elaboration of governing institutions appropriate to that autonomy. 'The aim should be to give the Governors the maximum responsibility for incurring expenditure within approved estimates which is reasonable and appropriate in relation to the particular circumstances of the college' (Circular 7/70). In addition, colleges with the greatest claim to institutional autonomy should have academic boards consisting of academic staff, both *ex officio* and elected, responsible for academic development within the college.

The creation of governing bodies has two potential effects on policy-making within the local education authority; first, it establishes an independent locus of power, focusing the demands of the particular institution; second, it introduces to decision-making individuals and groups owing no special loyalty to the local authority or the political party in majority control. Assessment of the positive advantage or hindrance to decision-making of these two major changes depends very much on the assessor's position in the structure of power and the values that he brings to bear. Superficially at least, coherence of further education provision in a local education authority will be advanced by the minimisation of competing, semi-independent sources of policy initiative; radical changes can be implemented with least resistance. Where policy is not laid down by fiat but emerges in some informal way from consensus among politicians, administrators, teachers and students, it may be argued that formally constituted governing bodies simply inhibit the free and speedy flow of information and consultation from idea to implementation. If governing bodies are responsible for the 'general direction of the college', it may be asked what there is left for the local education authority and its officers to be responsible for in the field of further education. By contrast, it is argued—and the argument evokes sympathy amongst further education teachers and students—that further education provision is so varied and so complex that there needs to be a deliberative and decision-making body whose task is to make sense of priorities between the workshop or lecture room and the offices of the local education authority. Governing bodies recognise the plurality of interests in further education; they provide a forum for detailed consideration of the needs and problems of a college and a position from which to assess the adequacy of the local authority's commitment to provision. The inclusion of representatives of industry, of professionals and of other sectors of the education service provide a counterbalance to the predominantly party-aligned local authority.

Whether governing bodies live up to these varying expectations is a matter for empirical inquiry. Their efficacy depend on the powers given to them and the use made of such powers. Circular 7/70 provided model Articles of Government, outlining powers for governors in respect of the preparation of estimates, responsibility for expenditure and maintenance of buildings, the appointment and dismissal of teachers, student discipline and so on.

Assessing the future resource needs of the college is clearly a responsibility that must be assumed by the governing body if there is to be any meaning to its concern for future development. But lay governors are largely in the hands of the professionals in analysing the implications of a particular set of estimates. Very often the estimates will have been prepared in theory by the principal, in fact by his administrative and academic staff jointly with the appropriate officers of the authority; many disagreements between college and local authority will have been settled at this stage. Major developments involving substantial new expenditure, whether on staff or on equipment, will be discussed and ratified by the governing body. It is unlikely that a governing body identifying with the college and composed in good part of senior members of the college staff will turn down proposals for new expenditure. Rather, it will add its weight to the competing claims on the local education authority.

Much the same may be said of the governing body's control of expenditure within an agreed budget, although here the potential exercise of virement requires some public accountability. Virement is the power to transfer money that was to be spent on one item to another under the same budget heading, or sometimes from one heading to another. Circular 7/70 envisaged quite extensive powers of virement for governors, to enable a college to respond flexibly to changing priorities through the financial year. Presented in this way, it seems an eminently sensible provision, but controllers of local authorities' finances tend to be much more sceptical, since its implication is that the resources agreed and allocated to a college for specific purposes may in fact be used for substantially different ends in the course of the year. In addition, there is the fear that expenditure incurred in this way in one year may effectively commit a local authority to similar expenditure in future years, without proper consideration of the consequences for the local education authority's policy overall. Expedients for striking the right balance between these two perspectives vary from one authority to another; some virement within budget headings is possible in all colleges. A finance subcommittee of the governors may be asked by the principal from time to time to allow expenditure on one consumable resource (such as stationery) to be increased at the expense of another; it is most unlikely that a governing body would be free to use finance originally allocated for quite other purposes to employ an extra member of staff. Any such obvious expansion of the college with long-term implications would have to be approved in turn by the governors and the local authority in the course of the approval of annual estimates.

Governors often have considerable discretion to approve items of building maintenance within the overall budget allocation. Circular 7/70 suggested discretion for individual items up to £500 in value, but many Articles have restricted this to a lower figure. Similar arrangements may be made in respect of supplies and equipment, although local authorities may resist these in favour of their centralised bulk-purchasing facilities. In these matters the initiative lies much more with the principal and his staff, enhancing their independent management of the institutions, than with the governing body itself.

The powers of governors over the appointment and grading of staff may have similar implications. Most of a college's expenditure is on staff, and it is the critical factor in determining the character and quality of the college's work. The more senior the post to be filled, the more likely it is that the governors will be directly involved. Lecturers may be appointed on the recommendation of the principal; the appointment of the principal himself will usually require a special committee of governors and local authority representatives. The governors will generally also have responsibility for recommending the dismissal of the principal to the local authority, just as they will have responsibility, through a disciplinary subcommittee, for student discipline and, through the Academic Board, for excluding academically unsatisfactory students.

Non-teaching staff, such as technicians, secretarial and manual employees, are more often the direct responsibility of the local authority. Their tasks, their rates of pay and their conditions of service will be common to many others employed in similar capacities in other parts of the local authority, and if day-to-day management is left to institutional discretion, there is considerable risk of the creation of anomalies and discrepancies between the experience of one employee of the authority and another. At the same time the support of non-teaching staff has increasingly become a critical factor in the effective pursuit of their duties by teaching staff in further education, and it can clearly present intractable difficulties of management if the college has little or no discretion over the deployment of a substantial and crucial element in its human resources. The ideal situation is one in which management decisions can be made within the institution on the basis of advice from an expert and responsive personnel service, economically provided within the central administration of the local authority. One polytechnic principal has acknowledged the theoretical adequacy of this solution but claims that experience demonstrates the inability of local authorities to provide quick, authoritative answers to problems of personnel management.

The tension between institution and governing body on the one hand and local authority on the other is most clearly seen in the controversial system for financing advanced further education. In locally maintained institutions, since the costs of all recognised higher education can be charged to a national pool made up of contributions from all local education authorities, those local education authorities monitoring, for example, polytechnics lack the spur which an increasing burden on the rate fund gives to a close examination of advanced further education expenditure. The Layfield Committee on Local Government Finance criticised the pooling of expenditure on higher education in the public sector because it did not provide a means of ensuring effective accountability: 'the net effect of the system is one whereby some providing authorities are able to precept all others for pooled services.' (Department of the Environment, 1976, p. 111)

Despite the disincentive, many local authority members and their finance officers take a close, if sceptical, interest in the budgeting and internal financial control processes of their polytechnic. The firm limitation on maximum disbursements from the pool announced for the financial year 1980—1, which means that any excess expenditure will fall entirely on the rate fund of the providing authority, has exacerbated local authority/institution relationships in many cases, as overall budgets have been slashed and internal institutional economies, including academic staff redundancies, are under discussion. Examples of apparently grossly wasteful expenditure in public-sector higher education are easy to find, but the responsibility for them is by no means always that of the institution and its governors. The thirty polytechnics were created by amalgamations and development of existing further education institutions in the late 1960s and early 1970s, and clearly any such processes produce short- and medium-term anomalies of staffing and other resources. At the same time these new institutions were called upon to embark on adventurous and experimental programmes of courses while remaining subject to the strongest academic demands for resources of manpower and facilities in order to obtain CNAA approval. While such rigour has been applied in approval of the form, content and resources for particular courses, the system of Regional Advisory Councils, in combination with the Further Education Inspectorate, has proved quite inadequate for planning overall provision in relation to student demand by the standards of the university sector of higher education.

But this is not the whole story by any means. For no sooner had the polytechnic amalgamations been constitutionally completed than the downturn in the birth rate from 1965 onwards led to a reappraisal of the scope and size of the teacher training colleges. Further amalgamations, sometimes with polytechnics, sometimes of previously separate colleges of education, took place in the mid-70s, accompanied by a diversification of college courses and redeployment of staff previously engaged in teacher training in other disciplines.

This history by no means excuses all the failures and waste of resources that can be found in institutions that provide advanced further education, but it does offer a powerful defence of their general record in the face of constantly changing demands from students, providing authorities and the DES. While senior management of institutions have borne the brunt of the problems posed from outside and all staff have shared in the consequences, it has been impossible for governing bodies to avoid participation in the debate, often acting as the nexus between all the parties concerned.

It will be clear from the above that the governing body may be little more than the 'dignified' part of the college structure, meeting three times a year at minimum to ratify formally the principal's report, the work of the academic board and the estimates as prepared and attending the college's ceremonial functions. But if the governors so choose, and they may, they can provide a concerned critical forum for discussion of the progress of the college and a valuable source of support in negotiation with the local authority and local industry and commerce. Locke (1975) has listed five distinct functions of governing bodies; they can act as a watchdog or fire brigade in case of problems; a mechanism to reconcile academic freedom and public accountability; a basis for public discussion about different educational values and priorities; an independent monitor of college work; and a legitimator of decisions. No doubt practice varies considerably, but these are important tasks. However, these tasks are carried out, statutory requirements do far more than delineate the constitutional activities of the governing body itself; they give formal structure to the process of educational policy-making within the college, intersecting and conflicting in various ways with the hierarchical staff responsibilities evolved over the years.

INTERNAL ORGANISATION AND ADMINISTRATION

There is no standard pattern of internal college organisation, since this depends in large part on the variety of activities and the varying size of different establishments. One can only propose a model resembling the commonest patterns of organisation, as in Figure 5.2. It is possible, however, to describe focal points of decision-making and key relationships, both internally and between colleges and other organisations, whose activities impinge on the work of the college.

Policies for future development may emanate from the local education authority, be instigated by the principal or simply follow a pattern consistent with national policy. On many occasions, however, expansion or a change in the priorities of provision will result from changes in consumer demand, as expressed by student or employer preferences. Structural change within the college depends to a great extent upon the principal. Principals are often men with substantial experience of industry or commerce, as well as of further education as former vice-principals or heads of department. Their major responsibilities encompass most appointments, discipline, academic and staff development, the maintenance and extension of buildings, the supervision and co-ordination of all resources which contribute to the functioning of the college and the welfare of students. As colleges

168

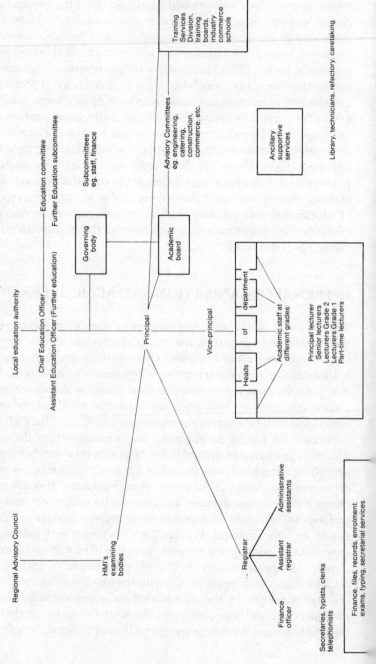

FIG. 5.2 The internal structure of a college and its major relationships

Local education authority
Chief Education Officer
Assistant Education Officer (Further education)

Education committee
Further Education subcommittee

Subcommittees
eg. staff, finance

Governing body

Academic board

Training Services Division, training boards, industry commerce schools

Advisory Committees
eg engineering, catering, construction, commerce, etc.

Ancillary supportive services

Library, technicians, refectory, caretaking

Principal

Vice-principal

Heads   of   department

Academic staff at different grades:

Principal lecturer
Senior lecturers
Lecturers Grade 2
Lecturers Grade 1
Part-time lecturers

Regional Advisory Council

HMI's examining bodies

Registrar

Assistant registrar

Administrative assistants

Finance officer

Secretaries, typists, clerks telephonists

Finance, files, records, enrolment, exams, typing, secretarial services have grown, many such tasks have necessarily been delegated to senior subordinates. The principal will be most concerned with resource planning in collaboration with the governors and the local authority, liaison with the DES through the Inspectorate and the representation of the interests of the college in the deliberations of the Regional Advisory Councils. In many cases the principal and senior colleagues will be deeply involved in the planning of new courses with and through professional institutions and subject boards of City and Guilds or the Royal Society of Arts. Close personal contact will also be maintained with local industrial and commercial interests, which may determine the viability of new and existing courses.

Since the fundamental changes in the structure of college government following Circular 7/70, academic boards have been involved in promoting, planning and maintaining the various college courses. The board normally has all heads of department as members *ex officio,* but there will be a substantial proportion of elected staff representatives. Boards now commonly control all procedures governing the running of course. At the same time heads of department undertake the organisation of teaching, timetabling, room allocations, the preparation of departmental estimates, including staffing and consumable resources such as stationery and books. Modification of departmental priorities may be imposed by the academic board or, perhaps, the governing body. Major departments often have advisory committees involving employer and trade union interests and, in some cases, training boards. Ideas about courses and resources may well be influenced by such bodies, which help to form the close links with industry, commerce and the community that all colleges need to sustain recruitment.

The head of department is much more powerful than the equivalent of his namesake in the secondary school. Such is the delegation of authority in colleges that his responsibilities bear comparison with those of the headmaster. The head of department may even have up to seventy full-time staff under him in a large college, and there will usually be half as many again employed on a part-time basis, not to mention the technicians, clerical and secretarial staff who may be assigned to a department.

The registrar often combines his role with that of the chief administrative officer and, if so, acts as clerk to the governors. He is normally responsible for the central administration of files, records, enrolments, examinations, internal correspondence, accounts, registers, inquiries and the submission of returns to the DES. These are but a few of the many procedures within the central administration. In larger colleges a finance officer and a chief administrative officer separately undertake responsibilities for these operations. The library is a common service and the chief librarian will be directly responsible to the principal and academic board, although there are inevitably constant interrelations with all departments. All other ancillary services in the complex organisation are subject ultimately to the control and direction of the principal. The principal, vice-principal, heads of departments and registrar in effect form the management team, but there is much delegation of responsibility to departmental level involving the head, section leaders and course tutors.

STAFFING: CONDITIONS OF EMPLOYMENT, ROLES AND TRAINING

The salaries of teachers in further education are agreed by the national Burnham Committee and made legally enforceable by statutory instrument. Conditions of service are governed by local agreement negotiated within the framework of national agreements which fix limits within which local variations may operate.

Up to the mid-1970s teachers' contracts were often loosely defined and varied considerably among employing authorities. Detailed conditions were largely dependent upon local custom, and many points were subject to common-law interpretation of duties, responsibilities, rights and benefits. For this reason, attempts by local authorities to extend the college operating year beyond the traditional thirty-seven or thirty-eight weeks found no support from the then Association of Teachers in Technical Institutions (now renamed the National Association of Teachers in Further and Higher Education) until local authority organisations agreed to negotiate conditions of service nationally. Teachers in further education, like most employees, now have a range of rights which have accrued from the Contracts of Employment Act 1972 and the Employment Protection Act 1975. These include a right to individual contracts which specify conditions of employment in terms of remuneration, holidays and the hours of service on the premises that can be required. Teachers now also enjoy benefits which have long applied to workers outside education (and, indeed, to non-academic employees within education). Regulations under the Health and Safety at Work Act 1975 came into operation in September 1978, so that many features of earlier employment legislation, such as the Shops, Offices and Safety at Work Act 1965, have become mandatory in all educational establishments. In 1975 the Council of Local Education Authorities and the further education teachers' organisations, predominantly the National Association of Teachers in Further and Higher Education, reached agreement over the conditions of service that were to form the basis of negotiations between the unions and individual local authorities. The maximum number of weeks which a member of staff would be required to teach and be present without a break of two weeks was specified as fourteen. Detailed holiday schedules for the academic year would be agreed and notified in the autumn term. Consultations with teachers' organisations would have to take place before changes in course lengths affecting the college year could be implemented. Thirty hours would be the maximum duration of duties per week, spread over ten sessions, each no longer than four hours with a break half-way through, some of which might be in the evening. The number of hours of student-contact time was specified in bands for each grade of staff. The higher the grade, the lower the class-contact time, since it was assumed that the more senior staff would have a greater administrative load.

The establishment of a college is determined by totalling student hours and weighting them according to the level of course followed, thereby determining the grade of the college. The proportion of senior to junior teaching staff, and sometimes the progression of individuals up the incremental scale or from one scale to another, depends upon the proportion of work at different levels, as does the grade of the department, which determines the head of department's salary.

Such detailed conditions of service in addition to employment legislation have created something of a minefield for those running colleges and for local authority administrators. No education department, let alone a college or polytechnic, can hope to assimilate all the nuances, and the legal and personnel resources of the whole local authority are increasingly brought into play. As indicated above, frequently a quick response to an immediate problem is needed; local authorities are not usually adapted to make such responses and problems are exacerbated by extended lines of communication and consultation. Without good will and common sense on both sides in planning and negotiating the use of staff, there are endless possibilities for disaster in the developing complexity of arrangements. The corporate consciousness of a college that may develop from the creation of stronger governing bodies and academic boards can provide a context in which the problems highlighted in the adversary context of union—management negotiations can be anticipated and largely forestalled.

This web of relationships and procedures both reflects and affects the attitudes and behaviour of staff. The study by Tipton (1973) of a quite typical further education college indicates the different attitudes brought to the college, as compared with those of the typical schoolteacher by the lecturer recruited in the main direct from industry and commerce: while an appreciation of the intrinsic attractions of the work is widely shared, teaching as a vocation hardly figures in the lecturer's analysis of his own motivations. For those with previous experience of teaching in school and for others dealing mainly with part-time students, teaching in further education can be a fragmentary and frustrating experience. The perceived main routes to promotion are generally seen as course development and the assumption of administrative responsibilities. The structure of opportunities for promotion within the college depends on student numbers and the level of courses taught; it is not surprising, then, that the staff studied by Tipton tended to divide for or against the introduction of higher-level courses according to the opportunities for advancement that such developments would offer them. In the building and engineering departments, which mainly provided craft courses, only one person, a graduate, was in favour of degree courses; while a majority of support was to be found in the general studies and management departments, where many more lecturers qualified to teach at degree level were to be found.

In the sample of lecturers from the college studied, just under half had no teacher training at all and only a third had one year or more teacher training, an accurate reflection of the national picture. Regardless of the perceived structure of advancement in further education teaching, national policy has increasingly encouraged opportunities for in-service training through specialist colleges and extra-mural centres offering full-time and part-time sandwich and day-release courses. Teaching staff in further education or students intending to enter colleges as teachers have been able to undertake a course leading to a Certificate in Education at one of four colleges of education (technical) situated at Bolton, Garnett College (London), Huddersfield (now part of Huddersfield Polytechnic) and Wolverhampton. Pre-service courses are provided on a one-year basis or, for in-service teachers, through a four-term sandwich course or day-release course over two years. The in-service course was also provided in many extra-mural centres. There were such centres in colleges at Nottingham, Sheffield, Grimsby, Chesterfield, Bedford, Ipswich, Norwich and Scunthorpe, for example, operating under or in conjunction with the Huddersfield College and leading to a Certificate validated by Leeds University. Wolverhampton had comparable arrangements at Coventry and Bristol Polytechnic, and Garnett at the Polytechnic of the South Bank. Since Circular 11/77 arrangements are being made for a more localised provision of initial training, co-ordinated on a regional basis. In Scotland further education teachers' training provision is centred upon Jordanhill College of Education, whose scope further encompasses training for primary and secondary education. Colleges are becoming more conscious of the need for deliberate staff-development policies, involving varieties of experience in the job and opportunities for the modification and improvement of qualifications, whether as teachers or subject specialists; but there is a long way to go before a career in further education is seen as other than the result of personal initiative, situational luck and the manipulation of the system.

REGIONAL CO-ORDINATION AND CONTROL

Most colleges serve a local catchment area; many will provide some courses to meet regional needs; very few will attract as students only residents in the area covered by the local maintaining local authority. For these reasons alone, some form of co-ordination of provision over and above that of the individual local authority has been thought necessary. Since the Percy Report (Ministry of Education 1945) government has required the coming together of local education authorities in the form of Regional Advisory Councils, modelled in general on the Yorkshire Council, which was founded as long ago as 1927. Membership of Advisory Councils includes representatives of the local education authorities, of industry and commerce, and of the universities and maintained colleges of further education. The Councils have full-time officers, some on quite a large scale, a Regional

Academic Boards and many advisory panels dealing with questions of fees, curriculum, teacher training and assessment. The Regional Staff Inspector from the Further Education division of Her Majesty's Inspectorate will have a seat on major committees of the Council. Sometimes the Regional Advisory Councils seem to participants to be little more than talking-shops; at other times they are the arena for bargaining between colleges and between local education authorities on the location and scale of new course developments, and any commitment to regional planning gives way to inter-authority horse-trading. At one time all new vocational courses proposed had to have the seal of approval of the Advisory Councils. Now only advanced courses have to be approved before being considered for final decision by the Secretary of State on the recommendation of the Regional Staff Inspector. It can seem to the larger urban authorities, who are the providers of most of the regionally and nationally significant advanced courses, that the Advisory Councils allow smaller local education authorities to exercise power with little responsibility, while adding only marginally to the expertise already available within colleges and major local education authorities. The universities, while willing to participate in regional discussions and to offer advice to the maintained sector, have never been willing to allow their own provision and development to be the subject of debate, despite the growing overlap between them and the further education colleges providing advanced courses. In the course of consideration of the reform of local government structure, one suggestion has been that further education should be administered at regional level, thus realigning power with responsibility in an appropriate frame of reference, but other pressures have successfully retained the 'seamless robe' of education in the control of the counties and metropolitan districts. The pooling system of financing advanced further education has, as discussed earlier, led to discussions about revised mechanisms for the control of that part of further education Strengthened regional bodies concerned with university resource allocations as well as public sector institutions have been advocated; the removal of the polytechnics and perhaps some other large colleges from local authority control and the establishment of a national body analagous to the University Grants Committee finds favour with some polytechnic directors. The reassertion of the responsibility of the providing authorities has also been considered: under the Conservative Government's new legislation a better articulated combination of national and regional bodies, with retained local authority responsibility, will, it is hoped, provide clearer, more manageable and more effective planning and accountability. Even so, the most characteristic feature of any further educatioin institution, a function of its variety of provision, will be its need to acknowledge many masters, including national and local government, examining and professional bodies, employers and students of every age, aptitude and interest.

CHAPTER 6

The Third Partner—
the Teachers

THE EMERGENCE OF TEACHERS' ASSOCIATIONS

Teachers have not always been considered an equal, or even a significant, partner in the education service. In 1863 Robert Lowe characterised the elementary school teachers' desire to have a say in policy and practice as the impertinence of 'chickens wishing to decide the kind of sauce in which they would be cooked'. Such a view was compatible with the reality of an education system which officially satisfied itself with the narrow and limited achievement of mass literacy and numeracy and which conceived of elementary school teaching as a mechanical process necessarily supervised by educated people but discharged by their social and educational inferiors. In many cases much more than this may have been achieved on the independent initiative of particular teachers or with the support of more ambitious sponsors. Within the schools providing for the children of wealthier and socially superior parents, much more came to be attempted in the course of the nineteenth century by teachers who were themselves more broadly educated and socially prestigious. Initiatives in adult education, motivated by a mixture of charity and political radicalism, gathered momentum in the latter part of the nineteenth century. The study of science, technology and vocational subjects was sponsored by the Department of Science and Art and stimulated further by scholarships and syllabuses introduced by the City and Guilds of London Institute (a product of enlightened self-interest on the part of the Livery Companies) and by philanthropists such as Quintin Hogg, who founded the Regent Street Polytechnic in the 1880s. These developments brought together large bodies of students of different ages and from a variety of social and educational backgrounds to leaven the lump of the officially constrained and submissive elementary school system.

But despite these many variants, for most pupils and for most teachers the characteristic learning and work experience was to be found under the Elementary School Code until the unification of the education system after 1944. The implementation of the Elementary Education Act 1870 eventually brought about a universal system of elementary schools in England and Wales (paralleled by earlier tradition and later equivalent legislation in Scotland and Ireland), but it did not bring to the average teacher security of tenure, nor uniformity of remuneration or conditions of service. For many a teacher summary dismissal, if he or she fell out of favour, was a very real possibility, and the predominance of Church-sponsored schools very often placed the teacher's future in the hands of the local parish priest. Even where standards of doctrinal and denominational purity were not applied with especial rigour, the 'moral' character of a teacher might be subject to scrutiny, and conscientiousness might easily be exploited by an overbearing employer. Most significant of all, remuneration responded to the local market rather than conforming to any agreed standard in respect of qualifications, experience or responsibilities undertaken. While qualification was discretionary and the minimum of academic attainment tolerated by employers was low, the bargaining power of the teacher was very limited, especially if, as was often the case, he or she was the only teacher employed and was therefore unable to band together with colleagues for collective strength.

The intervention of central government sometimes served to worsen the position of the teacher by making his livelihood even more overtly and mechanically dependent upon the narrowest criteria of educational success. From 1862 to the late 1890s 'payment by results' regulated the national grant payable to each elementary school according to the success of its pupils in annual examinations of basic skills administered by the Inspectorate. Although the initial rigours of the system were gradually modified and eventually eliminated, they threatened the security of the elementary school teacher, conditioned his remuneration and inhibited any broadening of his pedagogical horizons. In these circumstances it is not surprising that the training of elementary school teachers developed slowly and retained many of the characteristics of an apprenticeship, in contrast to the academic secondary and university experience of the

Inspectorate and some school managers. Pupil-teachers were for a long time the norm; that is to say, the more able elementary school pupil was given extra coaching and then used to instruct others, so that eventually he became a fully-fledged teacher. Under Kay-Shuttleworth, first Secretary to the Committee of the Privy Council for Education in the 1840s, pupil-teacher apprenticeship schemes were elaborated, codified and stimulated by examinations and scholarships, and teacher-training establishments came to be grant-aided. Much of the initiative in providing teacher training came from the Church sponsors of schools—established, Roman Catholic and nonconformist—consolidating the combination of non-academic training and submissive ethos among elementary schoolteachers.

Among the more prestigious, independent secondary schools a more aggressive ethos was created by headteachers entrusted, after a long struggle, with a virtual, if not actual, freehold right over the school property and its curriculum; in the case of endowed schools, one threat to the autonomy of the head might come from a second master, or usher, with independent powers to exploit; in the same way, pupil boarding houses developed by assistant masters might provide them with a bargaining position on remuneration, discretion and conditions of service that was not without strength. But most significant, in the late nineteenth and early twentieth centuries many secondary schools developed as single institutions that could afford to pay scant regard to the demands of the state, as opposed to those of their immediate clients, and were not part of a nationally *and* locally controlled system of schools, organised as a bureaucratic hierarchy from assistant through head teacher to local director of education, and subject to detailed supervision through Code and Inspectorate.

The valuation and orientation of pre-service training of teachers for secondary schools also developed along different lines. In the 1890s a number of the new civic universities set up education departments that combined the academic study of education with a one-year training course for graduates wishing to enter teaching. Even then, many able students went straight into teaching, a practice encouraged particularly by the more prestigious fee-paying secondary schools and indicating the value put on academic qualifications as against trained classsroom skill.

Although disadvantageously placed and often submissive, elementary schoolteachers took their opportunities to band together, at least for 'mutual improvement', as encouraged by the minutes of the

Committee of Council for Education that regulated teacher training, and increasingly for common advancement. When in 1852 Lord Derby's Government issued a minute giving clergymen the explicit right to dismiss a Church school teacher 'on account of his or her defective or unsound instruction of the children in religion, *or on other religious or moral grounds',* even the Metropolitan Church Schoolmasters' Association was among the teacher groups courageous enough to protest publicly. Although the Association's committee was repudiated by the membership after its patron, the Bishop of London, resigned at such a display of disloyalty to the Church, the minute was withdrawn within the year (Tropp, 1957, p. 48).

Much more serious for the growing self-esteem of the elementary schoolmaster was the introduction of 'payment by results' and other associated reforms, which increased his dependence on the good will of the school managers, reduced his remuneration and prospects and soured previously good relationships with the Inspectorate. A renascence of teachers' associations and collective political activity by teachers accompanied the campaign that culminated in the Elementary Education Act 1870. From that campaign and the subsequent legislation eventually emerged the National Union of Elementary Teachers and greater opportunities to influence the working conditions of teachers, to amend their status and to extend their role in policy-making.

These opportunities may be seen as three different sorts of strategy for advancement, overlapping but sometimes in conflict or at least requiring very careful reconciliation. The same differences of emphasis persist today and can be illustrated from contemporary political and educational debate.

As elementary schoolteacher numbers increased (105,000 in 1891), the cumulative voting system of the school boards, especially in the larger urban areas where teachers were often well organised, gave them the opportunity to support and to put forward candidates for election who would be sympathetic to teacher grievances. Gosden (1972) quotes the case of the schoolteacher dismissed by the Brighton school board whose union, the National Union of Elementary Teachers (NUET), intervened in the next school board election to return a majority pledged to his reinstatement. In the end the dismissed schoolteacher became chairman of the board. Similarly, the union sought to have sympathetic candidates elected to the House of Commons and eventually succeeded with the election of its general secretary, James Yoxall, as member for Nottingham (West) in 1895. Pressure on government to appoint experienced elementary schoolteachers to the Inspectorate can also be seen as part of a strategy to penetrate and take over the government of education.

Reconcilable in most respects with the above approach is the early and prolonged commitment to the ideal of an autonomous teaching profession. Among the first specific aims of the NUET was the 'proposal to raise teaching to a profession by means of a public register of duly qualified teachers for every class of school'. Such an aspiration was partly to a higher status and not necessarily endorsed by every generally sympathetic observer; Dr Temple, later Archbishop of Canterbury, commented to the Newcastle Commission in 1861 that the separate training of schoolteachers gave them 'too exalted a notion of their own position and of what they have to do and . . . they gradually acquire a sort of belief that the work of a schoolmaster is the one great work of the day and that they are the men to do it'.

Towards the end of the nineteenth century elementary schoolteachers came to see professional self-regulation, especially in respect of recruitment, not only as an element in status improvement but as a key to the most immediate practical problem posed for them by an excess of candidates for teaching posts.

> The impression that emerges of the teaching staff is of a small band of trained certificated teachers immersed in a growing flood of untrained certificated teachers, assistant teachers, additional women teachers, pupil-teachers and probationers. This flood of cheap, untrained labour was mainly female. The proportion of women teachers of all classes had increased from 53 per cent in 1869 to 75 per cent in 1899. (Tropp, 1957, pp. 117—18)

In seeking to use control of the supply of labour as an instrument of advancement, the NUET was adopting a classic trade union strategy. Its solidarity (18000 NUET members in 1891) and the strength of legal backing that it could provide for individuals and groups of members in dispute came in time to win the union consideration from anxious employers. In 1907, faced with the proposal of the West Ham Council to reduce teachers' salaries, the National Union of Teachers (NUT), as it had renamed itself, undertook a publicity campaign, blacklisted the authority, began to withdraw teachers from the schools and threatened mass resignations; eventually the West Ham Council capitulated. In 1910 teachers went on strike in Herefordshire, which had refused to establish a uniform county scale of salaries; in 1923 teacher strikes over salary reductions lasted eleven months, two and a half and three and a half months in, respectively, Lowestoft, Gateshead and Southampton. But the more common trade union practices—consultation and negotiation—predominated, always with the willing endorsement of the teachers' associations and, increasingly, with that of the officials of the Department of Education, most notably Sandford (1870—84) and Kekewich (1890—1903).

Secondary schools—that is, the seven great public schools and about 800 other endowed schools in existence in the mid-nineteenth century—first came together in 1869 at the Headmasters' Conference (HMC), which would, as Thring said in his opening address to the Conference, provide 'pronounced opinion from the most important profession in England' (quoted in Gosden, 1972 p. 7). The headmasters' social and professional pretensions were much more acceptable than those of their elementary school counterparts, and their means of influencing events were correspondingly different. Public campaigning might have its place, but the exploitation of social position and contacts were far more important. Indeed, the foundation of the Conference was inspired by the desire to consolidate the links between the great public schools and other secondary schools that had been threatened by the government's establishment of two separate Commissions of Inquiry into secondary education. Slightly less socially exclusive was the Headmasters' Association (HMA), founded only in 1890; according to Beatrice Webb (1915 p. 16), the HMA had 'from the first represented the ruck of endowed secondary schools', though it was (and is) closely linked with the Headmasters' Conference, and many leading headmasters are members of both. While the HMC heads may look to the leading public schools for inspiration, the membership and interests of the HMA have grown and been shaped by the development of state secondary education under the Education Acts of 1902 and 1944. Indeed, after the latter Act its doors were thrown open to new 'secondary' heads of modern schools and sectional meetings were held for them. It was claimed that members of the Assistant Masters' Association were being appointed to these posts and would be lost to the secondary associations unless welcomed by the headmasters.

The Assistant Masters' Association was established in 1891, with founding aims of advancing the course of education and protecting and furthering the interests of teachers. Its existence confirms the sectional divide, socially and administratively legitimated, between elementary schoolteachers and secondary schoolteachers that lingers on even today. Educationally, the separate grouping could originally be justified by the involvement of secondary schoolteachers in different curricula, different examination systems and correspondingly different problems and aspirations for their pupils as well as for themselves.

The most distinctive of the secondary associations in origin is probably the Association of Headmistresses. Founded as early as 1874, it was a hopeful anticipation of the expansion of girls' education. The few pioneers met at the house of Miss Buss, then head of the North London Collegiate School for Girls. Beatrice Webb (1915) suggests succinctly their dedication and distinctive horizons:

> In looking through reports of its early conferences, the student is struck with the wisdom of these pioneers—the care with which revolutionary methods in the physical and mental training of girls were combined with a quite genuine reverence for the religious, the domestic and even the social ideals of the middle classes.

Ten years later the Headmistresses' Association was in part the inspiration for the foundation of the Assistant Mistresses' Association, and by the end of the century the pattern of sectionalism in schoolteacher associations by sex, class and bureaucratic hierarchy was firmly established.

In other respects matters were less clear. The confidence of secondary heads in their own mission and social standing was confirmed by the new opportunities for expansion that the Education Act 1902 provided, but progress towards formal professional autonomy, the aim of elementary schoolteachers, was still thwarted in part by the very social and educational divisions of the teaching force itself. Political recognition of the NUT had been achieved; national consultation and parliamentary advocacy of teachers' interests were accepted, but many local education authorities failed to give the education service the financial priority that their employees thought it deserved. At the same time effective counteraction by teachers' organisations was often undermined by the ambivalence of members over their identity as 'trade unionists' or as 'professionals'. Belief in the validity of this distinction was widespread among employees and employers, as can be illustrated from the history of the Association of Teachers in Technical Institutions (now the National Association of

Teachers in Further and Higher Education), founded in 1904. Addressing a general meeting of the Association in 1907, the president declared:

> The authorities view our Association with favour, though they are a little on their guard lest we should develop into a Technical Teachers' Trade Union and become the TTTU instead of the ATTI. They need have no fear, I think, as if such an unfortunate result should come about there would be inevitably be a breaking up of the Association—a catastrophe we should all deplore. (Gosden, 1972, p. 15)

Leaving aside his moral evaluation, the president's prediction may be thought to have been proved wrong by the expansion of the Association's membership (1100 in 1911 to 46,000 in 1973) and the growth of its militancy, which may owe a lot to the industrial experience of many technical college lecturers.

Never far from the consciousness of teachers' organisations in Britain has been the desire to appear responsible and to be acceptable to employers. Such an emphasis may have been born of a prudent deference and an objective educational inferiority. But the interpretation of the goal of the traditional teachers' association, professional autonomy, includes a notion of respect for forbearance and vocation, which will eventually bring adequate material reward. Successive teachers' leaders have claimed compelling evidence of the reality of this progression but it has also been disputed by sceptics of 'professional' ideology.

As teachers' associations, especially the NUT, have become the accepted consultees of government, additional cogent reasons have been found for moderation and compromise in demands articulated. Most recent annual conferences of the mass teacher associations have amply illustrated the classic dilemma of trade union leaders of reconciling the maintenance of credibility with their grass-roots membership, impatient at delay and sceptical of excuses, with their own assessment, on the basis of privy information, of what is achievable without loss of highly advantageous access to government. The sectional organisation of teachers' associations has provided the opportunity for different emphases and grass-roots tolerance levels to be publicly represented, exposing membership divisions and weakening bargaining positions. Even so, the claims of the NUT to represent the desirable goal of a unified future for all teachers, regardless of educational and training background or school experience, was effectively challenged in 1922 by the formation of a breakaway union, the National Association of Schoolmasters (NAS).

The first men teachers' association as such was formed in Cardiff in 1913. Immediately after the First World War the question of equal pay for women teachers led to the breakaway of some 1500 men teachers from the London Teachers' Association (allied to the NUT); they feared that a common salary scale would depress the level of salary paid to men by reference to the common lack of dependence of women teachers on their pay as sole household income. Within two years relations between the NAS pressure group that disaffected male NUT members joined and the parent NUT were so strained that the NAS broke away completely and forbade its members to belong to the NUT.

The NAS's appeal has been to men committed to a full career in teaching, who are suspicious of the NUT's deferential leadership, its woman-teacher-dominated membership and its motives and capacities, and sympathetic to militant action in pursuit of its objectives. Its limited initial strength made its militancy often a matter more of rhetorical flourish and reaction than practical effectiveness, but its membership grew steadily during its first forty years of recruitment, especially as the NUT campaign for equal pay for women teachers drew to its successful climax in the 1950s. For many years the NUT and government connived at the exclusion of the NAS from any formally constituted national consultative or negotiating bodies in education, and NAS access to officials was sporadic and perfunctory when compared with other teachers' associations. But in 1961 NAS membership and self-projection was such that the Association was admitted to membership of the staff side of the Burnham Committee, which negotiates teachers' salary scales. Inevitably, with this formal recognition came much wider access to government, a further very substantial expansion in membership (from 22,651 in 1960 to approximately 50,000 in 1970) and an apparent change in militant tactics away from the stridency of the excluded towards a more subtle and no less effective outflanking of the NUT leadership in many national negotiations. What had always been public unanimity of the teachers' panel at Burnham under NUT leadership was successfully challenged by the new member, whose General Secretary throughout the period under discussion, Terry Casey, would hold press conferences to ensure that the NAS's distinct negotiating position did not go unrecorded.

With the fading of the equal pay issue, the NAS was at pains to stress its sympathy with the woman career teacher by encouraging the foundation of a sister association, the Union of Women Teachers; the two bodies, still growing in membership, have now amalgamated as the National Association of Schoolmasters/Union of Women Teachers.

The list of teacher unions is not complete without mention of the National Association of Head Teachers (NAHT), now some 19,000 members strong, drawn mostly from primary schools and outstanding as a defender of head teachers' autonomy within the school and the local environment.

THE STRUGGLE FOR PROFESSIONAL STATUS, INFLUENCE AND POWER

A picture of the work, the internal divisions on policy and strategy and the functions of teachers' associations in the wider context of educational government may most easily emerge from a consideration of issues and platforms that have been pursued and disputed. The search for professional status, the perpetual struggle over pay, the question of teacher supply and the reaction to secondary reorganisation will all serve this purpose well. The control of the curriculum nationally, locally and institutionally is examined in other chapters.

The College of Preceptors, founded in 1846, was the first attempt to create a professional regulatory body for teachers by private initiative. The model of professionalisation was that similarly exemplified by the founding of the Law Society (1825) and the Royal Institute of British Architects (1832). While the teachers' initiative did not achieve the same success, pressure mounted for legislative action that received some positive response from the Taunton Commission (1868). From then on the issue was on the political agenda either as a matter of status recognition or a means of raising academic standards. But the weakness of the teachers' claims lay most obviously in their division by class, education and conditions of work into those employed in proprietary schools, those in the endowed secondary schools and the mass of certificated elementary schoolteachers. In 1890 two registration Bills were before the House of Commons and were referred to a Select Committee. One Bill was confined to secondary teachers, sought to establish a council of established educational interests to control entry to the profession and went some way to integrate the College of Preceptors in statutory machinery. The other concerned all teachers, insisted on training as a condition of registration and would have excluded unregistered teachers from using the courts to recover tuition-free debts. Teachers' associations that gave evidence reflected their sectional bases in their support for or opposition to the various proposals before the Committee. While welcoming the principle of registration in its report to the House of Commons, the Select Committee came to no conclusion about the respective merits of the two Bills and further legislative action was deferred until the Bryce Commission (1895) reported in favour of establishing an Educational Council, which would have among its tasks the details of setting up and maintaining a unified register of teachers. The Consultative Committee created under the Board of Education Act (1899) followed the letter (though not the spirit) of the Act by proposing a single alphabetical list of all teachers, divided into two columns, one for certificated elementary teachers and another for graduates or their equivalents (with the promise of the list's eventual restriction to those possessing a teaching qualification as well). This compromise reflected and exacerbated the divisions amongst teachers over the acceptability of particular forms of register and antagonised in particular the members of the NUT as supporters of a single register both for secondary teachers and for its mass membership of elementary teachers.

The next twenty years saw little but frustration for the Union's endeavours to achieve professional status. The opposition of Morant, Permanent Secretary to the Board of Education (1903—11), despite a sympathetic Liberal Government from 1906, delayed the acceptance of possible alternative compromises but drew the teachers' associations into closer informal liaison than ever before. The distinct viewpoint of the national administrator could be seen in the evidence of HMI Fitch to the Select Committee of 1891, when he said:

> The public interests are the chief interests to be conserved and very important as the interests of teachers are, yet we all know that what are felt to be corporate and professional interests are not always absolutely identical with the public interests, the interests of parents and children. (quoted in Gosden, 1972, p. 242)

The General Secretary of the NUT, J. H. Yoxall, when addressing (significantly) a conference of the Headmasters' Association, expressed his suspicion that the Board of Education wanted to turn teachers into state functionaries. A commentator more sympathetic to such a policy, Beatrice Webb, described the secondary headmasters as self-characterised 'salaried servants of the public' (Webb, 1915).

A Registration Council was finally inaugurated in 1912, but it still had to face the difficulty of defining who was to count as a teacher, and it was without any control of initial teacher training or professional entry standards. Although the Council lasted throughout the inter-war period, it was rarely consulted on educational matters by the Board and achieved little standing among teachers. The provisions of the Education Act 1944 for the award of qualified-teacher status by the Minister aroused little dissent, and the Teachers' Registration Council was wound up in 1949.

The demand for professional autonomy was only dormant. The NAS called for a Teachers' Council again in 1954; the NUT renewed its demands at Conference in 1956. But approaches to government, such as the NAS made in 1958, evoked no positive response, although Sir William Alexander, Secretary of the Association of Education Committees, endorsed a Council that included educational adminis-trators and local Inspectors. In 1960 the NAHT took the initiative in calling together all the relevant teachers' associations to form the main committee of the Teachers' General Council Movement, which spent the next two years in internal negotiation.

Much that has been said of campaigns for professional autonomy in England and Wales is equally true of sentiments expressed and pressures applied in Scotland, where the complexity of sectionalised teacher organisations was absent. The Educational Institute of Scotland, unrivalled equivalent of the NUT, had long campaigned for the establishment of a Teachers' Registration Council. Problems of differing educational and training backgrounds among teachers were by no means as great within a smaller teaching force, all of whose members had undergone compulsory teacher training in a common set of colleges of education. A Committee on the Teaching Profession in Scotland (Scottish Education Department 1963) was set up by the Secretary of State for Scotland in 1961 as part of a conciliatory response to considerable agitation among Scottish teachers over the apparent lack of official consultation with them on educational matters. Three other working parties (Scottish Education Depart-ment, 1962a, b, c) made recommendations, on which government took administrative and legislative action as appropriate, for the involvement of serving teachers in teacher appointments, for arrangements for consultation between teachers' associations and local education authorities, for the establishment of formal consultative machinery between teachers' associations and the Scottish Education Department and for the eligibility of teachers to sit as co-opted members of local education committees (by analogy with English and Welsh practice).

But most significant by far was this recommendation of the Wheatley Report (para. 58):

> a change should now be made and . . . subject to appropriate safeguards, control of entry to the profession should be vested in a new body broadly similar in nature, powers and functions to the General Medical Council and other professional Councils. Accordingly we submit as our main recommendation that legislative action should be taken for the establishment of a General Teaching Council for Scotland.

The body that was established under the Teaching Council (Scotland) Act 1965 had forty-four members, made up of twenty-five teachers elected from among those employed in schools, further education and colleges of education; fifteen representing local education authorities, directors of education, universities, central institutions and the Churches; and four representing the Secretary of State. It proceeded to devise procedures and charges for registration and to make arrangements for exceptional admission to the register. By 1968 compulsory registration was in force, and some uncertificated teachers were actually dismissed. The application of the Act aroused substantial resistance, partly a response to teeething troubles and partly resentment of the necessity for annual registration, at a fee of £1, by existing teachers who could see little or no direct return for this. Teachers' action committees were set up to protest, and when the Secretary of State undertook a review of the constitution and function of the General Teaching Council (SED, 1969) they argued that the Council should become much more representative of 'practising teachers' or be renamed a consultative committee, to reflect its impotence, or that the whole project should be abandoned and previous practice, certification of competence, restored. Certainly, they argued, registration should be voluntary.

However, the more permanently entrenched representatives of

teachers, the Educational Institute, the Scottish Secondary Teachers' Association and the Scottish Schoolmasters' Association, were all content to maintain existing arrangements, subject to the reform of registration procedures and the extension of the representation of serving teachers.

The Council was increased in size to forty-nine by the addition of five more places for elected teachers, and the requirement for the substantial representation of head teachers among those elected was dropped. The proposal of the Scottish Schoolmasters' Association that teacher representatives should be nominated by the various teachers associated, at considerable saving of time and money, was firmly resisted by the Department, as it had been by the Wheatley Committee.

Scottish teachers have achieved all the outward manifestations of professional recognition found among doctors, lawyers, architects and the like, but there are many who doubt whether such professional recognition has or could transform the status and prospects of teachers, given their numbers and the nature of teaching as a mass occupation almost exclusively in the employ of the state.

The pressure of the English teachers' associations for professional recognition encountered much greater resistance from both Conservative and Labour Ministers of Education. Quintin Hogg, the first Secretary of State for Education (1963–4), failed to reply to the teachers' request for the establishment of an official working party before the 1964 General Election intervened. Labour's first Secretary of State, Michael Stewart, also failed to reply, but his successor, Anthony Crosland, agreed to meet a deputation. When Crosland refused to take the matter further no progress was made until a more sympathetic Minister, Edward Short (himself a former primary school headmaster), was appointed. On his initiative a working party was established in April 1969 and reported in February 1970.

As the report makes clear, the principle of a professional council was already implicitly accepted in the working party's terms of reference, and only detailed arrangements for operation needed to be discussed. The working party was chaired by a civil servant, Mr (now Sir) Toby Weaver, rather than by an independent outsider, as had happened in Scottish experience, and the recommendations show not only a wary eye to the controversies aroused by the first few years' activities of the Scottish General Teaching Council but also a concern to retain as much policy discretion and administrative oversight within the DES as possible. One major difference of substance concerned the recommendation that teacher members of the Teaching Council should be nominated by teacher associations rather than be elected. What had been an important matter of principle in Scotland was designated a mere matter of administrative detail and convenience in England. Another recommendation drew on Scottish experience in suggesting that a once-and-for all fee would arouse far less dissension than annual collection.

All such considerations proved superfluous. In September 1969, only two months after the Working Party had really got down to work, the NUT Young Teachers' Conference rejected the idea of a Teaching Council. Although the smaller teachers' associations and the local authorities welcomed the proposals on publication, there was no point in the new Conservative Secretary of State, Mrs Thatcher, taking any action until the long-established advocate of professional autonomy and the largest of the teacher groups, the NUT, had formally delivered its verdict. The reaction of local NUT branches had been mixed but mostly critical; in April 1971, at its annual policy-making conference, the NUT officially rejected the proposed Teaching Council as a useful way forward. By the time its long-sought objective had become realisable, the mood of the bulk of teachers, especially the large access of the late 1960s, had swung in favour of the other trade-union strategies for advancement.

However committed the teachers had been to formal professional recognition, there can be no doubting their central concern with questions of remuneration and conditions of service. In the minds of most members not only of teachers' associations but of all trade unions, whose membership is a consequence of conscious decision and not just habit, the motivation to belong, it might be argued, is born of the belief that collective representation in negotiations over salaries and conditions is the key to success and to the general protection of the individual employee against his employer. The further ideological commitment of the union activist, whether to workers' control or to professional autonomy, may be indulged by the mass membership as the just reward of the activist's successful pursuit of general material improvement. The dilemma for the union leadership, already noted above, is the choice between the elaborate formal machinery of negotiation developed since 1918 and the application of labour sanctions.

At the turn of the century there was no national and usually no local negotiating machinery. The school boards varied enormously in size, and, however controversial it might otherwise be, the Education Act 1902 did reduce the number of employers and increase their average size, so enabling the teachers' associations realistically to seek a general pattern of remuneration for the first time. Not that there was any sudden change; shortly before the First World War, the NUT's analysis of elementary school salaries showed quite clearly, in the words of Gosden (1972, p. 27) that: 'the higher salaries were to be found where the influence of the teachers' associations had been felt longest and where it had been stronger'—that is, in the large towns rather than in smaller towns and rural areas. Although the secondary school headmaster or headmistress was usually paid relatively well, assistants were more nearly in the position of curates, poorly paid but with reasonable grounds to hope for eventual preferment and financial security.

Although H. A. L. Fisher, President of the Board of Education in Lloyd George's Governments (1916—22), gave every encouragement to local authorities to improve teachers' salaries, it was direct pressure from the NUT that brought a successful initiative from the Association of Education Committees to establish national scales. Fisher made a 60 per cent central government grant available in respect of elementary teachers' salaries but with little effect. In 1918 and 1919 numerous local strikes were called by NUT associations throughout the country: the AEC, conscious of the shortage of teachers, outflanked the general local authority associations by endorsing a national salary scale as its annual meeting and calling on the Board of Education to arrange an immediate conference of the interested parties. The Standing Joint Committee with forty-four members drawn equally from employers' and teachers' representatives that was established in 1919 was soon paralleled by similar committees to deal with the pay of secondary teachers (the original Burnham Committee) and technical teachers. For the vast majority of teachers, national scales (there were, in fact, four scales agreed for elementary teachers) meant a very substantial restoration of their economic position prior to 1914; indeed, the commitment to the national scales and to Burnham became so firm that the NUT accepted a 5 per cent cut in salaries in 1923—4 under the 'Geddes axe' for fear of losing their national negotiating machinery. Salary negotiations in the inter-war period were characterised in part by political pressure to cut government expenditure, notably teachers' salaries, and the objective fact of a declining cost of living, but the negotiating machinery nevertheless remained intact and was strengthened by familiarity.

It is no surprise that the Education Act 1944 (Section 89) gave statutory force to what had previously been voluntary machinery and voluntary agreements on teachers' salaries. Logical but nevertheless somewhat surprising in view of central government's contribution to educational expenditure, in which teachers' pay featured largely, was the absence from the negotiating table of the Minister of Education or any of his representatives. The Committees, each under an independent chairman, consisted as before of equal numbers of teacher representatives (a majority were nominated by the NUT, and the NAS was excluded) and of the employing local authorities, led by the General Secretary of the AEC and including the main local authority associations. The various pre-war scales for elementary teachers, which had allowed a transition from local discretion to national standards, had gradually been eliminated but it was the structural changes in education brought about by the Education Act 1944 that permitted the final amalgamation of scales previously arrived at separately for elementary teachers and secondary teachers. Under the new Act a main committee to determine primary and secondary teacher salaries was established; in direct association were a further education committee and a farm institutes committee. Analogous arrangements were separately made for lecturers in teacher training colleges under the chairmanship of Sir Henry Pelham and later, for local authority advisers, organisers and inspectors, under Lord Soulbury. (Many years later similar arrangements were made for negotiating the remuneration of youth leaders and community centre wardens.)

If the trend of inter-war negotiations can be characterised as the removal of differentials between classes of teachers distinguished by qualifications, geographical location and type of school, culminating in the Burnham Agreement (1945), which authorised one scale for primary and secondary teachers, then a contrasting feature of the post-war period was the gradual re-establishment of differentials.

Teacher shortages, especially in some academic subjects and particularly in secondary schools, were answered first by increases in and the elaboration of the additional remuneration consequent on qualifications above the average. The strongest commitment to a common scale and to the minimum of differentiation had come from the NUT, almost all of whose members had worked in elementary schools and were now usually either primary schoolteachers or engaged in establishing the identity of secondary modern schools; judged by previous qualification and by school of work, few of them could hope to benefit from additional payment for a good honours degree or for commitment to work with the sixth form. The impetus for such financial recognition naturally came from the secondary teachers' associations, which bonded together for numerical strength and unity as the Joint Four on salary matters. Every third year, in 1948, 1951 and 1954, renewed negotiations in the Burnham Committee introduced additional differentiation, but the increased attractiveness of a teaching career to graduates satisfied neither the Assistant Masters' Association nor the Ministry. The former considered taking strike action for the first time in its history in 1954; in 1961, reacting to proposals from Burnham in the context of a general policy of public pay restraint, the Minister of Education argued that the total cost of settlement had to be reduced, but

to attract the highly qualified entrant, the rewards for higher qualifications and for higher posts of responsibility in primary and secondary schools require special attention. I therefore want to see the Committee's current proposals on differentials retained in full, or better still increased, in any revised scheme. (House of Commons, 1961)

The same period did see one further major achievement of principle for the NUT, however, as well as one financial defeat. The Government's Superannuation Bill of 1954, raising teacher contributions from 5 to 6 per cent of salary, aroused a storm of unavailing teacher protest; the only concession brought forward the date of operation of a new triennial Burnham salary agreement from 1956 to 1957, when the increased contribution would first be levied. The campaign for equal pay was perhaps the last in a long NUT tradition of mass petition and pressure on Members of Parliament and, through them, on Ministers. Between 1955 and 1961 the differential between men and women teachers was gradually eliminated—a substantial achievement when it is remembered that it had seemed necessary to include in the Education Act 1944 a provision prohibiting the formerly common practice of dismissing women teachers on marriage.

The limitations of the negotiating machinery were becoming apparent. For the teachers one was the omission of any facility for backdating awards; a delay in settlement involved economic loss. Another limitation for both teacher and management sides of Burnham was the lack of provision for arbitration in the event of failure to agree. Finally, the Minister's enormously increased general role in, and responsibility for, education was frustrated by his exclusion from salary negotiations. His only power was to accept or reject Burnham recommendations; he had no discretion to amend them. In 1961 complete impasse was avoided when the Burnham Committee agreed to revise its recommendations to suit the Minister; in 1963 no compromise proved possible, and the Minister imposed his own salary scales by special Act of Parliament (Remuneration of Teachers Act 1963) and promised to reform the Burnham structure. In this he was opposed by the local authorities, jealous of their prerogatives as sole employers, as well as by the teachers, but even a change of political party in power nationally did not prevent the implementation of reform under the Remuneration of Teachers Act 1965. Under this legislation, which is still in operation, retrospective payment and arbitration are both provided for. The authorities panel became the management panel, led still by the AEC but for the first time including officials representing the Minister; from 1963 onwards the Minister had to accept the recommendations arrived at unanimously by a Committee that included his own representatives. The local authorities and the Minister agreed informally that the former should have the greater say in the distribution of any increases in salary, while the total cost should be subject to the approval of the latter.

In the aftermath of the 1961 crisis the NAS and the NAHT, both representatives of teachers with a definite interest in differentials and in career prospects, had been admitted to the Burnham Committee. It is hardly surprising, then, that although some of the immediate post-war teacher shortages have disappeared and equal pay has long been achieved, the salary negotiations of the 1960s and 1970s have been as much about reward for responsibility, for qualifications and for experience as about increases in the basic scale that the NUT still prizes as one of the unifying factors of the teaching profession.

Although the Minister may have been satisfied by the structural reforms of 1963—5, there has been little evidence since that the traditional machinery is capable of bearing the pressure brought to bear upon it for other reasons.

First, the conflicting views indicated immediately above find expression within and between unions and are incapable of any final resolution; in particular, the NAS has been unwilling to submit its three members of the teachers' panel to the disciplines of confidentiality and unanimity in negotiation with the management side that the majority of teachers' panel members, representatives of the NUT, formerly accepted. The NUT has had to be, or to pose as, more militant in public and private than its immediate post-war tradition and perhaps its leaders' tactical sense would otherwise suggest. Even so, as the largest and most all-embracing teachers' association, it is constitutionally vulnerable to the astute outflanking manoeuvres of the NAS. The circulation of confidential negotiation papers, the holding of alternative press conference and the presentation of different cases in negotiations are all well documented activities, the effectiveness of which in inter-union politics is attested by the continuing growth of the NAS and the stagnation of NUT membership.

The NUT leadership has also, by its own account, been handicapped in recent years by the growth of an internal ginger group of young teachers, Rank and File by name, committed not only to the traditional aims of improving the basic scale, but also to a more radical conception of the union's function, and sceptical of the leadership's motives. Secondly, the Burnham structure has become less relevant to the teachers' associations as government economic policy has been extended to include more and more concern with pay in the public sector generally. It was the first 'pay pause', under Chancellor of the Exchequer Selwyn Lloyd, that precipitated the Minister of Education's unprecedented intervention in salary negotiations in 1961. Since then successive pay policies have turned the attention of teachers' associations from negotiations with the Ministry of Education DES and local education authorities to an alliance with other non-teacher unions. The NAS was the first of the schoolteachers' associations to decide to affiliate to the Trades Union Congress in 1968 (the Association of Teachers in Technical Institutions affiliated in 1967); it was followed by the NUT in 1970. Traditional teacher reluctance to associate with 'cloth cap' unions committed to the Labour Party was overcome as a result of experience of new government policy and the failure to sustain a 'white collar' and non-aligned alternative, the Conference of Professional and Public Service Organisations.

Finally, just as incomes policies and more extensive economic planning have placed the Burnham Committee in a secondary role in setting salary levels, so dissatisfaction with the results of Burnham and of incomes policies has promoted a search for special solutions to special cases on pay. Most outstanding has been the Houghton Committee which was set up to examine teachers' pay by the new Labour Government in 1974, in the interval between one pay policy and another. The arguments adduced and relativities then established have been used ever since as the standard against which to measure the achievements and failures of teachers' negotiators. Most recently, another mechanism for examining relativities (the Clegg Committee) has been set up by an outgoing Labour Government and retained (probably temporarily) by a new Conservative Government. As at May 1980, the Clegg Committee was still considering adjustments to teachers' pay additional to the Burnham settlement of April 1979, while the Burnham Committee was beginning negotiations for a new settlement as from April 1980. Neither the responsibility for nor the solution to such procedural problems lies with the Burnham Committee, which nevertheless cannot but look less adequate every year.

An equally vital element in the policy of teachers' associations has been the supply of teachers. While most unions are naturally concerned to limit supply as a sanction against employers and as protection against unemployment, teachers have been accustomed for several generations to campaign for an increase in numbers to meet increasing demand or to improve teacher—pupil ratios. Government has usually been willing to acknowledge the desirability of such aims, if not to endorse their immediate realisation. At the same time, the teachers' associations have been loath to allow any dilution of standards of entry to teaching by, for example, the creation of an auxiliary teaching cadre or delay in further training developments.

The primary post-war problems that had to be prepared for were the anticipated departure from teaching of many women who had been pressed into service during the war years and the increase in numbers required to maintain teacher—pupil ratios while raising the school-leaving age to fifteen in 1947 and to sixteen at a later, unspecified date. The emergency teacher-training scheme that provided some twelve months' intensive initial training and a subsequent course of part-time in-service study was completed by nearly 35,000 men and women, most of them on military demobilisation. The NUT, which had approved the scheme in consideration of a Ministry promise to eliminate uncertificated teachers, maintained its endorsement, despite the grass-roots criticism which was voiced as the access of emergency-trained teachers in the late 1940s appeared to take the edge off teachers' claims for a further salary increase. However, improved teacher supply was an essential component of improved working conditions for most teachers. The NUT maintained its delicate balance between the demands for quantity and for quality with such motions as that passed by its 1951 Conference, 'that the reduction to a maximum of thirty in all classes be the immediate and most pressing concern of our Union, but that this reduction be not effected by any lowering of the professional qualifications and standards of teachers'.

It was anticipated that teacher—pupil ratios could be substantially improved once the post-war baby bulge had passed through the schools and the secular trend to a lower birth rate had reasserted itself as anticipated. The opportunity could also be taken to extend the two-year training course of certificated teachers to three years. In 1949 the Ministry had set up a National Advisory Council on the Training and Supply of Teachers, composed of all the interested parties; in its Fifth Report (1956) the Council concluded that a temporary easing of demand would make it possible to lengthen the teacher training course either from 1959 or 1960. As it happened, subsequent data showed that increased teacher wastage would frustrate national targets for teacher—pupil ratios. The commitment to a three-year course was maintained, and further plans for an increase in teacher—training places were made. Once again, the danger of an over-supply of teachers had been averted but more by chance than through accurate forecasting and planning.

The 1960s gave further confirmation to the view that rising teacher qualification standards, an increased supply of teachers and improved salary levels could all be combined. Controversy concerned the acceptability of particular means of reaching agreed targets or the inadequacy of the targets set. The teachers' unions welcomed the Robbins Report on higher education, which offered the long-term prospect of an all-graduate profession as the training colleges, renamed colleges of education, gradually assimilated to the universities. The local authorities were discontent with teacher-training processes that neglected the fullest use of plant that a four-term college year might bring and with a profession that refused to contemplate the use of auxiliaries. Others resented the slow speed of expansion necessitated, it was claimed, by the exclusive association of teacher education with the universities. Such fundamental differences of view were beyond the capacity of the National Council to resolve alone, and in 1965 its chairman resigned after the publication of its Ninth Report. The Council was not reconvened.

The Council might have enabled the various interested parties to come to terms with the changes in demand for teachers that have since occurred. As it is, the DES has been able, by administrative fiat, to alter the institutional structure and terms of reference of the colleges of education, to cut teacher training places by about half and to turn the attention of local policy-makers from the consideration of ways of attracting staff to schemes for early retirement. On the other hand, the new Advisory Committee on the Supply and Training of Teachers, set up in 1972, does not seem to have been a serious impediment to the execution of national retrenchment policy.

Local education authorities and the Churches are the owners and maintainers of the colleges of education, but the Minister has the power to determine the numbers of trainees who may be admitted to a college and eligibility for grant aid. By ignoring and dismantling the regional consultative machinery for teacher education and by dealing separately with each institution, whether local authority or voluntary body, DES was able to prevent any systematic analysis of its overall plans and the construction of any coherent alternative. Successive waves of training-place reductions were met by opposing waves of protest, but the defenders of particular colleges were often in competition with each other for scarce resources or were ideologically in conflict. At the same time as teacher-training places were cut in some colleges and other colleges were scheduled for closure, the tantalising prospect of new courses other than teacher education was put before yet others, as was the less welcome possibility of amalgamation with polytechnics and colleges of further education.

The most important key to this radical change of policy was the belated public recognition of the implications of a fall in the birth rate each year from 1965 onwards. Even in 1969 one otherwise well informed study was claiming that 'both in Britain and in the United States, schoolteachers seem likely to be in short supply for the foreseeable future' (Kelsall and Kelsall, 1969, p. 177). To continue to produce teachers at the rate they were being produced towards the end of the 1960s, let alone to maintain the existing rate of expansion in teacher training, was to ignore the possibility of substantial teacher unemployment in the event of constraints on public resources for education. The demand for teachers is a function of the number of pupils to be educated and the desired teacher—pupil ratio, the amount of money that the public authorities are willing to make available for teachers' salaries and the average level of salary per teacher. The reduction in the birth rate not only made the achievement of substantially improved teacher—pupil ratios feasible without as large a commitment to training; it also signalled a shift in the age structure of the population that tipped the balance in demand for extra resources towards income supplementation and social services for the aged. A change in the political climate also left politicians less sympathetic to the demands of teachers for an unending improvement in teacher—pupil ratios; and the substantial improvements in teacher salaries that the Houghton Report brought about before the erosions of inflation, combined with economic and financial crisis, have made local authorities reluctant to contemplate further expansion in teacher employment.

It is perhaps a fatalistic realisation that the continued production of teachers for whom jobs cannot be found is not only demoralising for those concerned but also threatens the security and salary prospects of teachers in employment that has muted the actions of teachers' unions in opposing the curtailment of supply. The natural reaction of a union would be to welcome restrictions on supply as reinforcing a strategy of improved remuneration. Whatever recent problems there have been, the general picture is of co-operation between central government, local authorities and the leadership of teachers' associations in the pursuit of improved education as a corollary of increased teacher supply.

This co-operation has not been maintained at the expense of the target of a university-trained, graduate profession. Since the war the major teachers' associations have campaigned to establish the principle that successful completion of a teacher-training course should be a prerequisite for entry to teaching. The principle was applied to primary teachers recruited to maintained schools from the late 1960s onwards and to those, apart from science and mathematics specialists, who graduated after 1972 and wanted to go into teaching in secondary schools. No requirement is stipulated for teacher entrants to further education colleges, but an extensive programme of initial in-service training is provided. Teachers' associations welcomed the long-term opportunity to create an all-graduate profession presented from the late 1960s onwards by the introduction of degrees in colleges of education after the Robbins Report (1963). Many universities were prepared to validate courses leading to a B.Ed. degree that was offered in the colleges associated with them through the Institutes of Education. The James Report (1972) put forward a comprehensive plan for consecutive personal and professional education prior to entry to the profession, to be consolidated by a much expanded programme of in-service education. Some of the proposals were too radical to arouse widespread support, and even the attractions of their internal coherence were lost in the panic of college and course reorganisation of the 1970s, but such specific innovations as the Diploma in Higher Education, a general two-year course of higher education, have secured a toehold in the system.

Government's response to apparent public concern about teacher competence has served to confirm the desired trend towards an all-graduate profession. From 1980 entrants to courses of initial teacher training must have GCE Ordinary Level passes in English language and mathematics or their equivalents; they must also have at least two passes at GCE Advanced Level, as must matriculated university entrants. From this date there will be no demand for the three-year Certificate of Education course, since all trainees will have the minimum qualifications for entry to a degree course. The widely welcomed proposal of the James Committee for in-service training provision equivalent to one term's sabbatical leave in every seven years of teaching has yet to be realised. Some expansion, unevenly spread across local education authorities, has taken place despite the financial climate; but to achieve the James target some 3 per cent of the schoolteaching profession would be engaged in in-service training at any one time, whereas in May 1980 little more than 1 per cent of the profession was being released for such purposes.

Again, the James Report recommended an elaboration of the organised training element of the first year of teaching for the new entrant. One day a week was to be free of teaching commitment during this induction year and was to be used for in-service training appropriate to the probationary teacher. Two major pilot schemes have been undertaken in Liverpool and Northumberland; these, together with other local authority initiatives, provided in-service induction resources for the equivalent of 10,400 full-time teachers in 1978—9. Overall, provision for in-service, retraining and probation falls 50 per cent short of the targets set in the White Paper *A Framework for Expansion* (1972).

The teachers' associations may derive some satisfaction from the development that there has been in the raising of entry standards and the extension of the scope of in-service training, but the major influence appears to have been government's preoccupation with 'standards' and its interpretation of the opportunity that falling school rolls provide to emphasise quality rather than quantity.

ORGANISED TEACHERS AS PRESSURE GROUPS IN EDUCATION

The teachers' associations have always claimed to be as interested in educational improvement as in their own well-being, and much of their activity is testament to this. Pressure groups can usually be divided into those that are defending a vested interest and those that are 'promotional' (that is, those that support some cause of no direct benefit to their members). Teachers' associations are a hybrid. Some, like the Assistant Mistresses, originated as proselytising groups and have gathered together for mutual moral support; others, like the NAS, have been founded on the basis of clear self-interest that might otherwise remain unarticulated; yet others have bridged this conceptual divide—and all claim to have done so today. This double preoccupation can be covered by the rhetoric of professionalism, a recurring theme in teacher politics, but the practical manifestations of educational concern are often separated from overt trade union activity. Reconciliation is easier for the smaller secondary associations that federate on salary matters, since educational issues can often assume at least equal importance at their annual conferences; the head teachers' associations, each under two thousand strong, have hardly needed to hold formal public discussions about the intricacies of their salaries. The major issues within any salary settlement dominate an NUT annual Easter conference; educational discussions have found their conference outlet at Christmas sectional gatherings for teachers in different sorts of school. These meetings provided, immediately after the Second World War, a basis for discussion and support of multilateral or comprehensive schools, which were later to become one of the most controversial issues of post-war education. The interpretation of the statutory requirement of educational provision appropriate to the 'ages, ability and aptitudes' of children might be thought just the educational issue which the informed,

professional opinions of teachers, expressed through their representative associations, would resolve. But on this issue (very under-
standably, in fact) most of the teachers' associations maintained a
guarded neutrality for many years (Fenwick, 1976 Chapter 6).

Of course, teachers' associations are not the only promotional
groups in education; a satisfactory definition of the field and its
dynamics would that of Finer (1958, pp. 3—4):

> The term 'lobby' embraces all groups but only in so far as they seek
> to influence public policy. It recognises that most interest groups
> only seek to do so intermittently, and that most of their activity is
> domestic; it recognises that even when they do seek to influence
> government they do not necessarily use pressure; and it recognises
> that some promotional organisations do try to exercise pressure all
> the time.

Professor Fowler maintains it is possible to argue that organisations
representing particular interests are as effective as, or perhaps more
effective than, political parties in transmitting the political concerns
of the mass electorate to government, even though political parties
could be described as organised federations of interests. While
acknowledging their possible importance, he concludes more
cautiously that lobbying groups have 'had significant impact on
educational policy only when they have been swimming with the tide
of educational and political opinion' (Open University, 1974, p. 20)

Other groups, such as the idealistic New Education Fellowship,
were early promoters of a common secondary schooling. Some subject
teachers' associations hardly looked at the issue until the practical
implications of the reorganisation of schools forced it upon their
attention. Temporary campaigns were set up by opponents and
supporters, either nationally or when the issue arose in a locality.
Above all, political parties—first the Labour Party and later the
Conservative Party—took sides; perhaps because of this last
development the main teachers' associations trod warily and avoided
final commitment. Even the Headmasters' Association, whose
members, the heads of selective secondary schools, had most upheaval
to fear from any institutional change, claimed in retrospect that they
had been willing to countenance experiments with comprehensive
schools under suitable conditions. The reaction of the NUT in the
1950s was to keep the issue off the agenda of policy-making
conferences, while quietly encouraging the participation of the few

comprehensive schoolteachers there were in the union's educational activities and in the output of supportive material:

> By 1958 the basis of the tripartite system was being questioned. Within the N.U.T., the grammar schools' committee persuaded the education committee to send out a questionnaire to LEA's asking for their plans on forms of secondary education being provided and envisaged for the future; a panel was set up to analyse the replies. The initiative again came from the grammar schools' committee when the executive agreed to co-opt representatives from both comprehensive and bilateral schools in 1959. (Fenwick, 1976, p. 113)

Hedging bets was not so easy for the Assistant Masters. The mass union was anxious to retain and extend its membership, but its centre of gravity remained firmly the selective secondary schools, and it joined with the other secondary associations in a common platform of scepticism about reorganisation. Eventually, it had to make clear that it was not opposed to comprehensive schools for fear that it would be excluded from local authority discussions of reform where the principle had already been agreed. The NUT and the equally neutral NAS were in a better position to participate. As Fenwick (1976 p. 158) says: 'While teachers' organisations eventually moved towards acceptance of the comprehensive principle, they remained able to sidestep the main issue by concentration on the details of reorganisation plans and the consequences for teachers themselves.' In other words, teachers' associations adopted an interest-group rather than a promotional stance; it seems very likely that any other strategy, either in the 1950s or during the period of reorganisation in the 1960s and 1970s, would have split their membership with very little compensating gain. Nevertheless, the claims of teachers' associations to speak with authority on all major educational issues are necessarily invalidated by this history. Value-laden as every decision and every activity in education is, we can expect no more from teachers than informed participation in debate, and we must respect the caution of teachers' association leaders that occasionally causes them to remain silent in controversy.

This account of various strands in the history and policy priorities of the main teachers' associations has served to show the pretensions of the organised teachers to a partnership in the government of education and the reality of their absorption into formal and informal processes of consultation and negotiation. The last illustration demonstrates the constitutional limits on their active participation in policy discussion, but all in all, despite internal divisions and inter-union rivalries, the teachers' association leaders are as much a part of the government of education as the civil servants, education officers and party politicians of central and local authorities. The Scottish Education Department working party on consultation with the teachers' associations put the attractions and limitations of the position succinctly (Scottish Education Department, 1962c, pp. 5—6):

> We take it to be an acknowledged feature of the machinery of government that representative organisations should normally be consulted in all appropriate circumstances before effect is given to changes which concern them directly. The underlying object, as we see it, is twofold—to enable general experience to be brought to bear through the contribution which representative bodies can make in the development of national policies; and to ensure so far as possible the smooth working of administrative arrangements by establishing that particular proposals reflect informed opinion and are reasonably practical and acceptable.

CHAPTER 7

Conclusion

A BROADER 'PARTNERSHIP'

The world of British education is so various in detail across countries, across local authorities and across institutions that it is easy to lose sight of major landmarks and to fail to detect trends in policy and practice. This last chapter attempts to draw together themes and to illustrate the overall shape of the system of educational government as Britain enters a new decade.

However firmly political and educational power may be structured, the British political system is relatively open, and many individuals and groups have some real chance of having their views heeded. Outside the official organs of government teachers are, as Chapter 6 showed, the most powerful organised group, but they are by no means the only members of the education lobby, and many teachers unite with other interested citizens to publicise and promote causes and interests. Independent institutions such as the Advisory Centre for Education (ACE) exist to promote by example self-help in education and the advantages of greater educational information for the layman. The Society of Teachers Opposed to Physical Punishment (STOPP) has brought together teachers concerned to abolish corporal punishment in a campaign that has certainly not attracted universal public support and that divides the main teachers' associations internally. The Confederation for the Advancement of State Education (CASE), a product of the expansionist campaigning days of the 1960s, combines teacher and general public support. In some areas local branches may be teacher-founded and teacher-dominated; in others parents may be the dominant force, as parents may be in the majority. Any one such group—and the groups have proliferated with the expansion of the education service and the rising expectations of its clients—may exercise no more than a marginal influence on policy; taken as a whole, they represent a significant body in support of, or in opposition to, national and local policy-makers. The variety of positive and negative responses to secondary reorganisation in different local authority areas illustrates the ways in which vehement public opinion can be organised around issues and institutions that would have lacked salience for an earlier generation.

Most outstanding is the growth of organisations and channels of opinion for the parents of schoolchildren. The direct representation of parents on school governing bodies, although often only token, is now commonplace. Parent—Teacher Associations vary from groups of fund-raising enthusiasts to campaign groups for more public resources and greater accountability. Few local or national politicians fail to pay at least lip-service to parents' legitimate interest in schools. The common-law basis of teachers' power over children in school is summarised in the legal phrase *in loco parentis*; yet parents in fact have very few rights under statute, the emphasis being rather on their duties and the consequences of breaching them.

The law since 1876 has emphasised the obligations placed upon parents to cause their children to receive education. After 1880 children were required to attend school unless evidence of satisfactory alternative provision could be supplied; and parents had a duty to secure efficient instruction for their children in the three Rs. The 1921 Education Act made specific reference to the compulsory period of education and to the content of curricula. As the duty imposed upon local education authorities was extended in the 1944 Education Act, obliging them to provide education in accordance with the 'age, ability and aptitude' of children, accordingly parents seeking to educate their children outside the publicly maintained system had to abide by the same standards in order to meet their statutory obligation.

The most significant right enjoyed by parents up to 1944 (which has persisted) was the right to withdraw their children from religious education in any maintained school. However, critics would point out (with justice) the negative character of this right and the social pressures that diminish its effective exercise. Since the establishment of the 'dual' system, parents have been able to exercise choice over whether or not to allow their children to be taught in voluntary or publicly provided schools, at least in those areas where both types of school have been available. The deep, local religious antagonisms of the late nineteenth century often centred upon the lack of complementary facilities, which prevented parents from making such a choice. The compromise of 1944 enabled Church schools to continue to coexist with state schools and thus upheld the right of parents to choose between denominational schools and those prevented by law from providing religious education consistent with the doctrines and formularies of any specific religion. It is true that Section 76 of the 1944 Act required that the Secretary of State and local education authorities 'should have regard to the principle that children are to be educated in accordance with their parents' wishes'. (See Postscript for changes introduced by 1980 Education Act.) This right, however, is qualified substantially by the further statement that the principle is to be observed only 'in so far as is compatible with efficient instruction and training and the avoidance of unreasonable public expenditure'. In matters of dispute between an education authority and parents on this matter Section 68 enables the Secretary of State to decide the merits of appeals based upon this Section. In practice, the qualifying clause in Section 76 has rendered the right ineffective unless a particular Secretary of State has wished to uphold the plaintiff parent's cause when local and central government have been in conflict in matters of wider educational policy.

To comply with the 1944 Education Act registers of attendance had to be kept, and parents who failed to ensure the attendance of their children would normally be guilty of an offence under Section 39. However, arrangements for prosecution included an anomaly. Under Section 37 a parent could be served with an attendance order if the education authority was not satisfied with his or her child's attendance. The order enabled parents to specify the school of their preference, subject to the exercise of a veto by the Secretary of State. Some parents deliberately breached their statutory obligations in order to increase their child's chance of a place in the school of their choice. The loophole was recognised and exploited in the mid-1970s, with limited success, by parents who objected to their children's attendance at comprehensive schools or at particular neighbourhood comprehensives. The 1980 Education Act, Sections 10 and 11, amended school attendance provisions to ensure that parents who kept their children from school for long periods would not thereby enhance their chance of exercising a preference.

The responsibility of parents to ensure attendance has been accompanied since 1902 by an obligation placed upon local education authorities to provide transport to ensure the feasibility of mandatory attendance. In 1907 the concept of what constituted a reasonable walking distance was introduced. Section 39 of the 1944 Act clearly specified that parental responsibility to ensure attendance was dependent upon the provision of adequate transport beyond walking distance (defined as 2 miles for primary pupils, 3 miles for secondary pupils). Clause 23 of Education Bill No. 2 1979 attempted to revoke the education authorities' obligation, to allow them to determine charges and to make provision of transport as they thought fit. This, it was argued, placed children in rural areas at a disadvantage and also undermined the rights of parents to exercise choice concerning denominational education. Although the Government made some minor concessions on this Clause in the Commons to limit the discretion of authorities to charge more than a standard fare for transport within or beyond walking distances, the House of Lords refused to support the clause in any form. The majority accepted the argument of Lord Butler that to have done so would have constituted a breach of promise *vis-à-vis* the Churches, which had accepted the compromise of 1944.

Since the early 1960s there has been a growing feeling among determined groups of parents that their rights and interests with reference to the education of their children are ignored or unrepresented. Thus lobby groups such as CASE and organisations such as ACE have compaigned for more involvement by parents in their children's education. The growth of Parent—Teacher Associations and other bodies (the National Association of Governors and Managers, for example) are further manifestations of an increasing awareness and a more conscious demand for participation. In many respects the Taylor Report (1977) echoed the views of this relatively new movement.

Another factor that has focused attention upon parental rights and choice has been the reorganisation of the majority of schools on comprehensive lines, following a request by the Secretary of State to local education authorities to undertake this task in 1965. A decade later the 1976 Education Act required all authorities to submit plans for this purpose. The Wood v. Ealing London Borough Case (1966 3 All E.R. 514; (1967), Ch. 364) constituted an attempt to exercise rights under Section 76 to avoid comprehensive reorganisation. Although unsuccessful, this not only represented substantial minority disapproval of the reorganisation but also epitomised a feeling that choice once available to exercise preference for different types of school within a bipartite or tripartite system would now be eliminated. It is true that such choice was restricted to approximately 25 per cent of parents, whose children were deemed suitable to benefit from a grammar or technical school education, although proponents of comprehensive education argued that the exercise of such choice limited the choice of parents whose children were otherwise categorised. Nonetheless, the new system was perceived by many as restricting parental freedom. It is notable that Circular 10/65, which suggested alternative models for comprehensive reorganisation, included systems (albeit only temporarily acceptable) based upon parental choice. This suggests that the Government, however determined upon the reorganisation policy, was sensitive to the fact that parental choice was a significant factor to consider when planning the restructuring of secondary schooling.

In determining admission policies local education authorities have always faced the problem of reconciling the need to minimise differences of standard and status between schools of nominally .comparable character with the need to preserve the right of parents to exercise some degree of choice within the spirit of Section 76 of the 1944 Act. As the number of comprehensive schools has grown and the catchment areas of such schools has expanded, this conflict of objectives has become more apparent. The problem is accentuated where education authorities have sought to achieve a balanced intake for all schools in terms of numbers, social class and ability. The Inner London Education Authority, for example, allows parents freedom of choice among secondary schools while limiting the number of places available in each school for pupils of different levels of ability. A balanced intake created in this way may preserve much more opportunity for social and curricular choice within a school for the majority of children (and, by extension, for their parents) than the apparently attractive choice between schools. To achieve this same goal some local education authorities have zoned schools more strictly, a measure that has also diminished the opportunity of individual parents to have their children educated in the specific schools of their choice./In order to reassert the right of parents to choose literally between schools, the 1980 Education Act, Section 8, requires local education authorities to publish details of admission procedures and any other information concerning particular schools as the Secretary of State determines. What is more, the authorities and aided school governors are required to establish appeals committees, to which parents may appeal if their choice of school is not complied with. Section 6 of the same Act enables parents to express a preference for the school that they wish their child to attend, and both local authority and governors are obliged to abide by that choice unless the exercise of such preference would prejudice the provision of efficient education or the efficient use of resources. This right, which seems so similar to that afforded under Section 76 of the 1944 Act, goes further when one takes into account the appeals procedure, the inability of local education authorities to set limits on intakes and Section 6(5), which enables parents to extend their choice beyond local authority boundaries. Whether or not one considers that this legislation gives parents a more significant choice concerning the education of their children depends upon one's political philosophy and the priority one accords to the right of an individual parent as opposed to the rights of the totality of parents.

Until recently parents have never been prohibited from sending their children to non-maintained schools, and until 1975 it was possible for parents to educate their children in direct-grant grammar schools (fee-paying schools assisted by direct-grant funding) if such schools provided a specified proportion of places for selected children from maintained schools. In fact, from 1907—44 local authorities commonly bought places for children selected from elementary schools in non-maintained, fee-paying grammar schools as their major means of providing secondary education.

Assistance for such schools was withdrawn by regulation in 1975, and the schools concerned were given a choice of operating as maintained comprehensive schools or becoming independent. This action, together with Section 5 of the 1976 Education Act, which revoked powers conferred on local education authorities (Section 9(1), 1944 Education Act) to buy places in non-maintained schools was intended to eliminate support from public funds for fee-paying schools. (An exception was made for children who were particularly talented in the fields of music, ballet and art.) This was interpreted as a further erosion of parental rights by some, particularly the Conservative Party, which was committed to repeal this legislation when it took office in May 1979. Subsequently, Section 28 of the 1980 Education Act re-established rights conferred on local education authorities to buy places in the private sector. Without recreating direct-grant schools, the same legislation attempted to restore the *status quo* prior to 1975 by introducing an assisted-place scheme (Section 17) to enable participating independent schools to remit tuition fees which would be reimbursed by the Secretary of State. When the Bill was introduced it was anticipated that the proportion of pupils involved (2 per cent of the school population) would be comparable with the proportion of children previously subsidised in direct-grant schools.

The mandatory requirement that there should be parental representatives on governing bodies (one or two, depending upon the size of the school), stated in Section 2 of the 1980 Act, undoubtedly increases the legal rights of parents in general within the educational system. However, the involvement falls far short of Mr St John Stevas's unsuccessful attempt to amend the 1975—6 Education Bill, which would have required one-quarter of school governors to be parents (House of Commons, 1976). It disappointed many who expected more from the Conservative 'Parents' Charter' (1974), and although the number and proportion of parental representation proposed in Labour's 1978—9 Education Bill was never clarified, there was hope, before the Bill fell with the Government, that parental places on governing bodies might come close to the recommendation in the Taylor Report (1977) that parent representatives should constitute one-quarter of school governing bodies. As the vast majority of schools already had some parental representation on their governing bodies when the 1980 Act was passed, the gesture could be regarded as statutory recognition of a *de facto* situation.

The Taylor Report had raised hopes of the significant involvement of parents in the control of the education of their children. It stressed 'a need for each school to have its own governing body to ensure that the school was run with as full an awareness as possible of the wishes and feelings of the parents and the local community'. The 1980 Act has created separate governing bodies and allows for the grouping of schools only with the approval of the Secretary of State. It has also given parents the right to obtain information to enable them to exercise a choice between schools. Yet this fails to implement the Taylor recommendation to involve parents in their children's progress and welfare (Department of Education and Science, 1977, Chapter 5, section 23). Parental representation on governing bodies is widely regarded as a token recognition of Taylor principles, but perhaps equally significant is the omission of any reference to the assignment of powers to governors in relation to finance (Department of Education and Science, 1977, Chapter 7) and curriculum (Department of Education and Science, 1977, Chapter 6, section 23) to ensure that school government is meaningful.

The spirit of the Taylor Report was to establish through participation a degree of accountability of schools to parents, as well as to the community and the local education authority. Although current legislation has not realised these objectives, the Report has raised aspirations and established criteria that include the presumption that parents should be accepted as one of the partners in the educational system and that they should be participants in decisions about the character of education offered in schools to which they are, in effect, obliged to send their children.

It is perhaps surprising that politicians have been so slow to make a firm response to the claims of parents for recognition as a partner in educational policy-making. At best, reluctance may be based on the view that the education of the next generation is a matter of common public and not merely private sectional concern; at worst, politicians fear competition from a potentially coherent and effective pressure group. It may be equally surprising that parents did not recognise a common cause and mobilise accordingly on any scale before the 1960s. This in turn may be the result of enhanced expectations of the education system in the post-war period, initially appearing to be satisfied but latterly increasingly frustrated. There seems little doubt that there is growing disappointment with direct party political channels as means of satisfying educational demands, which reinforces prevalent scepticism of the overt political process as a whole.

POLITICS AND EDUCATION

It is the common reaction of the citizen to regard the connection of education and politics with distaste. A full analysis of the relationship is worthy of a substantial study in itself; all that can be done here is to try to pinpoint the range of connections and the variety of criticisms that may or may not be sustainable.

Politics is first and foremost about public power, the determination of collective values and priorities; it follows that the public provision of education is inevitably part of the political process. As education uses huge resources to provide a service that directly affects the lives of the whole population at some stage and indirectly thereafter, one cannot isolate education and political opinion in separate compartments. Classical philosophers such as Plato and Aristotle maintained that education and politics were inextricably interwoven. Alexis de

Tocqueville, (1946, p. 245) the early nineteenth-century political philosopher, put it more emphatically: 'Politics are the ends and aims of education.' Such writers indicate that politics is about acting on values, making value decisions, pursuing aims, valuing alternative policies, and that education is concerned at its broadest with inculcating values and aims in the young and, at least in part, with passing on the values of one generation to the next. Perhaps T. S. Eliot (1939, p. 36) puts it most distinctly in his understated comment: 'One would be surprised to find the educational system and political system of any country in complete disaccord.'

If this fundamental conception is once understood and accepted, it is possible to go on to look at the other ways in which the word 'politics' is used to describe public behaviour that may be to the advantage or disadvantage of education.

Some writers and philosophers of education, such as T. S. Eliot, see education as a trustee for civilisation, passing on a body of immutable knowledge and truths from one generation to another; while others have denied this implied autonomy of education and have perceived it instead as an instrument of social engineering. Either view fails to encompass fully a complex reality in which the transmission of cultural tradition is inevitable without gainsaying the possibility or legitimacy of its deliberate modification. The view from both poles underrates the interactive relationship between education and other aspects of social behaviour.

Many people believe that education is too precious to be influenced or buffeted by social and economic forces that permeate other facets of social life, and that it is the duty of those responsible, Ministers and civil servants, to shelter education from overt political intervention. At best, this must be a naive hope, the result of excessive zeal to cocoon education based on the false premise that education can be a completely neutral agent for the transmission of culture. Ideologically, it is associated most frequently with a wish on the part of its proponents to preserve existing practices, functions and roles throughout society as well as in education. While critics of the connection between politics and education may have in mind the general perspectives outlined above, it is much more likely that they will instance the behaviour of politicians and of political parties in making their case.

Criticism is often made (usually with the benefit of hindsight) of the undue haste of decision-making or policy formulation. Ministers are only in office for a very short period of time; education committee chairmen and council members often appear to come to important decisions on limited evidence and with the aid of inappropriate criteria. The parties are further indicted for espousing causes and supporting programmes of action without any real understanding (or even perception) of the issues involved. Thus the phrases 'comprehensive education', 'equality of educational opportunity' and 'deprivation' tend to elicit party-political responses that rarely go beyond mindless slogans. At the same time, an impression is given that great issues are steamrollered through processes and stages—a Bill through Parliament, a resolution through council — with the minimum involvement of those directly affected.

Even where it can be shown that the politicians have given time to discussion and thought about an issue, the tendency of parties to close ranks in order to defend policy when challenged or questioned by groups outside the formal political structures is widely noted and disliked. It reinforces what is perhaps a growing alienation between the governors and the governed. Those affected by decisions are rarely aware of the complex processes by which decisions are normally made. When lip-service is paid to public participation and consultation by involving only groups whose interests are formally recognised the alienation is almost complete. In these circumstances the political processes are cynically dismissed as methods of legitimising decisions already taken behind closed doors.

It is too easy to see the answer in comprehensive, party-policy statements making explicit one ideological commitment after another; for there can often be an adverse public reaction to the mindless striking of attitudes prompted by the belief that even before detailed arguments can be expounded, 'the party' should never be seen to lack a distinct view. Both Lord Alexander and Lady Plowden, former Secretary of the Association of Education Committees and Chairman of the Central Advisory Council (England) respectively, have expressed the deep concern of many that the polarisation of policies between parties could endanger the degree of stability that they feel to be a prerequisite for the growth of education.

Almost equally unsatisfactory to the public is the picture of politicians and parties as the source of extensive patronage, locally and nationally. The substitution of party loyalty and time-serving for ideological commitment as major criteria for the appointment of committee chairmen, school governors or members of advisory committees is difficult to justify when direct interest or relevant expertise would be more appropriate.

When people express the opinion that education should be above politics they rarely draw their conclusions from deep and explicit philosophical analysis. Their view is most often a manifestation of reasonable anxiety that party strife or political dogma may take precedence over the efficient provision of schooling for their children. The fear that education may be used as a means of totalitarian control is quickly aroused; correspondingly, there is a deference (perhaps misplaced) to professionalism, as adequate protection for the institution of the school; consequently, those wishing to modify the character of the school are easily caricatured as threatening its very existence. Most parents believe it desirable to maintain continuity of institutions and practices while their children are going through school. Thus if pedagogical or institutional change is to gain widespread support, it must display the characteristics of gradualism.

Paradoxically, during the period in which these criticisms have grown, it has also become common to think that the differences between the parties are of no great relevance to education. This may be one consequence of the bipartisan prosecution of consensus in educational policy for a long period after the war. In combination with scepticism about politicians' motivations and capacities, it is a powerful confirmation of the electorate's view that 'the government always gets in.' In fact, many shared perceptions of the 'governors' owe more to their reluctant recognition of the technical limitations on the direction, place and extent of possible policy change than to any decline in ideological differentiation. Of course, 'technical' factors are open to challenge, as they are ideologically based, but such challenge comes as often from politicians as from the common sense of the mass electorate.

THE PARTIES: CONSENSUS AND CONFLICT

There are, indeed, major proclaimed ideological differences between politicians of right and left on educational issues. Conservatives traditionally champion 'academic tradition', 'freedom of choice', the retention of priority for an academic elite, the use of tests of performance to maintain standards, the preservation of well tried educational institutions. The Labour Party espouses an egalitarian view, emphasising social justice, interventionism, universalised standard provision and the subordination of private preference to the 'public interest'. Both major parties claim a monopoly of concern about what they claim to be principles but which are often little more than emotionally charged slogans about 'opportunity' or 'parental rights'. At best, what they propound or defend are very often detailed interpretations of these slogans which then function as alternative operational guides to the assessment of different methods of achieving common aims. In these circumstances the centre of gravity of party policy can easily shift; the boundaries of what is acceptable can be so stretched as to become almost unrecognisable on occasions. The strength of a party majority, the ascendancy of leadership over supporters, the unity and coherence of purpose when key decisions are made can be critical factors in the determination of radical change in educational policy or its absence. Yet even when a party Government embarks on a new course of action some compromise within its internal coalition and with its external environment will be inevitable.

Clear ideological differences between the political parties are easier to find in the nineteenth and early twentieth century, when Conservatives and Liberals disputed the place of religious and Church interests in education. Contemporary disputants of marginal reductions in the state's direct commitment to educational provision rarely take issue with the principle of state involvement, as did their predecessors of a hundred years ago. It was a Conservative Minister in a coalition Government who pushed through the 1944 Education Act. Although a Labour Government championed comprehensive schools as an advance in secondary education, previous and later Conservative Governments allowed their introduction in some cases, and Conservative local education authorities are represented among the pioneers of common secondary schooling.

Political controversy in education has been associated with the radical left, but the Conservative Government elected in May 1979 has already proved determined to challenge educational consensus, if only to implement its overall commitment to reductions in public expenditure. Legislation was very quickly introduced to repeal Labour's Education Act 1976 (reorganisation of secondary education), to remove from local authorities duties in connection with school meals and school transport and to finance the transfer of a small minority of children from state to private schools. Radicalism, whether of right or of left, is the natural antithesis of consensus. It is by no means certain that its consequences as a strategy—leaving aside its particular content—are automatically as disastrous as the Conservatives would have us suppose. It is no longer possible for Conservatives to condemn those on the political left as unique advocates of potentially disruptive change.

Indeed, that charge has always been better levelled at Labour Party activists and a minority of backbench Labour MPs than at the leadership of a party that in Government or Opposition has seemed increasingly to seek the 'middle ground'. It was many years before the policy of common secondary schools became a major explicit plank in the campaign speeches of Labour leaders. In Government from 1964 to 1970, Labour preferred persuasion and financial pressure to legislation in leading local education authorities towards reorganisation; it was 1976 before statute confirmed comprehensive schools as the appropriate form of secondary education throughout the country, and even then the peculiar political divisions of Northern Ireland prevented serious practical change there.

By comparison with the Conservatives, the Labour leadership has seemed very responsive to party pressures. On the same issue of secondary school organisation, Conservative Governments have consistently allowed at least some comprehensive systems to be introduced, despite local and national party opposition.

Carrying the parliamentary party and Cabinet is easier for a Labour Minister if his policy echoes a manifesto commitment; in education commitments are often vague and uncontentious, allowing scope for ministerial discretion. Such discretion has been even commoner among Conservative Ministers of Education, whose Cabinet colleagues have often been happy to turn their minds to other matters; only under the present Conservative Government, with its policy of reducing public expenditure and with several specific commitments in education, can there be said to be continuous conscious evaluation of the political contribution of the Secretary of State for Education. A similar general political concern with education lay behind Mr Callaghan's appointment of a Minister as senior as Mrs Shirley Williams to the post of Secretary of State in 1976. The Prime Minister's influence on policy is greatest in the power to choose and replace Ministers. The personality and status of the person chosen often reflects the importance that the Prime Minister wishes to attach to the service. The choice of Mrs Williams was taken by many observers as a clear indication that Mr Callaghan was looking for action and was according the education service high political, if not financial, priority.

The Prime Minister's capacity for choosing able lieutenants will be tested not only against the lobby of teachers' associations and pressure groups outside Parliament but, most important, in the House of Commons itself. Ex-teachers of one sort or another are now the largest occupational group in the House; the majority of backbenchers will come regularly up against educational resource problems in their constituencies. Boyle and Crosland, both former Education Ministers, expressed concern about the state of backbench feeling and the education lobby within Parliament. One should not underestimate the potential of parliamentary questions or debates on the adjournment, let alone the new and powerful Select Committees. The Secretary of State must command the respect of the Commons to be effective, and legislation can founder or be delayed in Parliament, particularly at the Committee stage. The Labour Government Education Bill of 1970 was sufficiently mauled in Committee to prevent its completion before the General Election of June 1970 was called. More recently, the House of Lords deleted the Clause in the Conservative Education Bill No. 2 1979 that would have modified considerably the duty laid on local education authorities to provide free school transport, and Mr Carlisle, Secretary of State for Education, very quickly made up his mind not to try to reintroduce the Clause in the House of Commons, despite his party's numerical majority. The combination of closer scrutiny of government, an increased proportion of contested policy and a dwindling share of public resources may well test severely the calibre of Education Ministers in the 1980s.

THE CURRICULUM DEBATE: THE INTERACTION OF FORCES IN THE GOVERNMENT OF EDUCATION

An analysis of the development of government policy to provide more central direction of the curriculum tells us a great deal about contemporary government of education in operation, about the significance of party, politics, ideology and economic forces and the interactive relationship of Department, local authorities, parents, teachers and other lobby groups within the educational system.

Throughout the 1970s public attention was focused on standards of literacy and numeracy by industrialists and the mass media. Anxiety was expressed by politicians and professional commentators about the alleged inadequacies of comprehensive education, child-centred learning and discipline in schools. Similar points had been made more vehemently in the 'Black Papers', and evidence from opinion polls suggested that the public endorsed such criticism. Reservations were growing about ever-increasing expenditure on education, with no tangible evidence that this investment produced an effective economic return. On the contrary, from 1973 Britain's economic performance was reflected in high levels of inflation and unemployment unprecedented in the post-war era. Thus it was more difficult for politicians to assert that investment in education was critical for the growth of the economy.

The Labour Government, in office since 1974, was severely threatened by the changing mood as many popular criticisms concerned policies with which the party was associated, particularly the financial priority that successive Labour Governments had accorded to education. Naturally, quite apart from ideological considerations associated with the policies under attack, it did not wish to lose the initiative in an area that had been a vote-winner for so long. Aware of the mounting pressure, the Government needed to respond in order to counter political opponents and to ward off excessive reaction. This would help to explain why Mr Callaghan, soon after assuming office as Prime Minister early in 1976, called for a review of policy on education. Prior to this initiative, it had been regarded as an established convention that the Prime Minister's role in determining education policy was limited to the appointment and dismissal of Ministers and to ensuring that it had no cost implications inconsistent with the Government's overall economic strategy. Mr Callaghan was plainly associating the status of his office with a major reappraisal of education policy.

The result of this intervention was the production of a confidential report, referred to as the 'Yellow Book', which was conspicuously leaked to the press in October 1976. It then became known that earlier in the year Mr Callaghan had asked for a review of education with particular regard to curriculum and assessment, among other matters. The Report set the tone for development of policy, culminating in the establishment of a 'framework for the curriculum'. It embodied criticism of the Schools Council and its domination by teachers. It confirmed that there was widespread criticism of secondary education and a popular belief that standards were falling, which was associated with comprehensive schooling. Among many specific proposals, the Report recommended greater involvement of the Inspectorate in disseminating the work of the Schools Council and the expansion of the Assessment of Performance Unit which had just been established under the Inspectorate. The Department's influence was evident from the outset; it wished to see a firmer and more central direction of the curriculum and was already carrying out work with that end in view. The Permanent Secretary had stated in summer 1976, with reference to Section 1, 1944 Education Act: 'It means more than seeing that buildings, teachers and other resources are available. It must mean a much closer interest by the Department in the curriculum in its widest sense.' He added, 'The key to the secret garden of the curriculum has to be found and turned.'

There were other factors, however, that affected the reaction of the Labour Government. The 1976 Public Expenditure White Paper revealed that undertakings given to the International Monetary Fund would mean major cuts in all public expenditure, including education. Educational policy in the foreseeable future would be more concerned with content and structure as expansion was ruled out. This illustrates the importance of economic considerations in policies pursued by large-spending departments and the unforeseen consequences of major changes in a Government's economic policy. The OECD critique of the British education system (1975) and the Expenditure Committee Report of 1976 had both criticised DES planning and referred to a lack of central direction; they further highlighted excessive departmental secrecy and the lack of participation in policy-making, and they suggested that officials exerted power that often exceeded that of their political masters. Such criticism might well encourage a Government to make some gesture to refute the allegations, to demonstrate that government could be conducted more openly, with greater involvement of other interested parties. What is more, the Government would wish to prove itself capable of determining educational policy.

In October 1976 Mr Callaghan spoke at Ruskin College, serving notice on all involved in the provision of public education about the need for accountability. He expressed concern about standards and made passing reference to the possibility of introducing a 'core curriculum' but did not involve himself in detail, suggesting that

Mrs Williams, by then Secretary of State, was quite capable of taking over where he had left off. (Mrs Williams' appointment could be regarded as part of the policy, in so far as her seniority and popularity with the public conveyed an impression of the Government's concern about education.)

The following statements give some sense of the crosstream of views at the time, which the Government would be obliged to recognise as the policy developed. Toby Weaver, former Deputy Secretary at DES, speaking to the Educational Administration Society in the summer of 1976, commented: 'The public has called the bluff of the teaching profession. The Government in future will be under pressure to take more central control.' The Chief Education Officer for Sheffield, Mr Harrison, added: 'The 1944 Education Act said nothing about teachers being responsible for curriculum.' The major teacher unions responded with predictable anger. Mr Jarvis, General Secretary of the NUT, stated: 'The Yellow Book could totally change the basis on which the schools operate. It looks like the work of DES mandarins.' An NAS spokesman utterly condemned any rigid control of curriculum: 'It would prevent any development of individuality of either children or teacher.' The NAHT had similar but less strongly expressed reservations. Alex Smith, Chairman of the Schools Council, objected to the description of the Council's work as mediocre; while the National Confederation of Parent—Teacher Associations approved of anything which might improve standards, although it felt that professionals should decide on these matters. Clearly, the DES felt that deference to the profession and delegation of curriculum control had gone too far. On the other hand, the outrage expressed by teacher unions shows deep-seated interest in, and abhorrence of, any attempt to trespass within what they consider a professional domain.

The Prime Minister had stirred up a hornet's nest, particularly in the teaching profession, but as the *Times Educational Supplement* aptly commented on 15 October 1976; 'Mr Callaghan and Mrs Williams must defuse the time bomb of public anxiety.' This they attempted to do when Mrs Williams conducted a widely publicised series of 'debates' in regional centres throughout the country involving large bodies of representative interests. This display of open, apparently participatory government culminated in the publication of the Green Paper *Education in Schools* (1977), which revealed in style and content that the Government was only too conscious of the *Times Educational Supplement's* analysis of the situation. The document made oblique references to greater central direction of the curriculum by reference to the duty of central government under Section 1 of the 1944 Act not to abdicate from leadership on educational issues and the need to investigate the part that might be played by a 'core' or 'protected' element of the curriculum common to all schools. The need to tread warily, to allay public fears, to take account of professional sensitivity, to recognise the interests of local education authorities and, if possible, to steal the thunder of the Conservatives by providing a positive lead was evident throughout the Green Paper. Paragraph 2.19 indicates a willingness to provide leadership and to look for a common framework in conjunction with other partners. It was explained that the Secretary of State would consult with the Schools Council and local education authorities about their roles and that a circular would follow asking authorities to undertake a curriculum review in consultation with teachers. This review would form the basis for further consultation and would precede any advice which might then be issued on curriculum matters. There was no admission that standards had fallen, but it was conceded that higher standards might have been expected, given the increasing resources devoted to education. The Government obviously wished to show that it shared public concern, but it did not wish to do so by provoking the profession. Thus child-centred learning was approved in principle, but reservations were expressed about the expertise necessary to adopt the approach. Comprehensive education was stated to be at the centre of government policy, but concessions were made to critics by reference to strains placed upon teachers. The Paper also contained a strong suggestion that parents should be accepted as a major partner, but the Government (apart from issuing advice to local authorities on desired practices to involve parents) awaited the findings of the Taylor Committee. When the Report was published its main recommendations concerning parental involvement, though somewhat modified, featured largely in Labour's 1978—9 Education Bill.

The Conservative Party, although in opposition at the time, played no insignificant part in the formulation of the policy. Dr Rhodes Boyson, an Opposition Education spokesman, welcomed Mr Callaghan's initiative in the name of parents and 'Black Paper writers everywhere'. But the proposal by Mr Raison, another Conservative spokesman, that the literacy and numeracy of all children should be tested at the ages of eight, eleven and fourteen forced a response from the Secretary of State, who in the Green Paper rejected the view that 'individual pupils at certain ages should take external tests of basic literacy and numeracy.' The preferred method of monitoring performance was to continue the work of the Assessment of Performance Unit by conducting research on representative samples of children in terms of their work in English, mathematics and science in order to assess the effectiveness of teaching and schools rather than the individual abilities of children. In other respects the Labour Government's Green Paper (1977) and the Conservative Government's consultative document *A Framework for the School Curriculum* (1980) reveal a remarkable degree of accord between the major parties on the question of curriculum and a similar willingness to move slowly by consultation before taking any precipitate action. One might interpret this apparent consensus as a manifestation of the influence of the Department. When one examines the central themes of the two documents it is evident that despite a change of Government in May 1979, the policy remains largely unaltered. In fact, one gains an impression of an inexorable movement, partly instigated by the Department, that was able to sustain the momentum in spite of the change in the party-political complexion of the administration.

The policy was taken a step further in November 1977, when Circular 14/77 was sent to all local authorities seeking detailed information about their curriculum arrangements to enable the Secretary of State to assess how such arrangements were meeting national needs and affecting the employment of teachers and to assist her in preparation of future educational plans. From later developments—the DES report on Circular 14/77 (1979) and the consultative document *A Framework for the School Curriculum* published in 1980 — it becomes abundantly clear that central government intends to give a further lead to provide a common structure for the curriculum. By operating within existing legislation, central government demonstrates clearly that it is the senior partner in the decentralised educational system. Government leaves the public in no doubt that local education authorities have legal responsibilities for the provision of education stretching far beyond the provision of resources and that it expects them to operate within an agreed framework and to give account of their stewardship. Both later documents are greatly influenced by reports produced by HM Inspectorate on primary education in 1978 and on secondary education in 1979. In the consultative document the Government stated its intention of reserving final judgement on *A Framework for the School Curriculum* until the Inspectorate expressed its views, which it did in *A View of the Curriculum,* published in January 1980. This is a testament at least to government's awareness of the esteem in which the Inspectorate is held by the teaching profession. The differences between the Government's expressed views and those of the Inspectorate serve to confirm the latter's genuine independence, however close its day-to-day contact with the Department; correspondingly, where the Inspectorate's views do coincide with government's, those views may be found more palatable to teachers.

This analysis of a policy not yet come to fruition portrays current developments that could have profound effects on the curriculum, the nature of relationships between traditional partners and, indeed, the whole character of the education system. It also illustrates many salient features of the existing system: the ability of central government to exercise more control without seeking further legislative authority, the seemingly endless consultation and concern about the views of teachers and local education authorities, which suggests that the partnership is very much alive, although the balance of power within it may be changing. Furthermore, one can discern the interaction of powerful organised interests, changing public awareness and the exigencies of the economy as critical factors determining policy. One notes the ability of the Department to give substance to a policy and to keep it largely intact, notwithstanding a change of Government and the overt differences between the major parties. As the policy unfolds, it can be seen that party-political dispute is motivated largely by hope of electoral advantage rather than by ideological commitment. The statement by Mr Carlisle, Secretary of State, at the NUT Annual Conference on 8 April 1980 confirms this view of the situation. He assured Conference that he had no intention of prescribing details of curricula but added that official views and the Inspectorate's primary and secondary surveys had shown a need to look at school curricula. He continued: 'We are engaged in a positive exercise to try to establish a broad agreed pattern within which local authorities and schools can plan the curriculum for their pupils . . . This concern is not a party-political issue: it reflects interest and concern that has grown over the years.' The new framework, or central direction, is almost finalised in early 1980, but the tone and content of the Conservative ministerial statement echoes the Ruskin speech of 1976. The debate continues, not between parties but between the Government in office on the one hand and the profession and the public on the other.

Throughout the book and in this final review of one policy moving through critical stages of decision-making we hope to have shown that the government of education is a dynamic process. Although one can analyse functions and roles of responsible agencies, illustrate pressures, describe the legal framework and economic context of policy-making, it cannot be over-emphasised that the governmental process in education, as in any other sphere, involves a complex interplay of forces operating in a constantly changing environment. We have attempted to do only what is possible; that is, to take a snapshot picture of a system in motion and in evolution, a system above all of predictable stability for only a short period of time.

Postscript

Although reference has been made to the 1980 Education Act in this book, this postscript is included in order to update and, in some cases, to amend statements within the text written before the Act became law. The Act undoubtedly alters the legal framework of the educational system significantly and provides further evidence of polarisation between the major political parties on issues of educational policy.

The Sections of the Act dealing with admissions, establishment, awards and grants, and milk and meals have been resisted fiercely by the Labour Party, currently in Opposition. The Clauses of the Bill dealing with school transport, which would have given local authorities much greater discretion to provide, subsidise and charge for provision, have been eliminated following a defeat for the Government in the House of Lords. This defeat was inflicted by a temporary alignment of the official Opposition, Church interests (particularly those of the Catholic Church) and notable former Conservative Ministers, including Lord Butler and Lord Boyle, who both expressed disagreement with the Government on other Clauses but concentrated their opposition on this issue.

The Act does not detract from any of the central themes of the book, but the following short summary and commentary will, it is hoped, elucidate the most important change in the law of education since 1944.

THE CONTEXTUAL SETTING

The Act reflects the intention of the Government to implement a number of promises made in the Conservative Election Manifesto of 1979. As Mr Heseltine put it when introducing the White Paper *Central Government Controls over Local Authorities* (1979): 'It is Government policy to reduce controls over local authorities, allowing

226

them to become more efficient in their use of both money and manpower.' He pursued the theme by maintaining that the Government had reviewed the host of powers it had to make regulations and now intended to reduce them to a minimum. It had been the Conservative Party's declared policy to 'roll back the frontiers of the State'. As far as education policy was concerned, the Party had promised to give opportunities for a small group consisting of the most able children 'to enjoy the benefits of a selective education'. It was committed to enabling parents to exercise meaningful choice over the schools that their children should attend, and throughout the General Election campaign of 1979 the Conservatives made it clear that, if elected, they would reduce the level of public expenditure significantly. Education Bill No. 2 1979 did indeed reflect these various aspects of the new Government's commitments. An editorial comment in the journal *Education* on 2 November 1979 drew attention to the relationship between the Manifesto and the Education Bill in the following way: 'Few can have supposed that a pragmatic party like the Tories would be trying within weeks to apply its promises to the letter; this is the very essence of the doctrinaire in politics.'

Although the Bill and subsequent Act reveal obvious manifestations of party influence, it is also true to say that the new legislation provides evidence of the evolution of policy continuing across the lifespan of governments and of the influence of Advisory Committees, and attempts to adjust the legislative framework of the educational system in the light of changing circumstances.

THE 1980 ACT

School government: Sections 1—5 and Schedule 1

These sections provide for changes in the selection, organisation and nomenclature of school governors. The distinction between managers of primary schools and governors of secondary schools is abolished; thus former primary school managers will be known as governors. Section 3 does permit the grouping of two or more schools but subject to the approval of the Secretary of State (other than where provided for in the Act). Section 2 requires the inclusion of two elected parent representatives on the governing bodies of county and

controlled schools and one in aided or special-agreement schools. In
addition, there must be one or two teacher representatives, depending
upon the size of school. Changes in the governing bodies of voluntary
controlled schools reduce the 'foundation' representatives from one-
third to at least one-fifth, and in aided and special-agreement schools
the 'foundation' governors are to outnumber the other members by
two if the body consists of eighteen or less, or three if the body is
larger (one of these must be a parent representative). In county
primary schools serving an area where there is a minor authority one
governor will be appointed by that authority. Further governors may
be added to those required by the Act, and the Secretary of State is
empowered to make regulations as to the proceedings of governing
bodies arising from the selection of new representatives. Any
arrangements to discontinue or alter the character of an aided or
special-agreement school requires confirmation by a subsequent
meeting of governors.

These sections on school government in part follow proposals put
forward in Labour's Education Bill of 1978—9 (Bill 14) and the
Taylor Report (1977), whose essential recommendations were: to
provide a governing body for each school; to constitute governing
bodies so that they might equally represent the interests of parents,
school staff, the local community and local education authorities; to
give as much power as possible to governing bodies consistent with
the retention by local education authorities of overall responsibility
for schools in the area; to enable parents and, where appropriate,
pupils to be elected as governors through school-based elections. The
Act is broadly faithful to the concept of providing separate governing
bodies wherever possible, but it gives only token representation to
parents and teachers; although Section 2(3) allows for the inclusion of
community interests, they are not specified other than by the inclusion
of a representative of a minor authority where a primary school serves
an area covered by that authority. The Act makes no reference to the
powers and duties of governors, which remain as they have been since
1944 and are unaffected by Taylor recommendations.

Admissions to schools and school attendance orders: Sections 6—11 and Schedule 2

Section 6 enables parents to express a preference for the school that
they wish their child to attend, which may be located beyond the

boundaries of the local education authority area in which the parents are resident. Local education authorities and governors are bound to comply with parents' expressed preference unless the exercise of such a choice would provenly prejudice the provision of efficient education or the efficient use of resources. Other Sections and Schedule 2 establish appeals committees, their constitution and procedure. In cases involving a county school the appeals committees will consist of local education authority members, who will have a majority of one over lay members, and similar committees will be appointed by governors of aided and special-agreement schools. Those concerned with the original admission decisions cannot be involved, and the decisions of these committees will be binding. An amendment passed at the Committee stage in the Commons gave right of appeal to the local Ombudsman if injustice or maladministration is alleged by parents. Both local education authorities and governors are required to publish details of admission procedures and special arrangements, in manner and content as regulated by the Secretary of State, and the requirement extends to local education authority arrangements for provision in schools not maintained by them.

Section 8, which refers to the publication of information about Schools, differs only marginally from Clause 10 of Labour's Bill, although the admission by the Secretary of State that information to be disclosed should include results of examinations suggests a very different policy of implementation. One might conclude that Section 8 was a response to growing public concern about secrecy in government; the Section appears to support the belief that schools should be more willing to disclose information about their policies, expectations and performances. The DES has already issued Circular 15/77 to guide authorities on information which might be regarded as relevant. Section 9 establishes that the new arrangements will not apply to nursery schools.

Sections 10 and 11 amend the school attendance provisions of the 1944 Act and ensure that parents who keep their children from attendance in order to improve their chances of obtaining places for their children at schools of their choice gain no advantage over parents who have complied with the law. (A loophole in the law prior to the Act necessitated the elimination of this anomaly; see discussion above, p. 207.)

These sections on admission reflect in part the intentions of both parties to extend parental choice. One notes, however, a critical difference between the Act and Labour's 1978—9 Bill, in so far as the latter provided for limits to be set on the number of pupils in maintained schools to enable local education authorities to plan the operating capacities of schools which they maintained.

Establishment, discontinuance and alteration of schools: Sections 12—16

Local education authorities will be able to close or change the nature of schools without necessarily having to seek the approval of the Secretary of State. Sections 12 and 13 appear to nullify Section 13 of the 1944 Act, but closer scrutiny of the new sections suggests that the situation has not been as radically changed. Section 12 states that the Secretary of State's approval will be no longer necessary to open, close or change the character of a school. Where there are no objections two months after the publication of a notice of change or closure such change will come into effect automatically. On the other hand, local education authorities will be required to submit proposals to the Secretary of State before the publication of notices, and he retains the right of veto if there are objections. Furthermore, he will be able to call in any proposal by which national policy is affected, irrespective of local objections. Proposals concerning voluntary schools will still require the Secretary of State's approval.

Section 14 requires that proposed building plans be submitted to the Secretary of State as he thinks fit, which abolishes the requirement under Section 13(6) of the 1944 Education Act that authorities submit every major project for approval. This changes significantly the elaborate building programme procedures outlined in Circular 13/74, but building plans will have to be submitted if they fall outside cost and standard guidelines laid down by the DES.

Section 15 requires local education authorities and voluntary school governors who intend to reduce school intakes in any relevant age group by more than 20 per cent of the standard number that applies to publish proposals of such reductions, as regulated by the Secretary of State.

Awards and grants: Sections 17—21, Schedules 4 and 5

Section 17 gives details of the obligation placed upon the Secretary of State to establish an assisted-places scheme, which will enable participating independent secondary schools with whom the Secretary of State has reached a participation agreement to remit tuition and entry fees in whole or part for pupils selected by these schools, the cost to be reimbursed by the Secretary of State. The sum set aside for the scheme (£55 million) is referred to in the preamble of the Bill, and the scheme is intended to be introduced in stages, initially in September 1981. Section 18 enables the Secretary of State to provide for assistance to holders of awards under the scheme with respect to clothing transport, which appears anomalous, given the later provisions of the Act to reduce costs of ancillary services in the maintained sector and the abortive attempt to transfer the cost of school transport from public authorities to parents.

The assisted-places scheme proved to be one of the most controversial parts of a fiercely contested Bill. The Opposition spokesman, Mr Kinnock, promised immediate repeal by the next Labour Government. According to the journal *Education* on 2 November 1979: 'every single education association of standing has condemned the scheme save one, the Headmasters' Conference.' The scheme is similar in many ways to arrangements which had been possible under Section 100 (1)(b) of the 1944 Act, whereby 25 per cent of places were paid for by local education authorities in certain direct-grant grammar schools, which received further government assistance in lieu of fee remission, based upon parental income (details of arrangements were specified in Direct Grant Schools Regulations 1959, 5.1 1959, No. 1832). However, the Labour Government in 1975 issued the Direct Grant Grammar Schools Cessation of Grant Regulations, which obliged these schools to choose between independent and maintained status and, further, discontinued the system of local or central support for new entrants. This was opposed by the Conservative Opposition, as was the 1976 Education Act, which revoked the power of local authorities to take places in independent schools. The assisted-places scheme was an attempt to provide oportunities which had obtained previously in direct-grant grammar schools without reinstatement of this category of school. Mr Carlisle summed up the Government's view. It intended 'to restore opportunity to the child who is rich in intelligence but poor in cash'. The party-political divide on the issues of selective secondary education and subsidy to the private sector were highlighted by the scheme, and it was condemned by non-aligned educational interests, including the Society of Education Officers, which saw the scheme as divisive, threatening to the maintained sector and profligate in the light of the Government's stated intention in the Bill to make major cuts in the ancillary services.

By contrast, Sections 19, 20 and 21 provide evidence of consensus between the parties, in so far as these Sections are very similar to Clauses 15, 17 and 18 of Labour's 1978—9 Bill, illustrating the continuation of some policies despite the change of Government. Section 19 and Schedule 5 extend the Secretary of State's power to designate a course for mandatory award, which is organised jointly by United Kingdom and overseas institutions. Section 20 enables the Secretary of State to award industrial scholarships or to subsidise such scholarships provided by other bodies and gives statutory backing for a scheme of undergraduate national engineering scholarships. Section 21 enables the Secretary of State for Wales to provide grants through regulations that would contribute towards costs incurred in connection with the teaching of the Welsh language or of other subjects in Welsh.

School meals and milk: Sections 22 and 23

These Sections release local education authorities from the obligation under Section 49 of the 1944 Act to provide 'school meal service as regulated'; repeal the Education (Milk) Act 1971; and replace with a discretionary power the duty to provide free school milk to all pupils on grounds of age or health or in special schools. Thus local education authorities may make changes or withdraw services as they think fit except in the case of pupils whose parents are in receipt of family income supplement or supplementary benefits; for these children they must ensure that any necessary provision is made in the middle of the day, free of charge. Although authorities are legally enabled to pursue their own policies as outlined above, the financial presumptions in the preamble to the Bill reveal an expectation of saving £220 million, with strong implications that this will be reflected in subsequent RSG orders.

These Sections and, until defeated, the transport Clauses attracted most attention and, like the assisted-places scheme, were in the forefront of the party-political battle. The decision to alter mandatory requirements for milk and meals provision to discretionary powers was affected significantly by a Green Paper issued in July 1979 by the Association of County Councils, which proposed removing a host of mandatory obligations affecting milk, meals, transport and nursery education as an alternative to cuts across the board. By the end of July 1979 the DES admitted that the alternative approach suggested by the Association of County Councils could provide a saving of £200 million, and shortly afterwards the Government chose to achieve the cuts by this method.

The duty to supply milk under Section 49 (1944 Act) and regulations issued in 1945 stipulating that all children should be provided daily with free milk was modified by Section 3 of the Public Expenditure and Receipts Act 1968, which withdrew obligation to provide free milk in secondary and middle schools deemed secondary. This was part of a series of public expenditure cuts introduced by Mr Jenkins in an emergency austerity budget that cut across a host of Labour Party commitments. In 1971 Mrs Thatcher introduced the Education (Milk) Act, limiting free milk to pupils up to the age of seven, those in special schools and others in primary schools who could produce medical proof to justify such provision. In 1976 the Labour Party by then returned to office, enabled local education authorities to supply free milk to children in maintained schools. This part of the 1976 Education Act was a response to the hostility engendered by the previous Government's action and represented the fulfilment of another Manifesto promise. The implementation of the relevant Section, however, was deferred until April 1978, when the Government used an EEC grant to recoup the cost.

This outline of events is included to show that the contentious milk and meals sections of the 1980 Act are but the culmination of a series of actions by Governments (both Labour and Conservative) to erode the principle of the mandatory provision of these services. At the same time, these events, including the new legislation, show the Conservative Party to have introduced more drastic changes and with greater conviction.

Nursery education: Sections 24–6

Sections 24 and 25 arise as a result of the Government's having introduced an amendment to the Bill at the Report stage in the Commons in order to replace by a discretionary power the duty to provide nursery education for children between two and five years old, as stipulated in Section 8 (1)(a) of the 1944 Education Act. If local education authorities propose to discontinue nursery provision, such proposal will be subject to the closure procedure applying to

other schools; furthermore, it remains illegal to charge for nursery
provision, despite overtures made to the Government by the
Association of County Councils on this matter. The need to clarify
the position of nursery schools became apparent when Oxfordshire
tried to close nursery schools, whereupon the DES legal department
and the Attorney General advised that this move would be in breach
of the 1944 Act. This highlighted an embarrassing misunderstanding,
as the legal experts concluded that authorities had a duty to provide
nursery education when parents requested it, although few authorities
made provision for even half of their nursery-school-age population.
The amendment (now Section 24), despite altering a mandatory
provision to a discretionary service, did not allow arbitrary closures,
and, following a Cabinet decision in February 1980, local authorities
were not allowed to charge for the service.

Section 26 was part of the original Bill, and it empowers local
education authorities to provide educational facilities in day nurseries
through the appointment of teachers employed by them at such
centres (that is, nurseries provided under the National Health Service
Act 1977). By virtue of this, staff may be transferred by local education
authorities to day nurseries and may remain members of the teaching
staff of schools from which they have been transferred.

Miscellaneous: Sections 27—38

Section 27 extends the power of the Secretary of State to regulate
entry, standards of competence, physical fitness and other criteria
which may prohibit or restrict the employment of teachers in further
education on educational grounds. The Secretary of State had methods
of exerting control over many of these matters via the Inspectorate,
by collaboration with local authorities or, more generally, through
his power to control the training and supply of teachers, but these
new powers are more specific and give him much greater discretion to
take immediate and effective action. The Section also provides for
regulations to be made affecting medical standards to be applied to
teachers and ancillary staff who have regular contact with young
people under the age of nineteen and with respect of equipment and
materials that could be regarded as constituting a health hazard. The
Section is designed not merely for further education establishments
but also for schools and other establishments whose courses come
under the Further Education Regulations. Reference to the regulation

of fees in further education suggest the likely application of greater standardisation to all colleges.

The power to approve or discontinue advanced further education courses or to regulate the numbers and categories of students to be admitted, reinforces and somewhat extends powers already in existence, but such statements in statute reveal an intention to control student numbers and the provision of advanced courses in any college more strictly. Previous arrangements to approve advanced courses were more generally through Regional Advisory Councils and ultimately through the DES. It appears, however, that the need to control advanced further education by more coherent and more effective procedures endorses the view of the Oakes Committee, reporting in 1978, although it recommended that a separate national body, representative of the major partners in the educational system, should determine procedure and guidelines for provision.

Section 28 gives statutory effect to the administrative freedom already accorded to local education authorities to take up places at non-maintained schools that had been possible under Section 9(1) of the 1944 Act prior to the 1976 Education Act, of which Section 5 revoked this right.

Section 29 extends further discretion to local education authorities to provide and to charge for the provision of clothing for physical education. Section 30 allows local education authorities to continue to exercise discretionary power to provide services for physical social and recreational training; to charge fees for board and lodgings in maintained schools; to organise or to support conferences; and to conduct or to contribute towards research or to assist universities financially without obtaining the Secretary of State's approval.

Section 31 facilitates recoupment payments between authorities in order to improve opportunities for pupils to take up places in schools across local authority boundaries.

Section 32 and Schedule 6 amend existing pooling arrangements from 1 April 1980, so that claims on the advanced further education pool will be limited to an aggregate sum determined by the Secretary of State. This power to set cash limits on total 'poolable' expenditure has great significance for all institutions of further education undertaking advanced work, but most notably the polytechnics, many of which are financed almost totally from pooled resources because the vast majority of their work is designated advanced. Given the application of limits to 'poolable' expenditure, maintaining local authorities have to shoulder a far greater proportion of the costs of these institutions, which legally they maintain. The move has already caused serious retrenchment in most polytechnics, and in some, maintained by authorities with relatively limited potential to raise revenue from rate sources, there have been cutbacks of unprecedented proportions, which threaten the viability of courses and departments and, perhaps, the continuation of whole institutions. The Oakes Report had proposed firmer central control of pooling arrangements but, as stated above, via a national body, which, it proposed, should advise the Secretary of State and local education authorities about total provision and the allocation of funds for recurrent expenditure and should exercise further powers to oversee the development of maintained higher education and its cost effectiveness. Section 32 also allows for greater flexibility in the determination of expenditure that is to be pooled to meet other costs. This applies particularly to redundancy payments that might be paid to staff in former colleges of education as a result of former action by the Secretary of State to reduce the numbers entering courses of teacher training.

Section 33 provides that both the Sex Discrimination Act 1975 and the Race Relations Act 1976 will apply to local education authorities in the exercise of their duties under the Act, although a transitional exemption order may be made through regulations that the Secretary of State is empowered to draw up under Section 27.

Section 34 extends the definition of 'independent school' to all those that cater for children of compulsory school age but are not maintained by local education authorities (other than special schools). It further provides for the registration of such schools without exception. This measure both facilitates the introduction of the assisted-places scheme and enables direct-grant schools to obtain independent status more easily. In effect, it substitutes requirements for the inspection of independent schools under Section 70 of the 1944 Act by a power authorising the Secretary of State to order proprietors of independent schools to provide information as he prescribes. Control of the private sector is thus relaxed, and greater encouragement is given to the development of independent schools.

Subsequent Sections stipulate procedures and conditions to be followed by the Secretary of State in the issue of regulations and enable him to name the date on which the Act will come into force and to make any transitional arrangements that he thinks necessary.

The Act signals the end of consensus in the politics of education, at least as far as one can see into the future. It reflects the present Government's broader policies designed to extend the private sector of the economy and to reduce public expenditure very significantly. The replacement of duties by discretionary powers has a nineteenth-century ring and would appear to give local education authorities far more opportunity to develop their own policies; but as these changes are accompanied by very large reductions in central government subsidy for the education service, most authorities are hardly aware of much greater room for manoeuvre. The numerous references to powers to make regulations that are to be assigned to the Secretary of State means that local education authorities have been relieved of one series of central government controls only to be harnessed with a new set of different character but equal magnitude.

Bibliography and Further Reading

1 *A Historical Introduction*

Adamson, J. W. (1930), *English Education 1789—1902,* Cambridge University Press

Armytage, W. H. G. (1976), *Four Hundred Years of English Education,* 2nd edn., Cambridge University Press

Atkinson, N. (1969), *Irish Education,* Allen Figgis

Bishop, A. S. (1971), *The Rise of a Central Authority for English Education,* Cambridge University Press

Cruickshank, M. (1963), *Church and State in English Education,* Macmillan

Davies, J. A. (1973), *Education in a Welsh Rural County 1870—1973,* University of London Press

Dent, H. C. (1970), *1870—1970: A Century of Growth in English Education,* Longman

Eaglesham, E. J. R. (1956), *From School Board to Local Authority,* Routledge & Kegan Paul

Eaglesham, E. J. R. (1967), *The Foundations of 20th Century Education in England,* Routledge & Kegan Paul

Gosden, P. (1966), *The Development of Educational Administration in England and Wales,* Blackwell

Gosden, P. (1976), *Education in the Second World War,* Methuen

Lawrence, B. (1972), *The Administration of Education in Britain,* Batsford

Leese, J. (1950), *Personalities and Power in English Education,* Arnold

McClure, J. S. (1979), *Educational Documents—England and Wales, 1816 to the Present Day,* 2nd edn., Methuen

Murphy, J. (1971), *Church and State in Britain 1800—1970,* Routledge & Kegan Paul

Simon, B. (1960), *Studies in the History of Education: 1780—1870,* Lawrence & Wishart

Simon, B. (1965), *Studies in the History of Education: Education and the Labour Movement 1870—1902,* Lawrence & Wishart

Simon, B. (1974), *Studies in the History of Education: The Politics of Educational Reform 1920—1940,* Lawrence & Wishart

2   *The Central Government*

Bell, R., *et al.* (eds) (1973), *Education in Great Britain and Northern Ireland,* Routledge & Kegan Paul
Bernbaum, G. (1979), *Schooling in Decline,* Macmillan
Blackie, J. (1970), *Inspecting the Inspectorate,* Routledge & Kegan Paul
Bray, J. (1970), *Decision in Government,* Gollancz
Chapman, R. A. (1973), *The Role of Commissions in Policy Making,* Allen & Unwin
Corbett, A. (1978), *Much Ado about Education,* 4th edn., Macmillan
Crossman, R. (1975), *Diaries of a Cabinet Minister,* vol. I, Hamish Hamilton
Dent, H. C. (1977), *Education in England and Wales,* Hodder & Stoughton
Duverger, M. (1966), *The Idea of Politics,* Methuen
Edmonds, E. L. (1962), *The School Inspector,* Routledge & Kegan Paul
Edmonds, E. L. (1966), *The School Inspector of the Future,* Schoolmaster Publishing Company
Fowler, G. T., *et al.* (eds) (1973), *Decision Making in British Education,* Heinemann
Griffiths, J. A. G. (1966), *Central Departments and Local Authorities,* Allen & Unwin
Kogan, M. (ed.) (1971), *The Politics of Education,* Penguin
Kogan, M. (1975), *Educational Policy Making: A Study of Interest Groups and Parliament,* Allen & Unwin
Kogan, M., and Packwood, T. (1974), *Advisory Councils and Committees,* Routledge & Kegan Paul
Lawrence, B. (1972), *The Administration of Education in Britain,* Batsford
Locke, M. (1974), *Power and Politics in the School System: A Guidebook,* Routledge & Kegan Paul
McClure, J. S. (1979), *Educational Documents—England and Wales, 1816 to the Present Day,* 2nd edn., Methuen
Open University (1974), *Decision Making in British Education Systems* (E221): Unit 2, *Central Government of Education 1;* Units 3—4, *Central Government of Education 2*
Open University (1979a), *Finance of Education* (E322: Block IV)
Open University (1979b), *The Control of Education in Britain* (E222): Unit 2, *Department of Education and Science: Central Control of*

Education in Britain; Unit 3, *The Welsh Office, The Scottish Education Department and the Northern Ireland Office—Central or Devolved Control of Education?;* Unit 6, *The Politics of Educational Policy Making: Pressure on Central and Local Government;* Unit 7, *Finance for Education*

Political and Economic Planning (1960), *Advisory Committees in British Government,* Allen & Unwin

Raison, T. (1976), *The Act and the Partnership: An Essay on Educational Administration in England,* Bedford Square Press

Richardson, J. J. (1969), *The Policy Making Process,* Routledge & Kegan Paul

Taylor, G., and Saunders, J. B. (1976), *The Law of Education,* 8th edn., Butterworth

Official publications

White Papers

Department of Education and Science (1966), *A Plan for Polytechnics and Other Colleges,* Cmnd 3006, HMSO

Department of Education and Science (1972), *Education: A Framework for Expansion,* Cmnd 5174, HMSO

Ministry of Education (1956), *Technical Education,* Cmnd 9703, HMSO

Ministry of Education (1961), *Better Opportunities in Technical Education,* Cmnd 1254, HMSO

Scottish Education Department (1972), *Education in Scotland: A Statement of Policy,* Cmnd 5175, HMSO

Central Advisory Council Reports

CAC England (1947) *School and Life,* HMSO

CAC England (1948) *Out of School,* HMSO

CAC England (1954) *Early Leaving,* HMSO

CAC England (1959), *Fifteen to Eighteen* (Crowther Report), HMSO

CAC England (1963), *Half Our Future* (Newsom Report), HMSO

CAC England (1967), *Children and Their Primary Schools* (Plowden Report), HMSO

CAC Wales (1967), *Primary Education in Wales* (Gittens Report), HMSO

Department of Education and Science (1967), *Reports on Education, No. 37: HM Inspectorate,* HMSO

Department of Education and Science (1971), *Teacher Education and Training* (James Report), HMSO

Department of Education and Science (1973), *Adult Education: A Plan for Development* (Russell Report), HMSO
Department of Education and Science (1977a), *How the Department of Education and Science is Organised,* HMSO
Department of Education and Science (1977b), *The Educational System of England and Wales,* HMSO
Department of Education and Science (1978), *Report of the Working Group on the Management of Higher Education in the Maintained Sector* (Oakes Report), Cmnd 7130, HMSO
Treasury (1922) *Third Report of the Committee on National Expenditure* (Geddes Report) Cmd 1589, HMSO

Other reports and publications
Central Office of Information (1977), *Education in Britain,* 7th edn., HMSO
Civil Service Committee (1968), *Civil Service* (Fulton Report), Cmnd 3638, HMSO
Committee on Public Expenditure (1961), *Control of Public Expenditure* (Plowden Report), Cmnd 1432, HMSO
Committee on Higher Education (1963), *Higher Education* (Robbins Report), Cmnd 2154, HMSO
Department of the Environment (1976), *Local Government Finance* (Layfield Report), Cmnd 6453, HMSO
House of Commons, Select Committee on Education and Science (1968), *HM Inspectorate (England and Wales),* vol. I, HMSO
House of Commons, Expenditure Committee (1976), *Tenth Report: Policy Making in the Department of Education and Science,* HMSO
Organisation for Economic Co-operation and Development (1975), *Reviews of National Policies for Education: Education Development Strategy in England and Wales,* OECD

3   *The Local Education Authorities*

Birch, A. M. (1959), *Small Town Politics,* Oxford University Press
Bolam, R., Smith, G., and Canter, H. (1978), *'Local Education Authority Advisers and the Mechanisms of Innovation',* NFER
Byrne, E. M. (1974), *'Planning and Educational Inequality',* NFER
Duthie, J. H. (1975), *Auxiliaries in the classroom: a feasibility study in Scottish Primary Schools,* HMSO
Fenwick, K., and Woodthorpe, A. J. (1980), 'The Reorganisation of Secondary Education in Leeds: The Role of Committee Chairman and Political Parties', in *Aspects of Education,* no. 23, University of Hull
Goodwin, F. J. (1968), *The Art of the Headmaster,* Ward Lock

Greenhalgh, V. (1968), 'The Movement of Teachers' Salaries, 1920—69' in *Journal of Educational Administration and History,* vol. I, no. 1, Leeds.

Greenhalgh, V. (1974), *Local Educational Administrators, 1870—1974: the Emergence and Growth of a Profession,* unpublished Ph.D. Thesis, University of Leeds

Hennock, E. P. (1973), *Fit and Proper Persons,* Arnold

Kogan, M. and Eyken, W. van der (1973) *County Hall: the role of the Chief Education Officer,* Penguin

Lee, J. M. (1963), *Social Leaders and Public Persons,* Oxford University Press

MacMillan, K. (1977), *Education Welfare: Strategy and Structure,* Longman

Newton, K. (1976), *Second City Politics,* Oxford University Press

Ollerenshaw, K. (1969), *Education and Finance,* Institute of Municipal Treasurers and Accountants

Rendel, M. (1968), *Graduate Administrators in local education authorities,* Dillon's University Bookshop

Swinney, J. G. A. (1980), 'A First Examination of Numerical Data Relating to the Development of Local Advisory Services in England and Wales', unpublished MA dissertation, University of Leeds

Taylor, G., and Ayres, N. (1969), *Born and Bred Unequal,* Longman

Vaizey, J. (1958), *The Costs of Education,* Allen and Unwin.

Winter, G. (1977), *The Position of the Education Service Following Local Government Reorganisation,* Society of Education Officers

Wiseman, H. V. (1967), *Local Government at Work: a case study of a County Borough,* Routledge & Kegan Paul

Wood, B. (1976), *The Process of Local Government Reform 1966—74,* Allen & Unwin

Official Publications

Central Advisory Council England (1967) *Children and their Primary Schools,* HMSO

Department of Education and Science (1978), *Report of the Working Group on the Management of Higher Education in the Maintained Sector* (Oakes Report) Cmnd 7130, HMSO

Department of the Environment (1976), *Local Government Finance* (Layfield Report), Cmnd 6453, HMSO

Home Office (1968), *Local Authority and Allied Personal Social Services,* Cmnd 3703, HMSO

Ministry of Development (1970), *Review Body on Local Government in Northern Ireland: Report,* Cmd 546, HMSO, Belfast

Ministry of Housing and Local Government (1967a), *The Management of Local Government* (Maud Report), HMSO
Ministry of Housing and Local Government (1967b), *The Staffing of Local Government* (Mallaby Report), HMSO
Royal Commission (1960), *Local Government in Greater London* (Herbert Report), Cmnd 1164, HMSO
Royal Commission (England) (1969) *Local Government in England,* vol. I Report (Redcliffe-Maud Report) Cmnd 4040; vol. II *Memorandum of Dissent* by Mr D. Senior Cmnd 404—1, HMSO
Royal Commission (Scotland) (1968), *Local Government in Scotland,* vol. VII, Evidence of Scottish Education Department, HMSO (Edinburgh)
Scottish Education Department (1977), *Truancy and Indiscipline in Scotland* (Pack Report), HMSO

4   *The School*

Allen, B. (1968), *Headship for the 1970s,* Blackwell
Bacon, W. (1978), *Public Accountability and the Schooling System,* Harper & Row
Baron, G., and Howell, D. A. (1972), *The Government and Management of Schools,* Athlone Press
Barrow, R. (1976), 'Competence and the Head', in Peters (1976)
Bernbaum, G. (1976), 'The Role of the Head', in Peters (1976)
Burnham, P. S. (1968) 'The Deputy Head' in Allen (1968)
Duthie, J. H., and Kennedy, K. T. (1975), *Auxiliaries in the Classroom: A Feasibility Study in Scottish Classrooms,* HMSO
Hilsum, S., and Cane, B. S. (1971), *The Teacher's Day,* NFER
Hilsum, S., and Start, K. B., (1974), *Promotion and Careers in Teaching,* NFER
Hilsum, S., and Strong, C. (1978), *The Secondary Teacher's Day,* NFER
Jennings, A. (1977), *Management and Headship in the Secondary School,* Ward Lock
Lyons, G. (1976), *Head's Tasks,* NFER
Owen, J. G. (1973), *The Management of Curriculum Development,* Cambridge University Press
Peters, R. S. (1976), *The Role of the Head,* Routledge and Kegan Paul
Rutter, M., *et al.* (1979), *Fifteen Thousand Hours: Secondary Schools and Their Effects on Children,* Open Books
Sallis, J. (1977), *School Managers and Governors: Taylor and After,* Ward Lock

Sockett, H., *et al.* (1980), *Accountability in the English Educational System,* Hodder & Stoughton

Spooner, R. (1977), *Aims and Objectives,* in Jennings (1977)

Taylor, G. (1970), *The Teacher as Manager,* National Council for Educational Tecnology

Official publications

Department of Education and Science (1977a), *Ten Good Schools: a Secondary School Enquiry,* HMSO

Department of Education and Science (1977b), *A New Partnership for our Schools* (Taylor Report), HMSO

London Borough of Croydon (1971), *High Schools: Report of the Establishment Officer on the requirements for administrative and other ancillary assistance,* London Borough of Croydon

Ministry of Education (1944), *Principles of Government in Maintained Secondary Schools,* Cmnd 6523, HMSO

Ministry of Education (1945), *Administrative Memorandum No. 25,* HMSO

Northern Ireland (1976a) Department of Education: *Education in Northern Ireland, 1975,* HMSO (Belfast)

Northern Ireland (1976b) Department of Education: *Reorganisation of Secondary Education in Northern Ireland,* HMSO (Belfast)

5   *The Further Education College*

Alexander, W. P. (1969), *Towards a New Education Act,* Councils and Education Press

Argles, M. (1964), *South Kensington to Robbins,* Longman

Bristow, A. (1976), *Inside Colleges of Further Education,* HMSO

Cantor, L., and Roberts, I. (1978), *Further Education in England and Wales,* Routledge & Kegan Paul

Cantor, L., and Roberts, I. (1979), *Further Education Today: A Critical Review,* Routledge & Kegan Paul

Charlton, D., *et al.* (1971), *The Administration of Technical Colleges,* Manchester University Press

Cotgrove, S. (1958), *Technical Education and Social Change,* Allen & Unwin

Dean, J., *et al.* (1977), *Educational Provision 16−19,* NFER

Dean, J., *et al.* (1979), *The Sixth Form and its Alternatives,* NFER

Education Digest (1972), 'Further Education and Polytechnic Governors', 12 May

Education Digest (1974), 'Further Education Qualifications', 23 August

Further Education Staff College (1969, 1973, 1974), 'College Government', vol. 1, no. 13; 'Administration and Management of Polytechnics', vol. 6, no. 12; 'Management of College Departments, Change and Development', vol. 7, no. 2

Locke, M. (1975) *A Handbook for College Governors, Coombe Lodge Report vol. 8 No. 11,* Further Education Staff College

NATFHE (1980), *College Administration: A Handbook,* NATFHE

Robinson, E. (1968), *The New Polytechnics,* Penguin

Thompson, J. E. (1973), *Foundations of Vocational Education,* New Jersey, Prentice-Hall

Tipton, B. F. A. (1973), *Conflict and Change in a Technical College,* Hutchinson

Whitehead, A. N. (1923), *The Aims of Education and Other Essays,* Benn

Official publications

Central Office of Information (1977), *Education in Britain,* 7th edn., HMSO

Department of Education and Science, Circular 7/70, *Government and Conduct of Establishments of Further Education*

Department of Education and Science, Circular 7/73, *Development of Higher Education in the Non-University Sector*

Department of Education and Science (1966), *A Plan for Polytechnics and Other Colleges,* Cmnd 3006, HMSO

Department of Education and Science (1973), *Adult Education: A Plan for Development* (Russell Report), HMSO

Department of Education and Science (1977), *Reports on Education, No. 90: The Management of Non-University Higher Education*

Department of Education and Science (1978a), *Reports on Education, No. 94: Non-Advanced Further Education*

Department of Education and Science (1978b), *Report of the Working Group on the Management of Higher Education in the Maintained Sector* (Oakes Report), Cmnd 7130, HMSO

Department of Employment (1972), *Training for the Future: A Consultative Document,* HMSO

Department of the Environment (1976), *Local Government Finance* (Layfield Report), Cmnd 6453, HMSO

Manpower Services Commission (1977), *Young People and Work* (Holland Report), MSC

Ministry of Education, Circular 305/56, *Organisation of Technical Colleges*

Ministry of Education (1945), *Higher Technological Education* (Percy Report), HMSO

Ministry of Education (1956), *Technical Education,* Cmnd 9703, HMSO

Ministry of Education (1961), *Better Opportunities in Technical Education,* Cmnd 1254, HMSO

Ministry of Education (1964), *Day Release* (Henniker Heaton Report), HMSO

National Advisory Committee for Education in Industry and Commerce (1966), *Size of Classes and Approval of Further Education Courses* (Pilkington Report), HMSO

National Advisory Committee for Education in Industry and Commerce (1969), *Technician Courses and Examinations* (Haslegrave Report), HMSO

Open University (1976), *Report of the Committee on Continuing Education* (Venables Report), Open University Press

6 The Third Partner—the Teachers

Coates, R. D. (1972), *Teachers' Unions and Interest Group Politics,* Cambridge University Press

Fenwick, I. G. K. (1976), *The Comprehensive School, 1944—1970: The Politics of Secondary School Reorganisation,* Methuen

Finer, S. E. (1958), *Anonymous Empire,* Pall Mall Press

Gosden, P. H. J. H. (1972), *The Evolution of a Profession,* Blackwell

Hencke, D. (1978), *Colleges in Crisis,* Penguin

Kelsall, R. K., and Kelsall, H. M. (1969), *The Schoolteacher in England and the United States,* Pergamon

Open University (1974), *Decision Making in British Education Systems* (E221): Unit 2, *Department of Education and Science: Central Control of Education in Britain*

Tropp, A. (1957), *The Schoolteachers,* Heinemann

Webb, B. (1915), 'English Teachers and their Professional Organisation', published as special supplements to the *New Statesman,* 25 September and 2 October

Zabalza, A., Turnbull, P., and Williams, G. (1979), *The Economics of Teacher Supply,* Cambridge University Press

Official publications

Department of Education and Science (1965), *Ninth Report of the National Advisory Council on the Training and Supply of Teachers: The Demand for and Supply of Teachers, 1963—1986,* HMSO

Department of Education and Science (1970), *A Teaching Council for England and Wales,* HMSO

Department of Education and Science (1972a), *Education: A Framework for Expansion,* Cmnd 5174, HMSO

Department of Education and Science (1972b), *Teacher Education and Training* (James Report), HMSO

House of Commons (1961), Hansard, 1/8/61, col. 1409

Scottish Education Department (1962a), *Report of the Working Party on Appointments to Teaching Posts, Conditions of Tenure of these Posts, and Arrangements for Consultation between Education Authorities and Teachers,* HMSO (Edinburgh)

Scottish Education Department (1962b), *Report of the Working Party on the Appointment of Teachers in the Employment of Education Authorities in Scotland to the Education Committees of the Authorities,* HMSO (Edinburgh)

Scottish Education Department (1962c), *Report of the Working Party on Consultation between the Teachers' Associations and the Scottish Education Department on Educational Matters,* HMSO (Edinburgh)

Scottish Education Department (1963) *The Teaching Profession in Scotland* (Wheatley Report) Cmnd 2066, HMSO, Edinburgh

Scottish Education Department (1969), *Review of the Constitution and Functions of the General Teaching Council,* HMSO (Edinburgh)

7 Conclusion

Department of Education and Science (1977), *A New Partnership for Our Schools* (Taylor Report), HMSO

Eliot, T. S. (1936) *The Idea of a Christian Society,* Faber

House of Commons (1976), Debates, 1 July, C730, New Clause 31

Tocqueville, A. de (1946) *Democracy in America*

Index